KT-551-691

THE HIGH SCHOOL COOKERY BOOK

THE HIGH SCHOOL COOKERY BOOK

by

GRACE BRADSHAW

DIPLOMÉE OF THE CALDER TRAINING COLLEGE OF DOMESTIC SCIENCE, LIVERPOOL
FORMERLY H.M. INSPECTOR, MINISTRY OF EDUCATION
FORMERLY INSPECTOR OF HOUSECRAFT, LIVERPOOL EDUCATION COMMITTEE
FORMERLY HOUSECRAFT MISTRESS, MANCHESTER HIGH SCHOOL FOR GIRLS

With Preface by

SARA A. BURSTALL, M.A.

LATE HEADMISTRESS OF THE MANCHESTER HIGH SCHOOL FOR GIRLS

NEW EDITION, REVISED AND ENLARGED

LONGMANS

LONGMANS, GREEN AND CO LTD
6 & 7 CLIFFORD STREET, LONDON W1

THIBAULT HOUSE, THIBAULT SQUARE, CAPE TOWN
605–611 LONSDALE STREET, MELBOURNE C1
443 LOCKHART ROAD, HONG KONG
ACCRA, AUCKLAND, IBADAN
KINGSTON (JAMAICA), KUALA LUMPUR
LAHORE, NAIROBI, SALISBURY (RHODESIA)

LONGMANS, GREEN AND CO INC
119 WEST 40TH STREET, NEW YORK 18

LONGMANS, GREEN AND CO
20 CRANFIELD ROAD, TORONTO 16

ORIENT LONGMANS PRIVATE LTD
CALCUTTA, BOMBAY, MADRAS
DELHI, HYDERABAD, DACCA

New Edition 1948
New impression 1960

PRINTED IN GREAT BRITAIN BY ROBERT MACLEHOSE AND CO. LTD
THE UNIVERSITY PRESS, GLASGOW

PREFACE

It is now generally recognised that systematic teaching in the Domestic Arts should have a place in the curriculum of schools for girls, since we can no longer assume that training in household work and management will be given in the home itself. Even when this is done—and in the North at least, the tradition of good housewifery, both among rich and poor, has never died out—there are advantages in the systematic study of the principles on which sound practice depends.

The development of engineering education during the last thirty years has shown how much can be done by a wise combination of theory and practice: one cannot yet say that housecraft has gone so far. But it may do so: and the book which Miss Bradshaw has put forth is an attempt to help to such a consummation.

The material and the method of the book have been acquired and tested during her own wide and successful experience as a teacher in High Schools. In these, the amount of time given to any one subject is, too often, inadequate: four periods a week, as in languages or mathematics, is the least to allow for satisfactory work in cookery. But whatever be the allotted time, it will be spent to better advantage if a practical text-book be employed.

Such are the hopes and purposes of this endeavour. May they win some measure of achievement.

SARA A. BURSTALL

Manchester High School

PREFACE TO THE FOURTH EDITION

This revised and enlarged fourth edition has been prepared with the kind help of Miss H. M. McIntyre, formerly lecturer on the staff of the National Training College of Domestic Subjects, Buckingham Palace Road, London S.W.1.

AUTHOR'S PREFACE

This book has been written in the hope that it might be useful in secondary schools and training colleges which recognise the scientific basis of housecraft and which endeavour, as far as is practicable, to correlate the teaching of science and housecraft.

The book is adapted for the use of pupils preparing for such examinations as that of the First School Certificate Examination (Group IV) of the Joint Board of the Northern Universities, and the questions and practical tests will be found suitable for it.

While not written specially to suit the present war conditions, stress is laid throughout on the utilisation of food to the utmost, and the possible modifications of recipes with a view to economy are shown.

I must acknowledge my indebtedness first and foremost to two books, to *Economics of Modern Cookery* by M. M. Mallock and to *Bacteria, Yeasts and Moulds* by Prof. H. W. Conn, Ph.D. To the latter I owe the substance of the introductory chapter. If I have inadvertently omitted to make mention of my debts to other authors, I hope I may be forgiven. My grateful thanks are also due to various friends for much kind help and criticism.

GRACE BRADSHAW

CONTENTS

INTRODUCTORY

PART I. KITCHEN ORGANISATION

PART II. FOODS AND COOKERY

CONTENTS

INTRODUCTORY

CHAPTER I

THE BEARING OF MICRO-ORGANISMS ON FOOD AND COOKERY

Before we can deal adequately with the subject of cookery, it is necessary to understand something of the nature and activities of the minute organisms which abound in air, in water, and in soil, and which, sooner or later, thrust themselves upon the attention of every housekeeper.

These organisms are forces for good and evil in many departments of human activity, in commerce and in agriculture, as well as in the household. In the present instance we are concerned with their bearing on food, on its purchase, cooking and preservation, and on the management and cleaning of those parts of a house in which food is cooked and stored.

Nature of Micro-organisms. The minute plants with which we are concerned may be divided into three groups: (1) Bacteria, (2) Moulds, (3) Yeasts. Each of these differs in many respects from the others, but the plants in all three groups are colourless, lacking the green colouring matter or chlorophyll which most plants possess. This lack of chlorophyll has an important bearing on the kind of substance which the organisms are able to use as food. *Green plants* can use as food not only the simple inorganic or mineral substances they find in the soil and in water, but, in sunlight, can use also carbon-dioxide present in air. *Colourless plants*, on the other hand, can live only on organic substances, substances derived from animal or vegetable organisms. Micro-organisms, that is to say, require food such as we ourselves eat, and it is because they thus enter into rivalry with human beings that they are so important. When, in the struggle for existence, the micro-organisms win and feed on foods intended for the household, they bring about in the foods certain chemical changes, changes which are, as a rule, easily discerned.

These changes may be either beneficial or harmful. Thus *bacteria* are responsible for the flavour of cheese and are concerned in the manufacture of vinegar. On the other hand, it is due to bacterial action that milk goes sour, that fish and eggs putrefy and that all animal or vegetable matter sooner or later 'goes bad'. *Moulds*, though they are of use in the production of certain cheeses, are in the main to be discouraged; they grow readily on bread, fruit and other substances, spoiling them for use as foods. *Yeasts* are agents for good rather than for evil, causing the process known as *fermentation*, a process of immense value when it is employed to bring about the aeration or 'raising' of doughs, though less desirable when it results, as it sometimes does, in the spoiling of cooked fruit.

Since the activities of micro-organisms are so varied, it is advisable that the housekeeper should have some knowledge of their nature, of the manner in which they reproduce and distribute themselves and of the conditions under which they flourish.

Micro-organisms are difficult to deal with for three reasons:

(1) They are exceedingly small and exceedingly numerous.

(2) They reproduce themselves with extreme rapidity.

(3) They are present everywhere. In particular, they form the invisible matter of dust, and since dust is always present in air, it is almost inevitable that micro-organisms should find their way into food.

Structure, Growth and Reproduction of Micro-organisms

Bacteria, the simplest and smallest of the micro-organisms, are quite the most important. They are single, colourless cells, so small that it is necessary to magnify them some 800 times for satisfactory examination under the microscope.

The difficulty of realising the infinitesimal size of even the largest bacteria is only equalled by that of realising how rapidly they grow and multiply. One bacterium can produce literally millions of descendants in a few hours and though alone it could accomplish very little, by virtue of its offspring it becomes very powerful. Fortunately, the conditions are often unfavourable to the growth of bacteria, and they die in large numbers, one species destroying another.

Bacteria exist in two conditions: (1) an *active, growing* form in which they feed and multiply rapidly; (2) an *inactive, resting* form which some species assume under certain conditions and in which they neither grow nor multiply. Bacteria in this inactive condition are difficult to kill; measures which can be counted on to kill the growing bacteria are powerless to touch them, and they can resume active life when the conditions are once more suitable.

Moulds are visible to the naked eye as soft, fluffy masses of white threads on the surface and in the interior of the food on which they grow. After growing for two or three days they reproduce themselves, forming fine, powdery spores. When a piece of food on which mould is growing is moved, this coloured spore-dust is shed into the air. Air is thus full of mould spores, so small as to be indistinguishable, which, after floating for a time, settle on any exposed food, and if it is suitable, grow there and form new moulds.

Yeasts are much smaller than moulds, though not so small as bacteria. Under the microscope, the plants, each about $\frac{1}{2800}$ inch in diameter, are seen to be oval, colourless and almost transparent cells. Like bacteria, yeasts exist both in the *active and inactive* condition. When they are kept warm and given suitable food they grow and multiply rapidly; lacking these conditions they become inactive. They can exist thus for a long time without being injured and can grow and multiply when the conditions are once more favourable.

Conditions of Growth

In order that micro-organisms may grow and reproduce themselves, food, moisture and warmth are all necessary. Light and air also affect their growth.

(1) **Food.** *Bacteria* attack most readily foods rich in protein, the food-stuff familiar in white of egg and contained in such foods as meat, fish, milk. They feed also on fats and as most foods contain either proteins or fats, if not both, few are safe from their attacks. Foods which contain acids are protected to some extent, since bacteria feed more readily on foods which are slightly alkaline.

Moulds choose for their growth such acid foods as lemons and other fruits, and such foods as cheese, bread and cakes which are slightly moist. But almost any food will serve, provided it is kept in a warm, damp place. Organic substances which are not suitable food for human beings—leather, paper, cotton, woollen and silk materials—will also nourish moulds; their growth on these substances is less luxuriant than on foods and is known as mildew.

Yeasts require a fairly large quantity of sugar in addition to other food. But if they are given too much sugar, the plants over-eat themselves, so to speak, and their growth is checked.

(2) **Moisture.** All micro-organisms require a certain amount of moisture, and dry foods which are kept dry are therefore free from their attacks. *Bacteria* and *yeasts* both require a fairly large quantity of water. *Moulds* need only a small amount and either use the water in the food or obtain it from the air. Thus flour, a dry food, may be made musty by the growth of moulds if it is kept in a damp place.

(3) **Warmth.** *Bacteria.* Each species of bacteria flourishes best at a certain definite temperature. Most grow best at a temperature of 20°–35° C. (68°–95° F.). Heated above this point they become first inactive, then incapable of growth, until, if heated to a sufficiently high temperature, they are killed. Cooled below this temperature most bacteria cease to grow, but as some kinds flourish best at a temperature near freezing point, only a long application of a temperature *below* freezing point can be counted on to check completely the action of bacteria.

Moulds grow most vigorously if kept moderately warm. At temperatures near freezing point they grow either only very slightly or not at all. Heat destroys moulds, a temperature of 65°–70° C. (149°–158° F.) destroying the threads and that of 100° C. (212° F.) killing the spores also.

Yeasts grow readily at a moderate temperature, less readily at a low temperature and not at all if cooled to near freezing point. Cold therefore checks the growth of yeast plants, though they revive when warmed. Extreme heat also has ill-effects, first making the plants inactive and finally killing them.

(4) **Air.** Many species of *bacteria* cannot flourish at all if air is present, while others require air for their growth. Experience seems to show that food which is to be preserved temporarily in the larder usually keeps best when exposed to air. When food is bottled or tinned for permanent preservation, air is, of course, excluded; if it were not, bacteria would enter with it and so render useless the preliminary destruction of the bacteria originally present in the food.

Moulds. Practical experience shows that moulds grow best where air is stagnant. Possibly this is because the free movement of air dries the surface of the food. A familiar instance of the effect of stagnant air is the growth of mould on pieces of bread which are heaped up in a bread-pan.

Yeasts grow best when supplied with air.

(5) **Light** is a great safeguard against the growth of bacteria which flourish best in those dark corners in which dirt and dust

collect. Moulds grow either with or without light, but on the whole, grow best in darkness.

Light, by making it less easy to overlook accumulations of *dust* and *dirt*, also encourages cleanliness and the connection between lack of cleanliness and the growth of micro-organisms is a very intimate one. Bacteria, moulds and yeasts all form part of the dust normally present in air and food exposed to dust is also exposed to micro-organisms, while dirt consists for the most part of organic matter in a state of partial decay and affords excellent growing ground for micro-organisms.

Results of the Growth of Micro-organisms in Foods

When bacteria consume food they cause in it certain changes, changes familiar in sour milk, rotten eggs, decayed meat or fish. Some of the decomposition substances formed as the result of these changes are gases which pass off into the air; others are liquid, others again are soluble and dissolve in the water of the food. Food attacked by bacteria thus becomes soft and flabby and acquires new and often offensive odours and flavours.

It must be remembered that a food is not invariably unfit for eating because it contains decomposition products. If such were the case, we should not eat butter whose flavours are due to substances formed in the early stages of decomposition, nor should we eat game which is 'high', since its special flavour and tenderness result from the beginnings of decomposition.

Bacterial Food-Poisoning. In considering food-poisoning we may ignore (1) poisoning due to eating substances themselves inherently poisonous, e.g. deadly nightshade, (2) 'poisoning' which, as a result of personal idiosyncrasy, sometimes follows the eating of certain foods, e.g. strawberries, eggs. More important than these are cases of food-poisoning usually but wrongly described as 'ptomaine poisoning', which arise from eating food which is apparently perfectly normal in appearance, smell and taste. Such food-poisoning is due to certain bacteria which are quite distinct from (*a*) those bacteria whose products in the early stages do *not*, as we have just seen, invariably make food harmful to man; (*b*) those bacteria which form *ptomaines*, the name given to a group of substances often present in putrefying meat.[1]

[1] It is to be noted that (1) ptomaines represent the normal products of putrefaction in foods, and (2) ptomaines are not formed until putrefaction

Food-poisoning bacteria fall into two groups: (1) a group, much the rarer of the two, which cause the disease botulism; (2) a group first investigated by Gaertner, and therefore known as the *Gaertner bacilli*, which are responsible for most cases of food-poisoning. The chief source of the 'Gaertner bacilli' is the flesh (or milk) of an animal which is suffering from the disease set up by the bacilli. Beef (but not mutton), pork, ham, brawn, sausages, meat pies, tinned meat are most commonly infected, but milk, cream and ice cream with other foods have also been known to cause poisoning. The Gaertner bacilli are not formed in *wholesome* food, but it must be remembered that it is possible for food *originally* wholesome to be infected by contact with human beings or animals (e.g. fowls, flies) who act as 'carriers' of the bacilli. It is also important to realise that such infected food gives no indication of its dangerous nature, and that, though cooking may kill the bacteria, the *poisons* the bacteria have manufactured are not necessarily destroyed.

The prevention of food-poisoning caused by the Gaertner bacilli can only be brought about by (1) preventing the sale of the flesh or milk of animals suffering from infection, and (2) by a higher standard of cleanliness than at present exists in the preparation, distribution and sale of meat and of those meat-products which are known to cause this type of meat-poisoning. Extreme cleanliness in every particular after the food reaches the consumer is also obviously important.

Moulds. With the exception of certain cheeses, moulds have an injurious effect on food. They make it unsightly, spoil its taste and give it a peculiar musty odour. The food finally becomes quite uneatable, certain chemical changes taking place in it which cause its decay. In many cases decay is greatly assisted by bacteria.

Yeasts set up fermentation in sugary foods, splitting up the sugar into carbon-dioxide and alcohol. When jam or other preparations of fruit ferment they acquire a sharp, pungent taste.

When fermentation is set up in the making of bread, its results are very desirable, the dough being 'lightened' by the carbon-dioxide while the alcohol is dissipated in the baking.

is so far advanced as to make the food obviously repulsive. Further, there is little evidence that ptomaines are poisonous when the food is taken in the normal manner by the mouth, though they *are* highly poisonous when injected into the blood stream.

Prevention of Growth of Micro-organisms

Bacteria.

(*a*) *Application of Heat.* Heat is injurious to bacteria, first weakening their growth then killing them. Foods which are heated to boiling point or are otherwise cooked thoroughly are thus to a large extent, though not completely, sterilised. For though most bacteria are destroyed by a moderately high temperature, those in the inactive state can only be killed by boiling for several hours or by boiling under pressure. But prolonged boiling is harmful to many food-stuffs and boiling under pressure is not practicable in most kitchens. Complete sterilisation is therefore seldom achieved by cooking as ordinarily carried out. In spite of this reservation, the fact remains that thorough cooking does greatly assist in the preservation of food, and it is common knowledge that perishable foods will keep much longer when cooked than when raw.

(*b*) *Application of Cold.* We have seen that in order to kill bacteria by chilling them, a lengthy application of a temperature below freezing point is necessary. Such a temperature is not obtainable in ice-chests, still less in the ordinary larder. Cold as it can be applied in the household is therefore usually powerless to do more than weaken the vitality of bacteria, though to this extent it is valuable.

Cold storage depôts are cooled by artificial means to so low a temperature that food stored in them will not decompose for months.

(*c*) *Light, cleanliness and air* are all valuable preventives of bacterial action. No trouble is wasted which is spent on maintaining a high standard of hygiene in the kitchen, larder and storeroom, on having them well lighted, well ventilated, and spotlessly clean. Scrupulous cleanliness of utensils and of the hands in touching food is of enormous importance. Every precaution should be taken to keep dust from collecting on food. With dust come micro-organisms.

Moulds. Foods which are liable to become mouldy should be kept in dry, cool and well-lighted places; moulds grow best in damp, close atmospheres and in dark, airless corners. Not only should the ventilation be good, but the food should not be so covered up as to prevent free access of air to it.

Instances of the use of heat as a means of preventing or checking the growth of moulds are the drying of bread-crusts which are thus deprived of moisture and the re-boiling of jam on which moulds have begun to form.

Yeasts. The growth of yeasts which are causing fruits to ferment is most easily checked by heating the fruit to boiling point. This kills the yeast-plants and at the same time removes the alcohol formed as a result of the fermentation. Additional sugar must be added to replace that converted into alcohol and carbon-dioxide.

The means of promoting the growth of yeast, when it is required to produce carbon-dioxide for the aeration of doughs are discussed in Chapter XIX.

PART ONE

KITCHEN ORGANISATION

CHAPTER II

KITCHEN EQUIPMENT AND MANAGEMENT

Situation. The kitchen with the scullery and larder should form one compact block, preferably somewhat apart from the living rooms but not so remote from them as unduly to increase work or to cause hot food to be cooled before it reaches the table. On the other hand, the distance between the living rooms and the kitchen should be sufficient to prevent the noises and odours of cooking from penetrating to the former. Where the size of the house necessitates the kitchen being close to the living rooms much may be done by shutting the kitchen door systematically.

Lighting and Ventilation. The windows of the kitchen should face north or north-east to ensure coolness and light. Good light, both natural and artificial, is essential; it not only prevents mistakes in cooking but influences greatly the cleanliness of the kitchen. Where the light is poor, dust, dirt, and with them micro-organisms, are likely to accumulate unnoticed.

Kitchen windows should open top and bottom and should be open constantly so that the air never becomes impure, hot or tainted with the smell of cooking.

Furnishing. The kitchen should be so planned as to discourage dust and dirt and to facilitate their removal. In particular, the surface of ceilings, walls, floors, woodwork and equipment should hold dust and dirt as little as possible, and be easy to clean. The grouping of the necessary equipment in convenient well-lighted positions, and the heights of sinks, tables, shelves and store cupboards respectively need careful consideration, if unnecessary physical effort is to be avoided. Such furniture as is necessary should be of strong and plain construction and capable of being cleaned easily. A washable table with drawers for towels, etc., a cupboard to hold the groceries required for immediate use, one or two chairs and a clock are essential furnishings.

In recent years standard unit-equipment has been used for kitchen purposes. The housewife can have up-to-date furniture at a reasonable cost and a kitchen which is labour-saving in its planning, whether for a kitchen-workshop or a kitchen-dining-room.

COOKING EQUIPMENT

COOKING RANGES AND STOVES

The heat required for cooking may be obtained from oil, coal gas, or electricity.

Oil is inexpensive, but only simple cooking is possible with its use. Oil stoves and ovens combined are useful for cooking in summer or to supplement a small coal range in districts in which gas and electricity are not obtainable. A good quality of oil should be burnt, the burners of the lamps should be kept very clean and be fitted with safety extinguishers.

Coal and gas are both widely used. If cooking alone is considered, gas is by far the more convenient of the two. Gas heat is quickly available and is steadier and more easily regulated than that of coal. Gas stoves are cooler to work at, create less dirt in the kitchen and themselves require less cleaning than coal ranges. Soot does not collect on the pans, there is no smoke, while carrying of coal and stoking are unnecessary. Fumes arise from the gas, but if proper ventilation is arranged are not harmful.

Used with care, gas for cooking is, as a rule, less expensive than coal, and, of course, there is no necessity to burn it when the stove is not in use. The initial cost of gas stoves is less than that of coal stoves, and they can be hired at a very moderate charge. On the other hand, it must be remembered that a coal stove can simultaneously cook food, heat water for household use, warm the kitchen and assist in its ventilation, while if gas is used several pieces of apparatus are required to do all these things. Moreover, a gas cooking stove is useless for drying and airing clothes and for burning kitchen refuse.

Anthracite. This form of solid fuel is used for heat-storage cookers of which the Aga and Esse cookers are examples. The fire box is completely enclosed in the centre of the cooker and the heat is stored in the hot plates and in the walls of the ovens.

Electricity provides heat in a dependable and easily regulated form, free from smoke, fumes or smell; the cookers and ovens take up very little room, and like the utensils used on them, are easily kept clean.

The disadvantage of an electric cooker is lack of variation in temperature control, but the newer types are being fitted with thermostatic control which will give greater flexibility of heat range.

Electric stoves can be hired for quarterly payments, the charge, like that for gas stoves, covering maintenance and repairs.

Coal Ranges. The numerous coal ranges in existence have many features in common, and can be classified as belonging to one of three types:

Type 1. Ranges with an oven on one side of the fire and on the other a non-circulating boiler, fitted for self-supply or requiring to be filled by hand.

Type 2. Ranges with one or more ovens and a self-filling circulating boiler, either behind or at the side of the fire box. The boiler is connected with a system of pipes by means of which the water heated in it is distributed to other parts of the house.[1]

Type 3 (*a*) Ranges with one or more ovens, and a circulating self-filling boiler, devised to serve as a sitting-room grate when not required for cooking. These convertible kitchen-sitting-room ranges are useful in small houses or flats in which the kitchen is also the living-room. (*b*) Back-to-back ranges are sometimes installed, the coal fire in the living-room heating the cooking stove in the kitchen. Research is being carried out to improve this form of cooking stove.

Type 1 is interesting as being the type from which Types 2 and 3, now most commonly used, have been evolved.

Construction and Working of a Coal-Range. Certain points are of importance:

General. (1) The parts should be strongly made and should fit well. The spaces between them should be only just sufficient to allow for the expansion of the iron when the range is heated; if too large spaces are left, much heat is wasted.

(2) There should be ample openings and doors to facilitate the cleaning of every part of the range. The materials used in

[1] An independent boiler connected with the back boiler of the coal range, but capable of being heated by gas when the range is not required, is a useful device. In houses or flats where cooking is done entirely by gas or by electricity the boiler is sometimes put at the back of the living-room fire.

constructing and finishing the range should be as far as possible stainless and rustless, and capable of being easily cleaned. Stainless steel, nickel plating, tiles, vitreous enamel, all diminish cleaning. The only parts which may require black-leading are those in direct contact with the heat, e.g. front bars and the parts of the hot plate directly over the fire.

(3) Duplicates of parts which wear out quickly, e.g. fire-bars, should be obtainable readily.

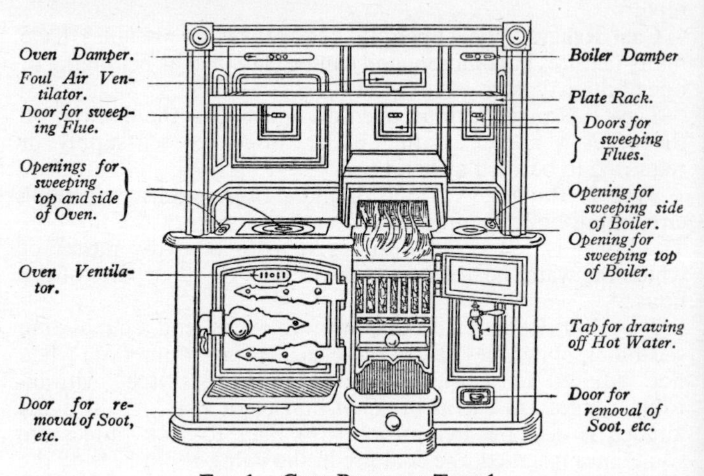

FIG. 1.—COAL RANGE OF TYPE 1.

Firebox. (1) When the boiler is at the back or side of the fire there should be easy access to it for cleaning (Types 1, 2 and 3).

(2) To economise coal (*a*) the bars of the front and floor of the box should be so close together that only the small cinders and ash can pass through; (*b*) there should be a cinder sifter between the firebox and the ashpan.

(3) In ranges of Type 2 the bottom of the firebox should be movable, so that the fire may be made large or small at will. The firebox should also be so constructed that it can be closed or open as desired. For cooking, the closed fire is to be preferred for several reasons:

(*a*) Since the draught is stronger and the combustion of the coal more complete, more heat is obtained in proportion to the amount burnt. (*b*) More heat is available for cooking and less escapes into the room. This makes cooking at the range cooler work. (*c*) The heat of the ovens is more even. (*d*) The hot plate holds more pans at a time, and heavy pans can be pushed

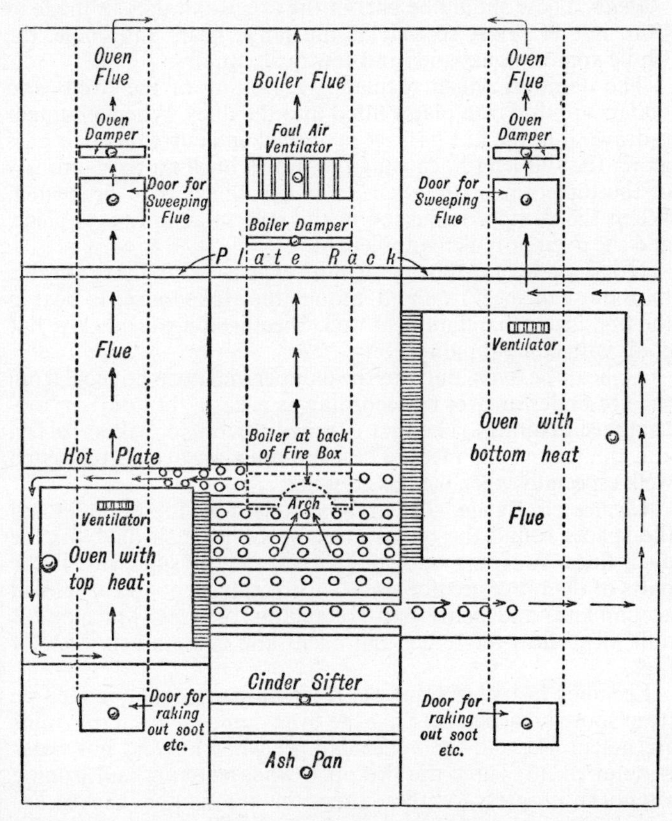

FIG. 2.—DIAGRAM OF COAL STOVE (TYPE 2) TO SHOW ARRANGEMENT OF OVEN AND BOILER FLUES.
(The arrows show the direction of the heat.)

instead of lifted from one part to another. (*e*) Soot does not collect on the pans or fall into them and their contents cannot become smoked.

The closed fire is also advisable for heating irons, but when clothes have to be dried or aired, the open fire is better. When cooking is done, the open fire burns the coal less rapidly and adds to the warmth and cheerfulness of the kitchen.

Flues. These should be part of the range and, like it, made of iron, not of brick, so that as the range heats and cools, the whole apparatus expands and contracts equally.

The dampers which regulate the heating of the ovens and boilers are thin iron plates fitted into the flues. When a damper is drawn out, the flue passage is opened and currents of air pass along the full length, causing the fire to burn more vigorously in the direction of the oven or boiler which is to be heated. When the damper is pushed in the reverse action takes place, and the oven or boiler is cooled.

Ovens made of cast iron are more expensive but more durable than those of sheet iron and, though they take longer to heat in the first instance, retain heat well. Sheet iron heats quickly, but cools with equal rapidity.

To heat the oven, pull out the damper and push hot coal from the fire under or over it, according as it has a 'bottom' or 'top' heat (see diagram). The first is suited for bread, cakes, pastry, and the second for meat. The oven must always be ventilated well, especially when meat is cooking.

Cleaning of Range.[1] The firebox, boiler flue, top of boiler and the spaces round the ovens must be swept each day; for the oven flues, sweeping once or twice weekly is sufficient. If the parts of the range are not swept thoroughly, soot and ashes will accumulate, and being bad conductors of heat, will make it difficult to heat the boiler and ovens and cause much waste of fuel.

Economy in Use of Coal. (1) Keep all parts of the range free from soot and ashes. (2) Shut the oven dampers when the ovens are not in use, and the boiler damper when no very hot water is required. (3) Have the fire open when cooking and ironing are not in progress. At these times the fire may be 'backed up' with sifted cinders and coal dust, which will burn only slowly. (4) Use the small and large coal equally; do not poke the fire oftener than is necessary.

[1] For the cleaning of coal and all other cooking stoves newspaper or other absorbent paper should be freely used to remove surface dirt, grease, rust, etc. It is convenient to have sheets of newspaper hung together by a string near the stove for use in removing grease and small amounts of liquid spilt during cooking.

Aga and Esse Cookers, etc. These are known as continuous burning or heat-storage cookers.

Construction. The stoves consist of:

(*a*) Two or more hot plates with insulated hinged covers to prevent escape of heat when hot plates are not in use.

(*b*) A roasting oven, simmering oven and a medium oven under the fire door. The advantage of this type of cooking stove is that it requires little stoking and is easily regulated.

Instructions issued by the makers for the use of these stoves should be followed carefully.

Gas Cookers. These are either (*a*) burners for boiling, grilling, etc., covered by a hot plate or (*b*) burners as in (*a*) combined

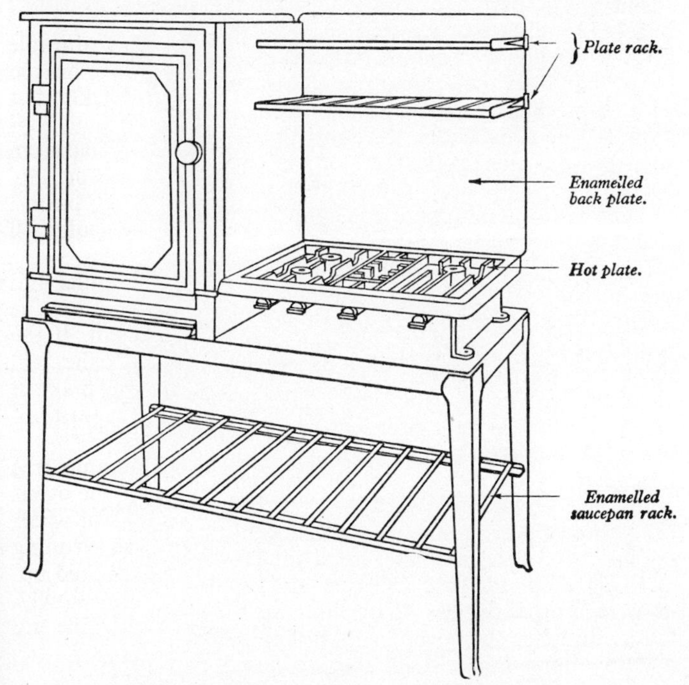

FIG. 3.—SKETCH OF 'EYE-LEVEL' GAS COOKER.

with an oven. The improvements in gas cooking apparatus which are constantly being made all aim at increased efficiency and economy by means of (1) accurate control of the gas supply, coupled with decrease in the amount burnt; (2) lessening the amount of cleaning required; (3) increased ease in manipulation. For example, gas cookers (i.e. combined hot plates and ovens) rest on enamelled stands which raise them from the ground, making it possible to clean the floor underneath and reducing or entirely eliminating the need for stooping to the oven. When the stand is only a few inches from the ground the hot plate rests on top of the oven, but in cookers of the 'eye-level' type (Fig. 3) the hot plate and oven both rest side by side on a stand raised some feet from the ground; below the stand is fixed a rack to hold pans and baking tins.

Burners.[1] These are constructed on the Bunsen principle, burning a mixture of gas and air. This mixture of gas and air gives a far greater heat in proportion to the amount of gas burnt than does the ordinary luminous gas, and does not leave soot, a product of partial combustion, on the outside of the pans. To be satisfactory the construction of a *burner* must be such that (1) the proportions of gas and air can be adjusted correctly to a given gas supply, thus producing the maximum of heat with the minimum consumption of gas combined with freedom from smell; (2) the flame is sent out at an angle which will enable it to spread well over the base of a pan placed over the burner; (3) the burners cannot be choked or the flame extinguished by the boiling over of contents of pans; (4) the burners can be cleaned easily and without interference with the gas and air adjustment; (5) the taps cannot be turned on accidentally. Further, the *bars of the hot plate* should be so arranged as to (1) leave sufficient space round the burner for the gas to burn correctly and without loss of heat such as would be caused by the flames striking the bars; (2) be capable of being cleaned and replaced with as little work as possible; (3) allow of pans being moved smoothly on them. In some cookers part of the hot plate is semi-solid for use with small pans.

To light the Burners. Cookers are usually fitted with gas-igniters or other devices which eliminate the use of matches and tapers. If, when the burner is lit, it 'lights back', i.e. burns with a yellow flame and a slight roaring sound, turn off the tap at once and re-light.

Before lighting the oven burners it is well to leave the door

[1] In the course of recent developments a silent, luminous flame has been tested for its advantage over the usual type of flame.

open for a moment, lest there should have been an accidental escape of gas, due, for example, to mistaking the oven tap for that of a boiler burner. If a light were applied to the oven burners in such circumstances, an explosion might occur.

Grillers must be heated thoroughly before food is put beneath them as the grilling or toasting is done by radiant heat from the red-hot plates and not by the flame itself.

Grillers are sometimes made reversible so that the flame can be directed upwards for boiling as well as downwards for grilling or toasting. These do not grill or toast as rapidly and evenly as those which are not reversible.

Construction of Gas Cookers.

The illustration[1] (Fig. 4) shows a modern gas cooker in side section. The oven is of the latest two-burner, bottom-flue type with welded wire grids and interchangeable grid supports (hangers) which are removable. They are thus not only themselves easily cleaned but leave the oven linings with plain flat surfaces for the same purpose. Fig. 4 shows a removable plinth, with toe space, to hide the burners and bottom framework.

The hot plate is covered by two semi-solid bars in which there are round holes to take the loose pot-supports. There are three boiling and simmering burners, a quick heating grill, a loose enamelled crown plate and a tray for spills.

All the hot plate fittings may be removed without undoing any screws and the space left completely free for cleaning purposes: the grill, for instance, is rigidly supported by a heavy bent wire loop held firmly in a slot from which it may be taken by simply tilting it upwards. All the taps are of the safety type and cannot be turned on inadvertently. The whole cooker is finished with vitreous enamel.

Heating Oven. Before cooking can be done the oven burner or burners must have been lit long enough to heat the entire oven case through. This usually takes 15 to 25 minutes, but the time must necessarily vary with the gas supply and with the size of the oven.

The heating of gas ovens is now thermostatically controlled and the heat controller or 'Regulo' automatically adjusts the supply of gas so that the temperature of the oven can be fixed to suit exactly the particular food or foods to be cooked. They thus need no attention during cooking.

[1] See p. 18.

Cleaning of Gas Cookers. To facilitate cleaning (1) surfaces and mouldings of the cooker should be as smooth and plain as possible; (2) the cooker should be made of material or be finished with material (e.g. stainless metal, nickel plating, porcelain enamel) which reduces cleaning to the minimum; (3)

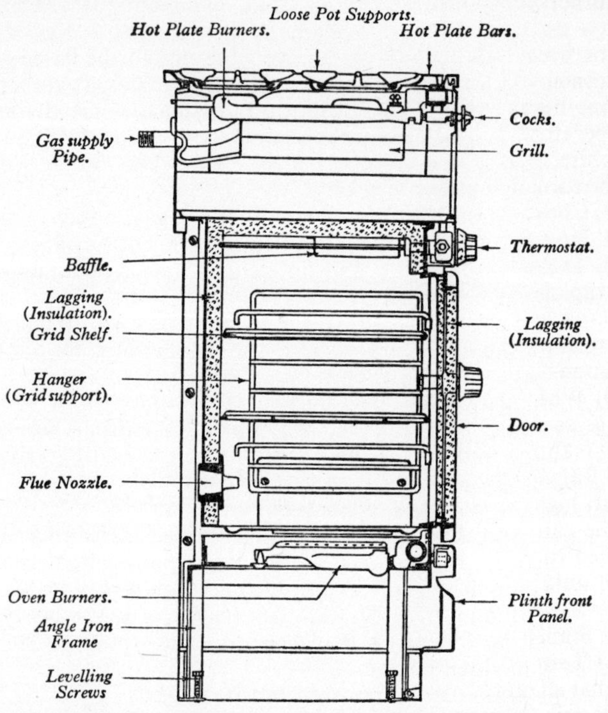

FIG. 4. A MODERN GAS COOKER IN SIDE SECTION.

burners, hot plate fittings and oven fittings should be of simple construction, easily movable and replaceable.

Every part of a gas cooker must be kept quite free from grease. Any grease or liquid must be removed at once, using for the former absorbent paper, followed by a cloth wrung out of hot, soapy water.

Gas cookers are most easily cleaned while still warm. As soon as possible after use, the enamelled parts, the tray for spills, etc., should be wiped with a cloth wrung out of, first, hot soapy water, then out of clean hot water or be washed if necessary and in both cases be dried well. *It is not desirable to use mechanical agents or abrasives* (see p. 27) for enamelled parts as they scratch and gradually destroy the gloss.

Burners, bars and griller plates are best cleaned by rubbing with a pad of paper or, if very greasy, with a rag or piece of cotton waste damped *very slightly* with paraffin or turpentine.

Economy in the Use of Gas. (1) When the boiling and simmering burners and the griller plates are heated to the required temperature, burn only sufficient gas to keep them at that temperature. Burner flames should never extend beyond the base of the cooking utensil.

(2) Choose broad, flat-bottomed pans and keep them free from soot. Do not use pans which have been used on an open fire.

(3) Light the gas oven at the appropriate moment, turning the tap on full. The tap should remain thus throughout the cooking as the 'Regulo' automatically controls the supply of gas to the oven. After lighting the gas, set the 'Regulo' at the required number.

(4) When the oven is to be used, arrange to cook as many things as possible in it, so that one heating suffices. When the oven is thus loaded, e.g. when a complete meal is being cooked, the 'Regulo' number must be raised accordingly, usually two points higher.

The card of instructions supplied by the makers should be studied carefully with regard to this and to the placing on the most suitable shelves of different dishes in the oven.

(5) Always shut the oven door *securely* to avoid escape of heat. Similarly, avoid opening the oven door unnecessarily.

(6) Turn off the gas the instant it is no longer required and see that all taps are turned off completely.

Electric Cookers. These may be (*a*) boiling plates (boilers), or (*b*) boiler-grillers, or (*c*) boiler-grillers combined with ovens as in gas cookers. A main switch by means of which the supply of electricity to the cooker can be switched on or off as required should be fixed near the cooker. When cooking is finished, and when the cooker is being cleaned, the main switch, as well as the switches belonging to the oven, boiling plates and griller respectively, must be turned off.

An electric kettle is a desirable addition to an electric cooker, and is sometimes supplied with it.

Cooker Hob. This, with the rest of the exterior of the cooker, is usually covered with vitreous enamel. The boiling plates have three-heat switches which can be turned to full (or high), medium or low as required. The plates may be (1) open showing the heating elements and giving radiant heat, or (2) enclosed, being covered by a solid metal plate which collects and conducts the heat to the pan placed on it. The open plate heats quickly, but cools with corresponding speed; the enclosed plate heats less rapidly than the open one, but retains heat longer, and is therefore the more suitable of the two for slow, long cooking. In a cooker hob with two or more plates, whether open or enclosed, the plates are so loaded as to give different amounts of heat. Both open and enclosed plates retain heat for a short time after the current has been switched off, and this should therefore be done before cooking is quite completed. When open plates are used, care is needed to prevent milk and syrup-like liquids from boiling over. If this occurs, keep the current on until the deposit has been burnt off; on no account remove it with a knife or spoon or other piece of metal while the current is on.

The *griller* has asbestos placed above it to prevent the escape of heat. It must be made thoroughly hot before use. A deflector is supplied which is used when food is to be cooked on the top of the boiler-griller, in order that all the heat may be concentrated on the hot plate.

Electric Kettle. The elements are in the base of the kettle, hence water heats more rapidly and more economically in a kettle than in a saucepan placed over a boiling-plate. Water for cooking vegetables, steaming puddings, etc., should be brought to the boil in the kettle and then be transferred to the saucepan. The kettle retains heat for a time after the current has been switched off, and for this reason should never be completely emptied of water immediately after use. A layer of water about half an inch deep will suffice to prevent damage to the kettle.

Oven. The oven has a double wall, the space between the two being filled as in a gas cooker with non-conducting material. The oven is ventilated, and a thermometer is often fixed to the door. The shelves and runners are usually fixed to an inner casing, enamel-lined, which can be lifted out bodily for cleaning. The oven elements are put behind the inner wall, either at the top and bottom or at the bottom and sides. The top of the oven is the hottest part.

Heating Oven. The oven switch can be switched on to give 'low', 'medium' or 'full' heat as required. When the switch is turned on at 'full' the oven heats rapidly. If the initial temperature is to be maintained throughout, keeping the switch at 'low' should suffice. Opening the oven door reduces the temperature, and when this is necessary, the switch must be turned on *momentarily* to 'full'. The current should be switched off for the last 15 minutes of the cooking as the oven retains heat well. When the oven has been in use for some time, the heat remaining will often suffice to complete the cooking of a milk pudding or stewed fruit. The residual heat can be utilised for drying crusts of bread.

Cleaning. This should be done regularly each time the cooker is used, preferably while it is still hot. First turn off all boiler, griller and oven switches and also the main switch. Remove grease and any food spilt on the cooker hob with pads of newspaper, followed by a cloth wrung *tightly* out of hot water. No water must touch the elements, either those of the boiling plates or those of the oven. Clean the interior of the oven, including the top and door, in the same manner. If cleaning of the oven has been neglected, a mechanical cleaning agent (see p. 27) or a cleaning preparation sold for the purpose may be needed.

COOKING UTENSILS

Iron, tin, copper, brass, aluminium, enamel, earthenware, glass and wood are all used in the manufacture of cooking utensils.

Iron is used chiefly for saucepans; wrought iron pans are the more expensive of the two, but are also the more durable. Iron rusts quickly and is liable to discolour foods; iron pans are therefore lined with tin or enamel, which do not rust.

Tin. In tin-lined pans, the tin-wash should be of good quality; a cheap tin-wash not only wears out soon but melts, forming roughness on the sides of the pans which make them difficult to clean. Even a good quality of tin melts unless care is taken, and flames must never be allowed to come up the sides of a pan which is filled only partially. Iron stewpans to be used for stews in which meat undergoes a preliminary frying or for 'deep frying,' in which a large quantity of fat is heated, should always be bought *without* the tin-lining.

Tin is a comparatively expensive metal and so-called tin

utensils, fish kettles, cake tins, etc., are made of iron dipped in molten tin. This tin covering, if it is not so thin as to be almost non-existent, easily wears through, exposing the iron foundation which rusts readily. Tin utensils must therefore be dried thoroughly after use and be kept in a dry place.

It is not advisable to use either tin or tin-lined pans for cooking fruit and other acid foods. If the coating of tin is not perfect, the acid may act on the iron and the food have a disagreeable flavour and colour.

Brass and Copper. Both these are more expensive than iron, but make very durable utensils. The drawbacks to their use are that (*a*) poisonous verdigris, recognisable by its green colour, quickly forms on them if they are not kept perfectly dry and that (*b*) they readily become tarnished and discoloured. Copper pans and moulds are often lined with tin, which tarnishes less readily. Care must be taken to renew the tin lining when the first signs of its wearing away appear lest verdigris form on the exposed copper. All brass and copper utensils must be kept dry, clean and bright.

Aluminium. This metal does not rust or tarnish, is not acted upon by weak acids and does not contain poisonous substances. It is a rapid conductor of heat and is not harmed by heating to high temperatures. Aluminium utensils are light, unbreakable and easily cleaned. Utensils of stamped aluminium are more durable than those made of cast aluminium.

Enamel. The drawback to the use of enamel for lining pans is that it does not expand equally with the foundation material. After being in use for some time the enamel first cracks, then becomes chipped, exposing a crumbling white substance under the glaze. It is not desirable that chipped enamel should mix with the food, if only because it may set up irritation in the body; moreover, cheap qualities of enamel contain a certain percentage of poisonous lead oxide.

Besides pans lined with enamel, a light, inexpensive pan with an outer as well as an inner coating of enamel, is obtainable. Such pans are not very durable and the foundation material is so thin that foods cooked in them burn easily.

Enamel pans are useful for such foods as milk which quickly absorb flavours, for foods which are easily discoloured and for foods containing acids, since these have no effect on enamel. Enamel utensils are easily kept clean and imperfect washing can be detected readily. For pie dishes, mixing-basins, etc., enamel is lighter and more durable than earthenware, though rough usage, by causing it to chip, makes it useless.

Fireproof glass and china utensils are clean, do not discolour foods, retain heat well and food can be both cooked and served in them. They may crack, however, if brought into direct contact with heat or subjected to sudden extremes of temperature. They must heat gradually and while hot must not come into contact with damp cloths, cold water or cold surfaces. Both fireproof glass and china can be used in the oven *only*.

CHAPTER III

THE CLEANING OF KITCHEN EQUIPMENT AND UTENSILS

In order that the cooking of food may be done under the most wholesome conditions, a high standard of cleanliness must be maintained in the kitchen departments. It follows then that the theory and practice of cleaning must be thoroughly understood. We shall have to consider:

(1) The nature of the substances which collect on utensils or other kitchen equipment and make cleaning necessary.

(2) The nature and action of the cleaning agents in common use.

(3) The principles underlying *all* cleaning processes, irrespective of the nature of the material which is to be cleaned.

(4) Practical points relating to the cleaning of different materials and utensils.

Cleaning is necessitated by:

(1) *The presence in air of*:

(*a*) *Dust*, with its invisible organic matter and grease.

(*b*) *Oxygen and carbon-dioxide*, which, in the presence of moisture, form respectively rust on steel and iron, and poisonous verdigris on copper and brass.

(*c*) *Compounds of carbon and sulphur* caused by the burning of gas and coal, with *various gases* arising from drains, sewers and manufactories. These tarnish polished metals, copper, brass, tin, etc., forming carbonates, sulphides, etc., of the metals. Copper and brass tarnish most readily; tin less readily.

(2) *Cooking processes* causing the formation on or in utensils of (*a*) soot, (*b*) condensed steam, often greasy, (*c*) grease or remains of food, the latter sometimes burnt, (*d*) stains on metals caused by acids, which form with the metals dark-coloured salts, e.g., stains on an (untreated) steel knife used to cut lemons, apples, all of which contain acids.[1]

CLASSIFICATION OF CLEANING AGENTS

A. **Grease Removers.**[2]

(1) *Hot water.*
(2) *Alkalis.* Soda, soap, soap-powders, ammonia, etc.
(3) *Solvents.* Paraffin, turpentine, methylated spirit, etc.

B. **Tarnish and Verdigris Removers.**

(1) *Mechanical agents* (see below).
(2) *Acids* (*a*) *Weak acids.* Lemon juice, diluted vinegar, etc.
(*b*) *Strong acids.* Oxalic acid, hydrochloric acid, etc.

C. **Mechanical Agents,** i.e. mineral powders and other substances which act mechanically by friction.

Examples. (*a*) Brickdust or powdered bathbrick, silver sand, whitening (precipitated chalk), salt, etc.

(*b*) Copper, brass and steel filings, steel wool (coarse or fine), etc.

(*c*) Prepared mechanical agents (home-made and manufactured) which usually contain both mechanical agents and alkalis.

D. **Preventives of Rust.**

On iron. (*a*) Blacklead, (*b*) enamel and other preparations for coating iron.

On steel (untreated). Sweet oil, mutton fat, tallow, vaseline.[3]

[1] Stainless steel cutlery is not, of course, affected.

[2] Paper (e.g. tissue paper, newspaper, blotting paper), though not a cleaning agent in the usual sense, is useful for absorbing and removing grease accidentally spilt.

[3] Rustless and stainless steel or steel which is plated with nickel or enamel or is otherwise protected does not, of course, require preventive treatment.

NATURE, ACTION AND USE OF CLEANING AGENTS

A. **Grease Removers.**

(1) **Hot Water** is much used in combination with alkalis for the removal of grease, by which dust and stains are often held. It prepares the way for the action of alkalis by melting the grease and by the speed with which it evaporates gives brightness and gloss to utensils washed in it.

Experiment. Take two greasy plates (*a*) and (*b*). Wash (*a*) in tepid water, (*b*) in water which is almost boiling, using a mop in both cases. Put both to drain, and compare the results. Notice that hot water alone is sufficient to remove small quantities of grease.

(2) **Alkalis.** These are necessary for the removal of grease in any but the smallest quantity. They form with the grease emulsions which are easily removable by water. A fat is said to be emulsified when it is broken up into very tiny globules, such as occur in the natural emulsion, milk.

Experiment 1. Shake a little oil and water together in a test tube, and leave undisturbed for a short time. The oil and water at first appear to mix, but soon separate on standing.

Experiment 2. Repeat, adding a little soda-solution. The addition of soda emulsifies the oil so that it is capable of being carried away by water.

Experiment 3. Repeat Experiment 2, substituting soap and soap-powder in turn for soda.

Soda is a strong and cheap form of alkali. It emulsifies grease, but it also destroys the colour and gilt of china and the colour of wood; it softens paint and varnish and has a corrosive action on the skin of the hands and on metals. Soda must not be used for aluminium utensils, since it attacks the protective film of aluminium oxide which forms on the surface, and roughens the aluminium, wearing it away. Soda should not be used for utensils of any kind unless it is really needed, and then only sparingly; it must always be removed by thorough rinsing.

Soap. A certain quantity of alkali is present in soap; when soap is dissolved in water, its alkali emulsifies grease, so that the dirt entangled with it can be removed. Soap has a strong taste and smell and must be applied sparingly, particularly to such absorbent surfaces as wood. Every trace of soap must be removed by rinsing utensils thoroughly.

Soap-powders. These have a basis of soda with the addition of small quantities of dried soap and other cleansing agents. Being in a finely divided form they act readily on grease, but apart from this they are no more efficient than soda and soap, and are more expensive. What has already been said as to the use of soda and soap applies also to soap-powders.

Ammonia is in the form of a gas dissolved in water. The gas escapes quickly, and ammonia is therefore less likely to injure utensils than the solid alkalis. It is too expensive to be used freely.

(3) **Solvents.** These do not emulsify grease but dissolve it. The removal of the grease is usually hastened and completed by friction, often assisted in the case of polished metals by mechanical agents.

Paraffin and Turpentine spread easily over the utensil to be cleaned, just as paraffin spreads over a lamp; they evaporate readily, giving a gloss to the surface to which they are applied. They have a strong taste and cannot be used for utensils which are brought into contact with food. Of the two, paraffin has the more powerful action on grease and dirt, but turpentine evaporates more quickly so that less friction is required to produce a polish.

Methylated Spirit, like all forms of alcohol, removes grease. Its taste is much less marked than that of turpentine or paraffin, and it evaporates very quickly.

All three solvents are highly inflammable. They are used with mechanical agents for the cleaning of metals which it is important to keep dry in order to prevent rust or verdigris, or on which a high polish is desired.

B. **Tarnish and Verdigris Removers.**

(1) *Mechanical Agents.* These rub off the polished metals the tarnish formed by atmospheric and sulphur compounds.

(2) *Acids.* (*a*) *Weak Acids.* Lemon juice (citric acid), vinegar (acetic acid) diluted with water and other harmless weak acids are used with mechanical agents when the latter alone are ineffective. The acid decomposes the tarnish, and the mechanical agent assists its removal. *Verdigris* is removed from copper and brass in the same way. Lemon juice is preferable to vinegar, but if either is used for cooking utensils, thorough washing at once in hot water with a little soda is essential.

(*b*) *Strong Acids.* Oxalic, hydrochloric and other strong acids are used to clean neglected brass and copper; all are poisonous and must be used with caution, and are best avoided for cooking utensils.

Metals cleaned with acids re-tarnish rapidly, unless the compounds formed by the acids are removed at once either by washing the metals or by rubbing them with powder which at the same time polishes them or by both processes.

Patent Metal Polishes. In addition to brickdust, rotten-stone, these often contain strong poisonous acids and paraffin or other inflammable substances. They must not be left where they could by any chance catch fire, and their use should be confined to non-cooking utensils. Patent preparations give metals a high polish and apparently leave them clean, but if they are rubbed with a white cloth, they are seen to be covered with a film of dark-coloured substance intended to protect the metal from atmospheric tarnish or stain.

C. **Mechanical Agents.** These assist in removing grease, tarnish, stains, rust and verdigris by increasing the friction. Their action is purely mechanical and is something like that of a fine file which grinds away the surface to which it is applied.

The agent must be chosen according to the nature of the material to be cleaned. Brickdust, for example, must only be used for substances which will not show scratches.

D. **Preventives of Rust.**

(1) *Blacklead* applied regularly to iron prevents the formation of rust by keeping out the atmospheric moisture. (Compare the rapid rusting of iron stoves or grates in an unoccupied house.)

To apply blacklead, mix it to the thickness of cream with a little water and add a few drops of turpentine to assist polishing. *Commercial grate polishes* consist of blacklead already prepared in this manner. The lid or cap of the container should be fixed on firmly after use to keep the grate polish from drying. All blacklead polishes should be used sparingly. If the range is very greasy from neglect, rub it first with turpentine: blacklead and grate polishes cannot be applied with success to greasy surfaces.

The only iron surfaces to which blacklead should be applied regularly are those parts of cooking stoves and similar pieces of apparatus which are in close and constant contact with heat, e.g. bars of the fire box, parts of hot plate directly over the fire. Objectionable as blacklead is, and frequent as must be its application, it seems at the moment the best means of protecting surfaces such as these from rust. Other parts of cooking stoves not in close contact with heat and not already protected from the action of the atmosphere by tiles, nickel-plating, etc., should be coated with 'heat resisting' enamel or similar preparations which do away with the necessity for constant blackleading. Thus treated, wiping with a damp cloth and polishing with a dry one will suffice. The coating should be renewed as required.

(2) *Sweet Oil* is used to moisten brickdust for the regular cleaning of untreated steel. It does not evaporate as do turpentine and paraffin, and a thin film of damp-resisting grease is left on the steel.

(3) *Mutton-fat*, *Tallow*, *Vaseline* are all used to coat untreated steel which is not to be in regular use for some time.

PRINCIPLES OF CLEANING

All cleaning processes, whatever the nature and material of the thing to be cleaned, involve firstly, the loosening of the grease, stain or tarnish, and secondly, the removal of the loosened substance by friction, a process sometimes completed by the use of water which finally carries away the dirt.

It is important to remember that:

(1) The agents used and the manner in which they are applied must be such as will not harm the utensil or, in the case of a cookery utensil, make it unfit for use by leaving an objectionable smell and taste.

In the case of metals the processes must be such as will leave the metals perfectly dry, and as far as possible in a condition to resist the action of atmospheric moisture and gases.

(2) The construction of some utensils, e.g., wire sieves, is such that special care is needed to remove completely all trace of soap or other agents used, and to ensure dryness.

(3) Much labour can be saved by (*a*) wiping up at once anything which is spilt, especially grease for which soft absorbent paper should be used; (*b*) wiping at once metals on which water has been spilt or which have been in contact with acids, so that rust, verdigris and stains respectively shall not form, and (*c*) by removing rust as soon as it is noticed.

(4) Utensils of all kinds last longer if they are *kept* in good order and not allowed to become so neglected as to require strong measures or prolonged cleaning.

WASHING-UP

A. **Preparations.**

(1) Collect and sort all utensils to be washed.

(2) *Pans*. (*a*) Remove any soot from the outside of the pans, using first an old knife, then a hard, dry brush; collect the soot on a piece of paper. (*b*) Pour off any grease and wipe the pans with soft paper; if still greasy, fill with hot water and soda and bring the water to the boil. (*c*) Scrape away any particles of food which still cling to the pans. Fill with cold or tepid water pans used for cooking (*a*) albuminous foods, e.g. raw minced meat or fish, eggs, milk; (*b*) starchy foods, e.g. cornflour and all cereals; (*c*) gelatine. Hot water would cause albumens and starches to cling more firmly to the utensils and would dissolve gelatine, spreading it in a thin film over the utensil where it would set as it cooled.

(3) *Plates, dishes, etc.* Scrape these to remove remains of food and grease still clinging to them. These make the washing water objectionable and entail unnecessary use of soap.

All scraps of food should be burnt as soon as is practicable.

B. **Washing.**

(1) Utensils should be washed as far as possible immediately after use. Pans, baking sheets and roasting tins, in particular, are most easily washed while still hot.

(2) Wash the cleanest things first, and wash all utensils both inside and out. Use plenty of very hot water, add more hot water as the first becomes cool, and change it whenever it becomes at all dirty. The use of really hot water diminishes the need for soda and other alkalis, and the washing is much less harmful to the utensil. If necessary, use pan-scrapers or brushes for pans, baking sheets, etc.; use scrubbing brushes for strainers and sieves.

(3) Rinse all utensils thoroughly, especially wooden utensils which have been washed with soap and sand, and metal utensils for which soda has been used.

(4) Drain and dry the utensils, using a dish-cloth wrung tightly out of clean, hot water to dry pans, baking tins, etc. To prevent rust and verdigris, complete the drying of all utensils of which metal forms a part by putting them in the sun or near the fire. Dry wooden utensils thoroughly and put them in the sun, when possible, to whiten them.

(5) When all the utensils are washed, rinse the brushes first in hot, then in cold water, the latter to stiffen the bristles. Wash dish-cloths, mops, pan-scrapers, etc., in hot soapy water, rinse and put to dry, preferably in the open air. Dish-cloths and mops should be kept exclusively for washing dishes and should be boiled whenever washing fails to keep them white. Towels used for wiping dishes should be dried after each time of using, and washed daily.

Too great stress can hardly be laid on the importance of the cleanliness of the water and also of the mops, dish-cloths and towels used in washing-up. If the last three are left soiled by the remains of food and grease, they acquire a disagreeable smell and provide excellent growing ground for bacteria, which they must inevitably transfer to the dishes for the so-called cleansing of which they are next used.

Additional Directions for Cleaning Cookery Utensils

Pans (Aluminium).[1] Wash with soap and water, not with soda; use whitening or other soft mechanical agent or fine steel wool to remove anything which sticks. After using these agents rinse the pans thoroughly. Wipe with a dish-cloth wrung out of hot water. These pans neither rust nor tarnish.

Pans (Brass and Copper). Wash in hot soapy water, scour with whitening or prepared mechanical agent. Remove tarnish and verdigris with salt and a lemon skin. Wash quickly and completely, dry thoroughly. Patent metal polishes must *not* be used.

Pans (Enamel). Wash in hot soapy water. Remove stains and burn marks with crushed egg-shells or salt, etc. Rinse and dry.

Pans (Iron and Tin-Lined). Scour with soap and prepared mechanical agent. Rinse and dry well, putting them near the fire to complete drying.

Pan Lids. Wash both inside and out with soapy water, scouring, if necessary, with a prepared mechanical agent or with whitening. Rinse, wipe and dry. Metal polishes must *not* be used.

Frying-basket. Wipe with paper while still hot, scrub with hot water and soda. Rinse thoroughly, wipe as dry as possible, and put near the fire to complete the drying.

[1] Shelves for holding pans should be made of strips of wood so that air can get to the pans and prevent their becoming musty. If the shelves are made of one piece of wood only, the pans should be placed so that they project a little over the edge.

Griller Pan, Trivet and Deflector Plates. Wash after use and remove stains with a prepared mechanical agent or with whitening, or other soft mechanical agent.

Egg-beaters and Wire Whisks, etc. Wash in warm water, giving special attention to the junction of the wires and the handle. Dry carefully and put near the fire.

Strainers, Potato Mashers, Sieves. Scrub in hot soapy water. Use a *wooden* skewer to remove any food collected in the joints. Scrub the woodwork of sieves. Rinse, wipe and dry out of doors in the sun or near a fire.

Mincing Machines. Remove any food, if necessary, before taking the machine to pieces. Wash in soapy water, rinse and dry well.

Cake and Patty Tins. Wipe while hot, first with paper, then with a dish-cloth wrung tightly out of hot water. Dry near the fire or in the oven. If cake, jam, etc., clings to the tins, soak them in warm water before washing.

Knives. Wipe greasy blades with paper. Wash the blades in soapy water, using a mechanical agent, if necessary, to remove stains. Wipe the handles only; putting them into hot water loosens the resin which holds the blades in place. Stainless knives need no further treatment. Polish knives of untreated steel with emery or knife powder, wipe first with a knife cloth, then with a soft towel.

Wooden Utensils. Scrub with plenty of warm water, using as little soap as possible. Use silver sand occasionally to keep the wood white. Rinse well, first in warm, then in cold water, and take care to remove every trace of sand used. Rub as dry as possible to prevent discoloration, and put in the sun to bleach.

Pastry Brushes. Wash in warm soapy water, avoid soda, rinse in cold water to stiffen bristles, dry and twirl between the hands to separate the bristles. Dry in the sun or near the fire.

CONSTRUCTION AND CLEANSING OF SINKS

Treatment of Sink.

Dirt of any kind which is allowed to collect in the sink or waste pipe is certain to contain some organic matter, which in due time will decompose and betray itself by unwholesome smells. Hence it is essential to keep both the sink and the waste pipe thoroughly clean and to see that the pipe does not become blocked up.

The following are the measures to be taken:

(1) Small pieces of food, e.g. tea-leaves, potato peelings, must be collected in a sink basket and must not be allowed to remain in the sink or to go down the pipe. Fat, also, must never be poured down the pipe. It hardens there and is very difficult to remove.

(2) Cleaning water containing brickdust and silver sand or other gritty material in any quantity, dirty water used for

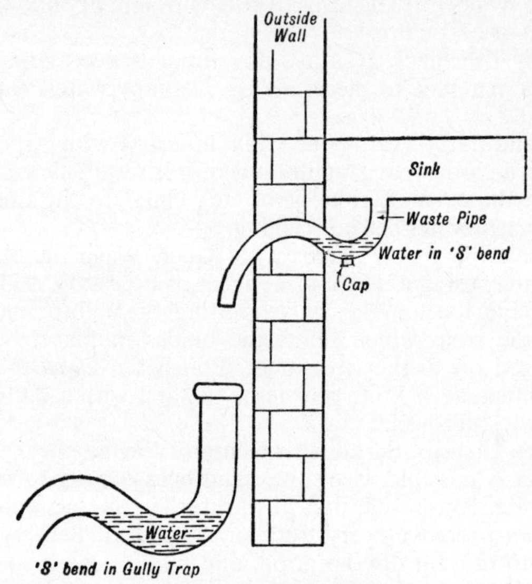

FIG. 5.—SECTION OF SINK.

scrubbing floors must be poured straight down the outside gully and not down the sink.

(3) Strong-smelling water in which cabbage and other green vegetables have been boiled must also be poured straight into the gully, and should first be allowed to go cold.

(4) After washing up, clean the sink and send down clean water so that the water in the bends of the pipe and gully is clean.

At the end of each day flush the sink and the waste pipe with (a) boiling water and soda, the former to disinfect the pipe and trap as far as possible and the latter to emulsify grease; (*b*) hot water to remove the emulsified grease; (*c*) clean cold water to remain in the bend. Empty the water from a can at a short distance above the sink. Its force will cleanse the pipe far more effectually than that of a gentle flow of water.

Once a week, in addition to hot water and soda, pour down the sink some strong disinfectant, such as carbolic acid.

If the waste pipe should become blocked up, unscrew the cap and remove the obstruction with a pliable cane or wire.

Treatment of Kitchen Refuse.

All kitchen refuse, except such inorganic matter as ashes, tins, should be burnt speedily, especially in summer. Animal or vegetable refuse, though useless as food for man, nourishes bacteria, which cause it to decay rapidly, to give off offensive smells and to become a danger to health.

Such decomposing refuse is a double source of danger in that it encourages the presence of flies, both house-flies and blue-bottles, which, after coming into contact with every kind of objectionable material, enter houses and settle on food. Apart from this, flies are highly undesirable; they act as bacteria-carriers, carrying not only those species which cause food to decay but also those which spread disease, notably typhoid fever, and the summer diarrhoea which accounts for so much loss of life among very young children.

Burning is the safest way of disposing of organic refuse not suitable for pigs or poultry or for the garden compost heap. Otherwise, providing they are no longer usable, bones from meat and fish, fat from meat, dripping, together with waste vegetable leaves and parings, egg-shells, etc., should be burnt, if a suitable fire is available, while the fire is still hot. If the grate is closed and the dampers pulled out, the rubbish will burn quickly with the minimum of smell.

Dust Bins.

Should it not be possible to use organic refuse as suggested above and should there be no facilities for burning, it should be stored for short periods of time only, pending its removal by the sanitary authorities. The bin should be made of galvanised iron and fitted with a lid. It must never be filled so full that it cannot be covered closely. If it is left uncovered, the refuse will attract flies, and sun, air and rain will all hasten its decay. Many medical officers of health advise wrapping the rubbish in paper before putting it in the bin, a plan which reduces the fly pest considerably and makes the emptying of the bin into the scavenger's cart much less objectionable.

Dust bins must be cleansed frequently, especially in summer, by means of very hot water, soda and an old broom; after rinsing, they should dry in the sun. These measures should prevent smells, but if they fail, some strong disinfectant must be used.

PART TWO

FOODS AND COOKERY

CHAPTER IV

THE BUYING OF FOODS

The buying of food is a very important part of housekeeping, and if indifferently done involves much waste, not only of money, but also of time and labour. Care and discrimination are especially necessary in the buying of perishable foods. Conspicuous among these are meat, which accounts for so large a proportion of the average household's expenditure on food, and fish, the freshness of which is extremely important.

BUYING OF MEAT

Among the general signs of good quality in meat are the firmness and elasticity of the flesh; if pressed, the mark quickly disappears. Good meat is quite free from disagreeable smell, and any fluid on the surface is watery and not viscid.

Meat with a moderate amount of fat is best. Very lean meat is often tough and flavourless, while very fat meat is wasteful. In choosing joints, the proportion of bone and fat to lean should be considered.

The Hanging of Meat.

Meat is hung by the butcher in a cool, dry, airy place for some days before it is cooked, the time being regulated by the season of the year, the weather and the nature of the meat. During the hanging the stiffening of the muscles, which comes on soon after the animal is killed, passes away, and the meat becomes tender and well-flavoured. It remains in this state for a short time, then bacterial action and, consequently, decomposition set in. Lamb, veal and pork are hung for a few days only, as the changes succeed each other rapidly; beef and mutton are hung for a week or longer unless the weather is warm or close. The length of time for which meat has been hung may be judged by the darkening of the colour of the lean and fat and by the condition of the cut surface. As the meat hangs, the surface becomes drier; if it becomes more moist, it is a sign that the meat has been hung too long.

Imported Meat. This has to be kept at a low temperature for the time necessary to bring it to this country. When the meat is taken out of the refrigerator it begins to thaw and the surface appears moist. It does not keep as well as home-produced meat.

Mutton. *Signs of Good Quality.*

Fat, hard and very white. Lean, dull red where it is newly cut, reddish-purple where it is seen through the skin, as in parts of the leg. Flesh, plump, fine-grained and dry.

The usual method of cutting up a sheep is shown in the diagram.

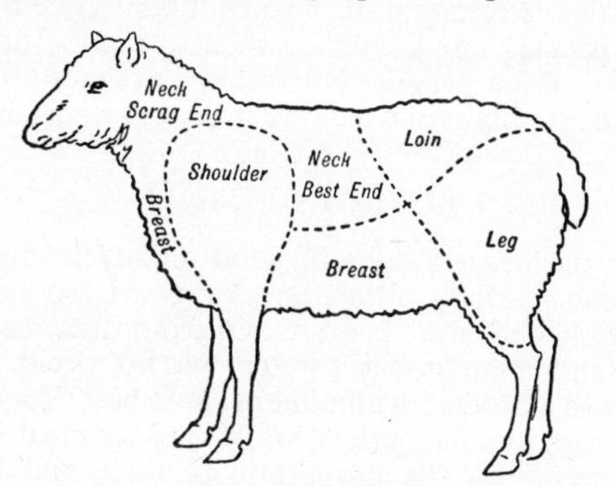

FIG. 6.—JOINTS OF MUTTON.

Joints of Mutton. *Leg of mutton* contains the greatest quantity of meat in proportion to bone and fat, and is a good roasting piece. *Shoulder* has a larger proportion of bone than the leg and is often rather fat. Both legs and shoulders should be short and plump. The meat of the *loin* is juicy and tender, but the large proportion of fat and bone makes it an uneconomical joint; if the kidney is taken out and much of the suet which surrounds it left in, the loin is still more wasteful.

The weights given in the table on p. 37 are the average weights of joints of mutton of ordinary size. Larger joints can be got, but the meat is of coarser grain and contains more bone and fat in proportion to lean.

The weights of joints cut from small Welsh and Scotch sheep correspond roughly to those of lamb.

Methods of Cooking Mutton.[1]

Joint	*Average Weight*	*Average[2] Price per lb.*	*Possible Methods of Cooking*
Shoulder.	6 lbs.		Roast whole, *or* bone, stuff and roast. To make a small joint, remove the piece under the shoulder blade and use for 'made' dish.
Neck (Scrag).	2 lbs.		Stew, *or* make into broth. If a portion of best end of neck is attached, it makes a small joint suitable for boiling.
Neck (Best)	3½ lbs.		Roast whole, *or* divide into cutlets and fry or grill, etc.
Loin	4½ lbs.		Roast whole, *or* bone, stuff, roll and roast. *Or*, cut best end (near neck) into chops and fry or grill; make the remainder into stew or curry, or into a pie.
Leg	8 lbs.		Roast or boil whole. *Or*, cut into two across the bone, roast the upper or broader end and steam, boil or stew the lower portion. Slices or fillets may be cut from the upper end for frying or grilling.
Breast	1½ lbs.		Stew *or* make into broth.

Lamb. *Signs of Good Quality.*

Fat, hard and white with a faintly bluish tinge. Lean, pale pink colour.

Joints of Lamb. Lamb is cut up in the same way as mutton. When it is first in season and very small, it is often divided into two *forequarters* (shoulder, neck and breast) and two *hind-quarters* (loin and leg). The average weight of a leg of lamb is 5 lbs., of a shoulder 4 lbs.

Beef. *Signs of Good Quality.*

Fat, cream or faint yellow colour. If the fat is a bright yellow, the animal has probably been fed on oil-cake and the meat will

[1] These tables are given here for convenience. The principles underlying the choice of the cookery process for each piece of meat are explained in subsequent chapters.

[2] The current prices may be inserted here.

be coarse and greasy. If there is very little fat, the animal is either old or underfed. Lean should be a bright cherry-red colour and more moist on the surface than mutton. A 'marbled' appearance of the lean, due to the presence of fat between the muscle fibres, is a sign of particularly good quality.

Joints of Beef. *Sirloin* is divided into three pieces. The 'middle-cut' is best since it has the tender fillet or 'under-cut'. *Ribs* are cut according to the weight desired; cuts of ribs are more wasteful than cuts of sirloin. The three-cornered piece nearest the sirloin, the 'wing-rib', is a good joint with only one short bone.

Rump provides the best quality of steak. Steaks are also cut from the *shoulder* and from the *round.*

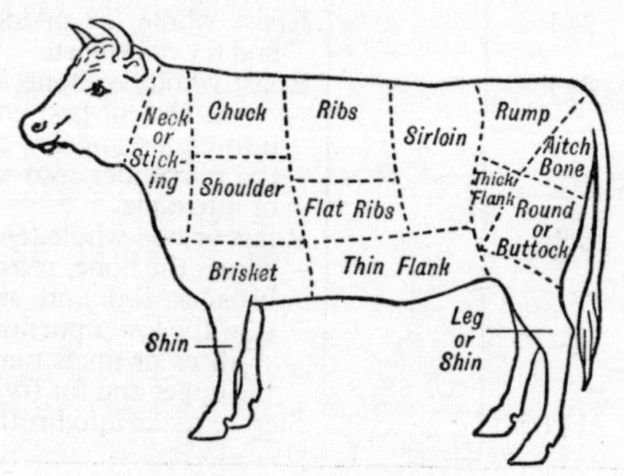

FIG. 7.—JOINTS OF BEEF.

Aitchbone. This joint has bones which make it an awkward shape and difficult to carve; it is therefore low-priced. The proportion of bone is rather large, but the joint is otherwise economical and the meat tender and of good quality, though somewhat lean.

Round is divided into two parts, the innermost, the 'thick' or 'top' side, and the outermost, the 'thin' or 'silver' side.

Weights of Cuts of Beef.

Cuts of Sirloin and Round	- -	4-14 lbs.
„ Ribs	- - - - - -	2½-12 lbs.
„ Brisket	- - - - -	4-12 lbs.

Methods of Cooking Beef.

Joint	*Average[1] Price per lb.*	*Possible Methods of Cooking*
Brisket		Pickle and boil ***or*** bone, spice and boil for 'pressed' beef.
Shoulder (steaks)		Use for 'made' dishes, e.g. pies, puddings, stews, and for making into potted meat.
Ribs		Roast whole *or* bone, roll and roast.
Flat Ribs.		Roast, *or* pickle and boil.
Sirloin		Roast whole, *or* bone, roll and roast. *Or*, remove fillet, then bone, roll and roast.
		Roast fillet whole *or* cut into slices and grill or fry.
		The thin end of the sirloin may be cut off and pickled, boiled and served cold.
Rump		Roast upper portion, *or* cut into steaks and grill or fry.
Aitchbone		Roast or boil *or* use part for potting and part for stew or 'made' dishes.
Round (Topside)		Roast or boil *or* salt and boil; use for 'made' dishes or for making into potted meat.[2]
Round (Thin Side)		Salt and boil *or* use for 'made' dishes.
Leg (Gravy Beef)		Use for cheaper stews and for good quality of stock.
Shin		Use for stock.

Veal.

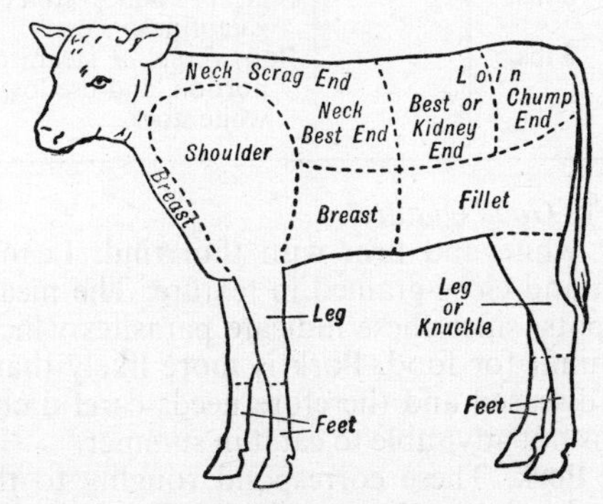

FIG. 8.—JOINTS OF VEAL.

[1] The current prices may be inserted here.

[2] A process best described as cooking meat in its own juices is admirably suited to the cooking of small pieces of topside. See footnote on p. 93.

Veal. *Signs of Good Quality.*

Fat, white, firm and more transparent than that of mutton or beef. Lean, pale pink, fine-grained, very dry and rather less firm and close in texture than that of other meats. Veal which is damp and flabby or which shows yellowish-green spots is unwholesome.

Joints of Veal. The *fillet* is the best and most economical part for roasting, for cutlets and for pies or other 'made' dishes. *Loin*: chump end has more bone than the kidney end.

Methods of Cooking Veal.

Joint	*Average Weight*	*Average*[1] *Price per lb.*	*Possible Methods of Cooking*
Shoulder	7 lbs.		Roast whole *or* bone, stuff and roast.[2]
Neck (Scrag)	3 lbs.		Stew *or* use for broth.
Neck (Best)	4 lbs.		Roast whole *or* divide into cutlets and fry.
Loin (Chump)	3–4 lbs.		Roast.
Loin (Kidney)	3–4 lbs.		Roast whole *or* bone, stuff and roast *or* cut into chops and fry.
Fillet	Any weight		Roast, *or* bone, stuff and roast, *or* cut into fillets and fry. Use for all 'made' dishes.[2]
Breast	6 lbs.		Boil, *or* bone, stuff and roll for galantine *or* stew.
Knuckle	3 lbs.		Boil whole, *or* steam or stew upper portion, and use lower portion for white stock.

Pork. *Signs of Good Quality.*

Fat, very white and firm with thin rind. Lean, pale pink colour, firm and close-grained in texture. The meat should be free from spots, since these indicate parasites which make the meat quite unfit for food. Pork is more likely than any other meat to be diseased and therefore needs careful choosing and cooking; it is not advisable to eat it in summer.

Joints of Pork. These correspond roughly to the joints of mutton. The *leg*, *loin* and *spare rib* (the part above the shoulder) are most used and are generally roasted. The loin provides chops.

[1] The current prices may be inserted here.
[2] See also recipe on p. 93 for veal cooked in its own juices.

Ham and Bacon. A ham is the hind leg of the animal, gammon the fore-leg; both are preserved by salting and smoking. Bacon is the flank similarly prepared.

Suet is internal fat and should be fresh and free from any suspicion of taint. That from round the kidneys is best. Beef suet should be pale yellow, mutton suet very white, firm and dry. 'Kernels' or glands, veins and any part which, when the suet is cut through, is seen to be discoloured with blood, should be removed at once or the suet will become tainted. If it acquires a slight smell, it should be clarified at once according to the directions on page 189.

BUYING OF FISH

Fish should be bought when it is in season, since it is then cheapest and its flavour is at its best. Fish so quickly becomes unwholesome that it is important that it should be very fresh when bought. Herrings and mackerel in particular keep fresh only for a very short time. Cod and turbot are by some people considered to be better for being kept a day or two.

The *freshness of fish* may be judged by:

Smell. This should be fresh and not at all disagreeable.

Colour. This should be even and not mottled. Flat fish should be examined on both sides; the dark-coloured skin shows signs of staleness sooner than the white. In plaice the spots should be bright red; if they are a dull, orange colour the fish is stale. When haddocks and whitings are fresh, the skin is silvery.

Flesh should be plump and firm with smooth, unwrinkled skin. The scales of herrings, etc., should be plentiful. Marks of pressure on the flesh should disappear at once; any flabbiness shows the onset of decay. When the fish is cut the flesh should be close-grained, firm and dry.

Eyes should be bright and prominent. Fish with the eyes or heads removed may be stale and should be examined carefully.

Gills should be red, except in the case of herrings where the redness increases with the staleness of the fish.

BUYING OF VEGETABLES

These also are best when they are in season and should be very fresh; stale vegetables are never economical.

Green vegetables and salad plants should be a bright green colour, firm and crisp; pods, leaves and stalks should snap sharply when broken. Limpness and discoloration are signs of staleness.

Medium-sized vegetables are best; large vegetables are usually tough and woody. *Root vegetables* should be firm, not flabby, and should not show signs of sprouting, since the young shoots are fed at the expense of the parent plant. *Potatoes* should be of medium size and regular shape and should have smooth skins.

CHAPTER V

THE STORAGE OF FOODS

It will be clear from what has been said in the introductory chapter that perishable food should, as a rule, be bought in just such quantity as will suffice for immediate use and that it should be cooked and eaten as soon as possible after it has come into the house. But, for a variety of reasons, such a course is not always practicable, and arrangements have to be made to keep the food for a short time and to keep it in as fresh and wholesome a condition as possible.

The Arrangement and Management of the Larder.[1]

It will be obvious that the larder must be so planned and kept as to *reverse* the conditions which are favourable to the growth of the micro-organisms which attack food. Warmth, dampness, lack of air, of light and of cleanliness, using the word in its widest sense, all assist the work of bacteria and moulds.

The **essential conditions for a larder** are therefore:

(1) **Coolness.** The larder should face north or north-east so that it is cool. It should be within reasonable reach of the kitchen, but not so near as to receive its warmth.

Stone or tiled floors, shelves of slate or stoneware all make for coolness and are easily kept clean. There should be at least one slate or stoneware shelf, on which milk, which rapidly becomes sour, can be put.

(2) **Dryness.** This condition is in the hands of the architect

[1] Substitutes for larders, e.g. food safes, should provide as far as may be the same essentials of coolness, dryness, ventilation, light, cleanliness. Their arrangement, management and cleaning should follow as closely as possible the lines suggested for a larder.

The use and management of *refrigerators* is described on pp. 45, 47.

and builder rather than in those of the housekeeper, but she can at least see that the shelves and floors are dried thoroughly after cleaning.

(3) **Ventilation.** In order to allow of the free circulation of air, the larder should have two or three outside walls. Cross-currents of air should be admitted either by two windows or by a window and ventilating bricks. The window should be open constantly, night and day. A good plan is to use perforated zinc for the window space and upper part of the door.

(4) **Light.** The larder should be light, not only because light tends to prevent the growth of micro-organisms, but because light is also an incentive to cleanliness.

(5) **Cleanliness.** (*a*) *Surroundings of larder.* The air which enters the larder must come from a pure source; drains, gullies, etc., from which bad smells might possibly arise, should not be near the larder.

Flies are a great menace to the preservation of food. In this connection the sections on the treatment of kitchen refuse and the use of dust bins (page 33) should be re-read. All possible measures should be taken to kill flies, especially the blue-bottles which attack meat. In the summer months flies multiply with extreme rapidity, passing through the stage of maggots which should, of course, be destroyed at once. Sticky fly-papers and other similar devices are useful, but much more can be done by maintaining a high standard of cleanliness in all premises, both inside and outside the house.

(*b*) *Interior of Larder.* The larder should have no uneven surfaces or cracks or crevices in which dust and dirt can collect. Painted and varnished or tiled walls give a smooth and easily washed surface. If the walls are lime-washed, as is frequently the case, the wash, with that of the ceiling, should be renewed three or four times a year.

(*c*) *Cleaning of Larder.* Wipe the shelves daily with a clean damp cloth which will collect dust without distributing it. Once a week scrub the shelves and the floor. If the walls are varnished or tiled, wipe them with a damp cloth from time to time.

Keeping of Food in the Larder.

Soup and Stock. Keep in earthenware or enamel bowls covered with muslin.[1]

[1] All muslin used to cover food must, of course, be washed and boiled frequently, and should be dried in the open air to purify it.

Milk. Keep in shallow basins rather than in jugs; cover with muslin. Place on the stone or slate shelf, away from cheese and other strong-smelling foods; milk readily absorbs flavours. The basins must be washed thoroughly with boiling water and soap then rinsed well in cold water; if this is neglected, bacteria which make milk sour will collect in the vessel and new milk put in it will speedily become tainted.

Butter. Cover with muslin and keep on the cool shelf. In hot weather put butter in a basin, put the basin in a second basin containing cold water and cover with muslin, placing it so that the ends are in the water; by this means the muslin will always be damp. An inverted plant-pot may be used instead of the muslin.

Bread. Keep in a covered bread pan so that it does not become dry. Either the pan or lid must have air holes; without air bread becomes mouldy. Scraps and crusts of bread must not be allowed to accumulate. The pan must be wiped out two or three times a week and be washed weekly to keep it from becoming musty. Thorough drying is necessary after washing.

Meat. Use muslin or gauze covers to protect meat from flies. Raw meat keeps best hung from the ceiling, so that air can circulate round it. It should be hung cut side uppermost. Meat which cannot be hung up should be turned and put on a clean dish every day.

Fish. Cover with muslin and keep in a current of air.

Vegetables. Put in a vegetable rack or in baskets on the floor of the larder, so that they keep cool.

Parsley, Watercress and Cress. Put the stalks in water. If they become slimy they are unfit for use.

Lettuce. Wrap in paper or keep in an air-tight tin.

Prevention of Decay in Foods.

In the summer, when the warm and often close weather helps on the work of micro-organisms, it is frequently necessary to heat foods to prevent or arrest decay. The food must be heated *rapidly*, not by slow degrees, since most bacteria grow best in foods which are lukewarm. *Milk, stock, soup, gravy, etc.*, should be brought quickly to the boil each day to prevent their turning sour. They must then be put at once into a cold place, so that they cool rapidly and do not remain for some time in a tepid condition. The same applies to all cooked foods which are not to be eaten at once.

Meat requires careful examination during hot weather. If its keeping good is at all doubtful it should be cooked immediately, and should be heated rapidly, not slowly. When the condition of meat is doubtful, it may be tested by means of a knife put in near the bone and left for a moment or two; if the knife, when withdrawn, has only a slight smell, the meat may safely be used, provided the bone is taken out and the meat washed in water coloured with vinegar. Vinegar acts as a preservative, since bacteria attack alkaline substances most readily. Permanganate of potash may be used instead of vinegar, using sufficient crystals to colour the water faintly.

In hot or sultry weather, both meat and bones may be sprinkled with vinegar and also with pepper, the latter to ward off flies.

Refrigerators.

In the modern house or flat a refrigerator is sometimes installed to take the place of the larder, but the actual capacity of the refrigerator is very limited, and other food storage space is usually necessary for the average -sized family.

Management of Refrigerators.

(1) *Gas refrigerators*: these should be serviced at regular intervals in order that they may be kept running efficiently.

(2) *Electric refrigerators*: the motor should be oiled to ensure a smooth-running refrigerator.

(3) Keep the door of the refrigerator closed, and de-frost the ice box once a month. These two points are essential if the cost of running the refrigerator is to be kept to a minimum. Instructions for de-frosting are supplied with the refrigerator.

(4) Do not place hot food in the refrigerator, as this will cause the cooling box to be less efficient.

Use.

(1) Usually a chart is supplied with the refrigerator, showing how to arrange the food.

(2) The coldest part is round the ice box, the top of the compartment being the warmest.

(3) All foods should be wrapped or covered to avoid flavours penetrating from one food to another.

(4) Keep salad plants in the glass container supplied with the refrigerator.

Daily Inspection of Larder.[1]

The larder should be inspected regularly before ordering the day's meals. By means of such inspection the housekeeper can assure herself that there is no waste of food through decay and can arrange that food left from previous meals is used to the best advantage.

The following should be set aside in clean vessels for further use:

(*a*) Remains of gravy, savoury sauce and soup; use gravy and sauce for meat and fish réchauffés. Add remains of clear soups to thick soups. Use quickly soups which contain milk and vegetables; such soups soon become sour. Sauces containing milk should also be used as quickly as possible.

(*b*) Remains of meat, game, poultry; trimmings of ham, tongue, bacon; use these for réchauffés. Ham and tongue may be used for savoury dishes, e.g. Macaroni and Tomato (p. 144), Stuffed Tomatoes (p. 167).

(*c*) Bones of meat, game, poultry; use for stock.

(*d*) Fish-bones and remains of fish; use the bones for fish-stock for fish sauce or soups; use fish for réchauffés.

(*e*) Remains of raw and cooked vegetables; use raw vegetables for stew or stock, cooked vegetables for salads or réchauffés.

(*f*) Pieces of raw or cooked fat; prepare these for frying (for directions see pp. 189–190) and for use as 'shortening' for pastry, buns and plain cakes.

(*g*) Pieces of cheese; use for such savoury dishes as Macaroni Cheese (p. 144), Cheese Cauliflower (p. 166).

(*h*) Pieces of stale bread; cut into dice, dry in the oven and serve with soup; or, use as a foundation for suet puddings (see p. 215) or for forcemeat. If not required for other purposes, convert into dried crumbs. To do this, cut the bread into small pieces and dry in a cool oven, then crush with a jam jar or a china rolling pin, sift and store in air-tight bottles. Dried till they are a pale golden brown colour, these crumbs form the 'raspings' required for savoury dishes; dried without colouring, they can be used to coat foods to be fried.

(*i*) Pieces of stale cake, sweet biscuits, teacake, etc., use as a foundation for puddings of the 'trifle' or 'cabinet' type (pp. 76, 77).

[1] Chapter XXI should be studied in this connection.

Daily Inspection of Refrigerator.

(1) Daily inspection of the contents of the refrigerator is necessary and all bits of food must be utilised.

(2) Wipe the walls and the shelves and replace any food not being used.

(3) Clean thoroughly inside and outside each week.

(4) Keep sauces, gravy, etc., in screw-top jars. See 'Daily Inspection of Larder', p. 46 for the way in which foods left over may be utilised.

CHAPTER VI

THE PROCESSES OF COOKING FOODS

Cookery processes may be classified as follows:

I. Cooking by Direct Heat.

1. Roasting.
2. Fire-grilling.

} Radiation of heat from surface of fire.

II. Cooking by Indirect Heat.

A. Heated Grillers. Grilling by gas or electric grillers; radiation of heat from plates of griller.

B. Heated Ovens. Baking: (*a*) *Coal range oven*: radiation of heat from the oven case assisted by conduction of heat from the shelves; (*b*) *Gas oven*: cooking mainly by convection currents, air being heated by the gas flame, assisted by conduction and radiation; (*c*) *Electric oven*: cooking by radiant heat from oven case, assisted by conduction from shelves and by convection currents.

C. Heated Mediums: mediums heated by convection.

1. Frying:[1] medium of oil or liquefied fat at 171°–204° Cent. (340°–400° Fahr.). (2) Steaming:[2] medium of steam. The steam is obtained from boiling water and is at the same temperature, 100° Cent. (212° Fahr.). (3) Boiling: medium of water or other liquids at boiling point. (4) Stewing:[3] medium of simmering water or other liquids, as illustrated by tests

[1] In shallow frying (see Chapter XVI) the amount of fat used is so small that cooking is done largely by conduction of heat from the pan.

[2] Braising is a combination of steaming and baking.

[3] A process best described as cooking meat in its own juices is described on pp. 92, 93.

given on p. 49. Except in the case of steaming, the heat is applied to the surface of the food and reaches the inner layers by conduction.

COOKING BY DIRECT HEAT

Roasting.[1] Meat or poultry to be roasted is placed in a roasting-jack in front of a bright clear fire, whose rays are directed on to each part of the meat in turn by the continual revolutions of the jack on which the meat is hung. Air moves freely round the meat, but a draught so great as to check cooking is prevented by a bright metal screen which, by reflection, heats the part of the meat momentarily away from the fire. Free circulation of air as the meat cooks distinguishes roasting and grilling from other processes.

Fire-grilling is in essentials precisely similar to roasting, but the food is held over the fire and the contact with the source of heat is much closer.

COOKING BY INDIRECT HEAT

A. **Heated Grillers.**

The food is held under the plates of the gas or electric griller, which must be red-hot in order to radiate heat.

B. **Heated Ovens.**

Baking. The oven should be clean, well ventilated and at the temperature which is best suited to the food to be cooked. The temperature should be noted before the food is put in and should be maintained and regulated, if required, while baking is in progress. If a culinary thermometer is not available and there is no thermostatic controller the temperature may be gauged with a fair degree of accuracy by placing a small piece of white bread in the oven for five minutes exactly. If the oven is moderately hot, the bread will be biscuit-coloured by the end of that time; if hot, golden brown; if very hot or 'quick', a more decided brown colour.

C. **Heated Mediums.**

The use of heated mediums for the cooking of foods makes it possible to regulate the temperature to a more exact degree and

[1] For 'roasting' joints and poultry the oven is now almost always used instead of the roasting-jack: though baked in the oven the joint or bird is still described as 'roasted'.

to do so more speedily than in other processes. The convection currents (see p. 50) set up in the medium ensure even distribution of heat over the food.

Frying. There are two varieties of frying:

(1) *Shallow frying*: cooking in a small quantity of fat. (2) *Deep frying*: cooking in a quantity of fat sufficient to cover the food completely. Both methods are described fully in Chapter XVI.

Mediums of Steam or Water

Before considering the cooking of foods by means of steam and water, it is necessary to understand how water is affected by heating.

Effects of Heat on Water

Experiment 1. Heat water in a beaker or saucepan, noticing the changes which take place in it. Take the temperature with a thermometer, holding it so that the bulb is under water without touching the bottom of the vessel.

Stage 1. Small bubbles form, rise and shake the surface of the water very slightly. These bubbles are formed by the expansion and expulsion of air dissolved in the water. The water at the surface is still so cool that the bubbles contract and sink again.

Stage 2. The bubbles grow larger. These are bubbles of water vapour, the invisible gaseous form which water takes as its temperature rises. As the bubbles come upwards they cause gentle movements of the still cold water on the surface, contact with which causes them to condense, or to become reconverted into water. At this point tiny bubbles are seen to reach the surface *from time to time* bursting there. The water is now said to be simmering, slowly or rapidly, according to the amount of movement the water shows.

Stage 3. The bubbles become still larger and finally reach the surface in large numbers, their contents escaping as steam.[1] The water is said to boil and is at a temperature of about 100° Cent. (212° Fahr.).[2]

[1] Steam is water vapour in a state of partial condensation, If a kettle of fast-boiling water is watched, nothing is to be seen quite close to the spout, but about ½-inch beyond it is a cloud. The space near the spout is filled with invisible water vapour, which as it cools is converted into minute drops of water, forming the cloud of steam.

[2] The temperature at which water boils varies under certain conditions, e.g. when salt is added, but the temperature of the steam remains the same.

Experiment 2. Increase the heat so that the bubbles form more rapidly.

An increased quantity of steam forms and is removed by the air. The temperature registered by the thermometer is unchanged, showing that the additional heat employed serves only to form *an increased amount of steam*. If boiled for a sufficiently long time, all the water will eventually disappear as steam. Fast boiling, therefore, does not give increased heat and unless required for a definite purpose e.g. to 'reduce' or thicken a sauce, is waste of fuel.

Experiment 3. Let the water boil gently, cover the vessel closely with a lid, so that very little steam escapes. Notice that after a time the lid becomes warm and its inner surface covered with drops of water. The steam condenses when it comes into contact with the cold lid and in doing so gives up its heat to it.

In order not to waste heat, food should, as a rule, be cooked in covered pans.

Experiment 4. Put some cold water in a flask or saucepan with a few grains of rice or some tiny pieces of blotting-paper. Heat the flask and notice that the water at the bottom rises up the middle, while an inrush of cold water takes place from the sides and upper surfaces. It is by these *convection currents*, as they are called, that the whole of the water becomes heated and thus the heat is distributed evenly over the surface of food cooked in the water.

Cooking in Double Pans. We may notice here that water may be the indirect as well as the direct means of cooking foods. When food is cooked in a double pan, such as a porridge pan, or its substitute, a jar or jug placed in a saucepan, it is put in the inner of the two vessels and surrounded by a jacket of heated water which passes on its heat to the food. As the water evaporates, more water at the same temperature must be added, lest the outer pan 'boil dry'.

This device makes it possible to cook foods at a uniform temperature for long periods of time with very little attention. The water in the outer pan cannot, under ordinary circumstances, be heated above its boiling point and the passage of its heat to the food in the inner pan goes on very slowly, so that there is very little risk of over-heating the food. Moreover, as long as the outer pan contains water, the food cannot burn.

Steaming. By reason of its *latent heat*, steam has a greater heating value than the boiling water which produces it.

We saw in Experiment 2 that though water which boils quickly does not register a higher temperature than that which boils slowly, it *does* produce a greater quantity of steam. That is to say, the additional heat used to make the bubbles of water vapour form more rapidly converts more and more water at boiling point into steam at the same temperature. The heat or energy used thus to turn water into steam is not registered by a thermometer, and for this reason is called 'latent' or hidden heat; it is recovered or released when the steam, on condensing, again becomes boiling water. We saw that condensation takes place when the steam comes in contact with a cool substance and that as the steam condenses it gives up to the substance its latent heat.

When steam is used to cook foods it penetrates them thoroughly, condensing and giving up to the food its latent heat. Steam re-converted into water takes up much less room than it did as steam, so that spaces are left in the food into which more steam pushes its way. This continues until steam has penetrated the whole mass, and very thorough cooking is thus ensured.

Though the heating value of steam is greater than that of boiling water, steaming is a longer process than boiling, taking from one-third to one-half as long again. This seeming contradiction is explained by the fact that the amount of steam used to steam a pudding, for example, would, if re-converted into water be far less in bulk than the water required to boil it.

Apparatus. The apparatus for steaming must be so arranged that no water except that formed by condensation of the steam comes into contact with the food. The most convenient apparatus is the regulation steamer whose construction is shown in the diagram on p. 52.[1]

The separate compartments make it possible to cook different foods at the same time without intermixture of their flavours and with no more fuel or space than would be required to cook one.

To use the Steamer. (1) Have the water boiler three-quarters full of boiling water and keep it boiling steadily; pour in more boiling water as required, so that the pan does not boil dry.

[1] A potato steamer, a tin vessel with a perforated bottom, placed over a pan of boiling water, can be substituted if necessary, or a colander placed over a pan of boiling water will also serve.

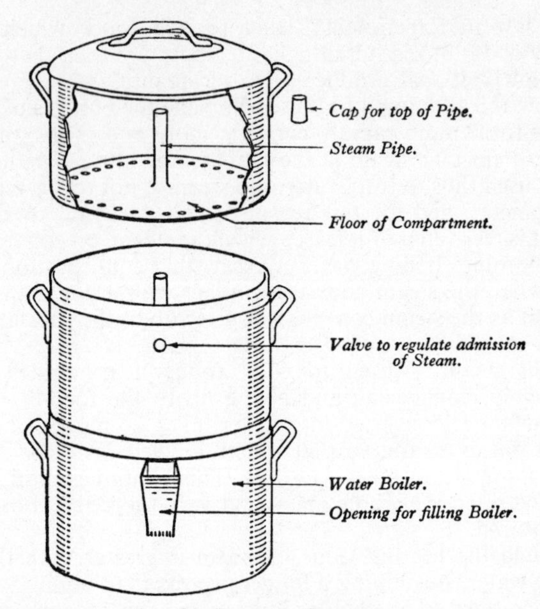

FIG. 9. PUDDING STEAMER.

(2) Put the foods which require most cooking in the lowest compartment.

(3) Pull out the valves to allow steam to enter the compartments, putting the cap on the top of the pipe in the topmost part of the steamer.

(4) See that the lid fits tightly and remove it as seldom as possible, so that the minimum of steam is lost.

(5) When food is sufficiently cooked but is not to be served immediately, push in the valve so that the food keeps hot without further cooking.

Foods may be steamed in two ways:

(1) By *direct contact* with the steam. This method is used for such firm, solid pieces of food as meat which keeps its shape and can be lifted easily out of the steamer. Such foods are put in the steamer without protection or covering of any kind, so that the steam surrounds and penetrates them.

(2) By *indirect contact* with steam. This method is used for foods or mixtures of foods too soft and fragile to keep their

shape without support. Such things as puddings, mixtures of minced meat or fish are put in a greased mould and covered with paper made waterproof by greasing it, so that the condensed steam cannot soak into the food and make it sodden. In this method the steam gives up its latent heat to the vessel, which by conduction passes on the heat to the contents.

Processes allied to steaming. There are two methods of cooking foods in which steam plays a part and which, though not, strictly speaking, steaming, are often spoken of as such and can be substituted for it if necessary.

Process 1. The food is put in a mould and placed in a covered pan containing sufficient boiling water to come half-way up the sides of the mould. The mould is thus heated partly by steam and partly by the water in which it stands and as before, the food is cooked by conduction. As in steaming proper, the lid of the pan must fit closely, the water must boil steadily and be replaced as it evaporates by more boiling water.

Process 2. The food is put between two greased plates and placed over a pan of boiling water, the steam from which heats the plates. This method is much used for fillets or cutlets of fish and thin pieces of poultry, e.g. the breast of a chicken. For thicker pieces of food a plate covered by a basin can be used.

Boiling. There are three varieties of boiling:

(1) The food itself, e.g. milk, sauce, is cooked at its boiling point.

(2) The food, e.g. meat, fish, is cooked, though not, strictly speaking, 'boiled' by direct contact with water or other liquid actually or nominally at boiling point; the liquid, as a rule, covers the food completely.[1]

It is to be noted that in this case the term 'boiling' is inaccurate, not only as regards the food, which does not reach boiling point, but frequently also as regards the liquid medium which in some cases, e.g. 'boiling' meat, boils only for a few minutes, and in other cases, e.g. 'boiling' fish, not at all.

(3) The food is cooked by indirect contact with boiling water and is cooked (*a*) in a covered bowl or basin, completely surrounded by boiling water, e.g. boiling suet pudding, or (*b*) in a double saucepan with boiling water round but not over it, after the manner described on p. 50 for Double-pan Cooking.

[1] As little water as possible should be used to reduce the solvent and extractive action of the water to the minimum (see p. 284).

Stewing differs from boiling in several important particulars:

(1) The liquid medium moves more gently than when it is boiling.

(2) As a rule, large pieces of food are cut up before cooking, in order to expose a large surface to the action of the heated liquid. In comparison with the size of the pieces of food, stewing takes much longer than boiling.

(3) The liquid used is considerably less in quantity than that required for boiling and is invariably served as part of the dish.

The stew may be cooked in a pan placed at one side of the fire or over a very low heat on a gas or electric cooker or in a casserole in the oven. If a pan is used on the fire or cooker it will be found that a *double pan* gives the best chance of maintaining the steady, even temperature which is so essential. Without this much care is necessary to prevent overheating. However the stew is cooked, the vessel must be covered closely to retain all the flavours of the food.

CHAPTER VII

FOODSTUFFS AND FOODS

Before we can practise the processes of cookery described in the last chapter it is necessary to consider the nature of the foods with which we have to deal.

The tissues which form the body of a human being are composed of certain complex substances. During life the tissues are constantly wearing away and food is necessary to renew them, to build new tissues, and to give the body the energy required to warm it and to enable it to do work.

The complex substances of which the tissues of the body are made are of the same kind as those which form the tissues of plants, and food is necessary to the life of plants just as it is to the life of animals. But here the likeness ends, for plants can use as food materials which would be quite useless to animals.

As we have seen, green plants, those which have chlorophyll, exist on the comparatively simple inorganic materials which they take direct from soil and water, and on the carbon dioxide of air, which the presence of sunlight enables them to use

Animals cannot do this; with the exception of water, they can use as food only materials which have already been changed from inorganic to organic matter. Human beings, that is to say, depend for their life on plants, and feed either on plants, or on the flesh and products, e.g. milk, eggs, of other animals, which in their turn have been nourished by plants. Most human beings live on a mixed diet, and eat both plant and animal substances.

The Nature and Functions of Food. The constituents of foods fall into the following classes: (1) proteins, (2) fats, (3) carbohydrates, including cellulose, which serves as 'roughage', (4) mineral salts, (5) vitamins, (6) water. These are distributed among the different plant and animal substances used by man as food, and each has its special function to perform in the body. Human beings need a 'mixed' diet of food of good quality, containing these constituents in quantities adapted to the particular needs of each person. Further, the food must be so prepared and eaten as to have its highest value. Beyond this point the body takes charge, digests and assimilates the food and proceeds to use it as a source of energy and as material for the creation of tissues.

Proteins, which are distinguished from other foodstuffs by the fact that they contain nitrogen, are found both in animal and vegetable foods, but more abundantly in the former, for example, in meat, fish, eggs, milk and cheese. All plant substance has some protein, but with the exception of certain storage organs of plants which hold reserves of food, the amount is very small. Vegetable proteins are most abundant in the legumes, peas, beans and lentils, and to a less extent in some cereals, e.g. wheat, oats. Plant proteins are less digestible than those found in animal foods, being contained in cells of a tough vegetable fibre known as cellulose.[1]

Chemically, proteins consist of amino-acids united together; one protein differs from another in the number, nature and arrangement of these amino-acids. One protein may contain some twenty different amino-acids, another a few less than

[1] *Soya bean flour* is a valuable plant protein with a good amount of protein and fat, vitamins A and B, and carbohydrate in the form of sugar It lacks starch and so cannot thicken mixtures. It is used in *conjunction with wheat flour* to increase the food value of pastry, puddings and all flour mixtures. It can also be added to soups and to the gravy of stews, mixing one part of soya flour with two parts of wheat or household flour.

In making pastry, puddings, batters, cakes and biscuits, use 1 oz. to each 7 oz. wheat flour.

twenty, a third only three or four. Again, in one protein a given amino-acid may preponderate, in a second protein another. Yet again, two proteins may consist of the same amino-acids put together differently. Just so may a boy use the parts of his 'Meccano' outfit to build many different structures, or a girl use the same stitches to embroider a variety of designs. It is important to realise that these variations determine the suitability of individual proteins for nutrition.

Proteins are essential to life. From their amino-acids the body builds up and replaces or repairs, as the case may be, its tissues. In the normal healthy grown-up the wear and tear of every day must be made good; in the child new tissue must also be made, while the convalescent needs proteins to replace the tissues lost. Further, proteins supply the materials the glands of the body need for making their secretions.

Not all proteins are equally valuable. Animal proteins which can most readily give the body the amino-acids it needs are 'A' or 'first-class' proteins, and are said to have a 'high biological value'. Many authorities consider that such proteins should always be included in a diet, especially in the diet of growing children and of convalescents. Other proteins are of slighter value. For example, certain proteins lack some of the tissue-forming amino-acids, and so are valueless by themselves for this purpose, though they are a useful addition to other proteins. Such are gelatin (obtained from the connective tissues of animals) and one of the proteins of maize. Yet again, proteins may have tissue-building amino-acids, but also a high proportion of amino-acids useless for this purpose. Proteins of these two types should not, however, be cut out of a diet, for, though they may be wholly or partly useless for making tissues, they are burnt in the body and the resulting energy is used for heat or for muscular work. Proteins thus share with carbohydrates and fats the work of giving the body the heat it requires, but are able to give a more rapid output of heat than the same amounts of carbohydrates and fats. When protein is thrown on to the body's fire, so to speak, it has the same effect as that of paraffin thrown on to a coal fire; both body and fire are stimulated to greater activity. This is particularly true of the body in hot weather and in hot climates. Under such circumstances supplies of protein should be lessened. It is worth noting that vegetable proteins are less stimulating than animal proteins.

We shall see later that the proteins differ in their properties as well as in their make-up, but that nearly all are coagulated by heat or other agents.

Fats are of both animal and vegetable origin. Animal fats are found in yolk of egg, meat, fish, milk, butter, cheese; vegetable fats in olive oil, nuts and 'nut-butter'. Some cereals, such as oats and barley, contain fats.

Chemically, fats are compounds of simple fatty acids and glycerin. Their consistency and melting points depend largely on the proportion in which the three types of fat, stearin, palmitin and olein are present. Fats with a high proportion of stearin, e.g. mutton fat, are hard and firm, those with a high proportion of olein, e.g. olive oil, are soft or even fluid. The latter are the more easily used by the body.

Fats, particularly animal fats, are excellent sources of vitamins of classes A and D. With carbohydrates and proteins they supply the body with the energy required for work, and for the production and maintenance of heat. Weight for weight, fats give two and a quarter times as much heat as either of the other two. Up to a point fats and carbohydrates can be substituted for each other, but not entirely. Fats slow down digestion in the stomach, and it is for this reason that a meal with fats is more satisfying than one without them.

Carbohydrates. With a few exceptions (e.g. glycogen, found in the liver of most animals), carbohydrates are obtained wholly from vegetable substance, more particularly from the storage organs of plants.

(1) *Starches* are contained in large quantities in cereals, in rather smaller quantities in legumes, and in roots and tubers.

(2) *Dextrins* as such are not found in foods, but are formed when starch is digested or is acted upon by heat, as in baking or frying.

(3) *Sugars*. Sugars are found chiefly in fruits (where they form as the fruits ripen) and in root vegetables, e.g. carrots. Grape sugar (glucose) from fruits and honey, cane sugar (used in cooking or at table) from the sugar cane or beet, with milk sugar (lactose), and malt sugar (maltose), obtained from sprouted barley and used in malt extracts, are all familiar forms.[1]

[1] (*a*) *Golden syrup and treacle* obtained in the process of refining cane sugar are useful sources of sweetness for cooking and table use.

(*b*) *Saccharin*, though not a food, as is sugar, has sweetening properties, 3–4 tablets replacing 1 oz. sugar. It has a somewhat unpleasant taste and is

(4) *Cellulose*, or 'roughage', forms the fibres of plant substance.

Carbohydrates form about two-thirds of the average diet, and fortunately are relatively cheap. In the body they are quickly digested, absorbed and assimilated; and with proteins and fats (whose combustion they help) provide the body with energy. In excess, carbohydrates have their dangers, especially for young children, in whom rickets may develop.

The indigestible cellulose which forms the fibres of vegetables, fruits and cereals is the main source of the 'roughage' necessary in a diet, the precise quantity varying markedly with the individual. Roughage acts mechanically, making the alimentary canal active, and so preventing constipation and the poisoning of the body which results from the absorption of the products of bacterial decomposition.

Mineral Salts are present in most foods; milk, cheese, eggs and green vegetables all give valuable supplies, while common salt (sodium chloride) is added to many foods in cooking or eating or both. Though only small amounts are needed they do important work. Calcium and phosphorus help to form bones and teeth, iron is used in the red colouring matter of blood, while chlorine is required for all tissues of the body.

Vitamins.[1] Recent research has shown that vitamins, found in minute quantities in many, though not all foods, substances of as yet unknown nature and chemical composition, are necessary for normal growth and health. If the diet lack vitamins the general health suffers, insidiously at first; at length, and more rapidly and fatally in children than in grown-ups, disease develops, affecting particularly the nervous system, the skin and mucous membranes, the joints and the growth of bones and teeth.

Human beings cannot make their own vitamins, and obtain them either at first hand from plant substances, or second hand from the flesh or products of animals fed on plant substances.

best used to 'fortify' sugar, 30 finely crushed tablets being mixed with each ½ lb. of sugar. This 'fortified' sugar can be used to sweeten stewed fruit, pudding mixtures, etc., half the quantity normally used being sufficient.

Where it is practicable as, for example, in stewing fruit, it is as well to delay adding the crushed saccharin tablets or the fortified sugar, as the case may be, until cooking is completed. If cooked for any length of time saccharin develops a bitter flavour.

[1] Many vitamins can now be artificially produced but it is thought that their value is not quite so great as that of natural vitamins.

The grass-fed cow, for example, stores vitamins in its fat, and the vitamins of fish-oils are presumably got in the first instance from the tissues of sea-water green plants.

So far at least six, or possibly more than six, classes of vitamins grouped according to (*a*) their functions in the body, (*b*) their distribution among food stuffs, are known.

(1) *Vitamins of Class A*. The fat-soluble A vitamins, found mainly in the common animal fats, assist growth and development. Without them growth is slow and may even stop, while eye disease may develop; there is also susceptibility to infection. Fortunately, quite small amounts of the vitamin protect the body from these evils.

Vitamins of Class B. The vitamin hitherto known as B has now been divided into at least two, vitamin B_1 and vitamin B_2 (or F), as they have been termed. Both are essential to health and it is possible that without them the body could not use satisfactorily certain of the foodstuffs with which it is nourished.

Vitamin B_1 preserves the health of the nervous system (hence the name anti-neuritic) and so of the body as a whole. Vitamin B_1 is found mainly in the husk and germ of wheat, in peas and beans, in yeast and yeast extracts, and in eggs. In this country, the disease beri-beri, due to complete absence of the vitamin, is rare.

Vitamin B_2 *(or F)*. This, as has already been noted, has now been separated from vitamin B_1. Like B_1 it is essential to health. It is probable that B_2 is present in many common foodstuffs and that the vitamin in vegetables and milk, formerly called B is in reality B_2 (or F).

This vitamin has been described as the anti-pellagric vitamin. 'Pellagra', a disease of which 'rough skin' (hence the name) is a marked feature, is common in Spain, Italy and the southern states of the United States of America. The disease is aggravated by sunlight, and it is possible that sunlight is concerned in its development.

There is much yet to be learnt about the vitamins of Class B, their number, functions, and distribution. In the meantime, we may think of B_1 and B_2 together, noting (so far as this is known) in which of the common foodstuffs they are found and remembering that, as we shall see later, B_2 is less easily affected by high temperatures than B_1.

Vitamins of Class C, soluble in water, are obtained mainly from fresh citrous fruits, oranges, lemons, grape fruit and some other fruits, also from fresh green vegetables and salad materials. They preserve the general health and without them the disease scurvy develops.[1]

Vitamins of Class D. Lack of this 'anti-rachitic' vitamin causes in young children the deficiency disease rickets and prevents the proper development of the teeth. Vitamin D is present in many, though not all, of the foods which contain vitamin A.

Until recently vitamin D could be got only from living substance. Now, however, by means of the action of ultra-violet rays on ergosterol, a waxy substance found in most fats, it has been found possible to make a synthetic vitamin D, minute quantities of which have been shown to cure rickets very rapidly. An abundant and cheap supply of this synthetic vitamin D is now available and it is thought that very small amounts are sufficient to preserve health.

Sources of Vitamins. The table which follows will make it clear that any well-balanced and sufficiently varied diet provides in itself the necessary vitamins. Where, however, as a result of lack of means, lack of knowledge or other difficulties, a diet is ill-balanced and limited, a partial lack of vitamins may result, with consequent damage to health, especially in early life.

Table showing the Chief Sources of Vitamins

(*Note.*—The numbers must *not* be taken as indicating the relative value of the different sources.)

Vitamins of Class A (anti-infective).

Found in: (1) Animal fats, e.g. beef, mutton fat, especially suet, but not lard.

(2) Margarine prepared from animal fats, but not that prepared from lard or from vegetable fats.[2]

(3) Milk and milk products of cows fed on grass: e.g. cream, butter, cheese.

(4) Liver.

(5) Oily fish, e.g. herrings, mackerel, salmon, eels.

[1] It is important to ensure that babies fed artificially are supplied with vitamin C by being given daily 1–2 teaspoonfuls of orange juice or tomato juice. The juice of raw swedes, obtained by grating the swede finely, wrapping the pulp in muslin and squeezing out the juice, may be substituted if needful.

[2] *Synthetic* vitamin A and also *synthetic* vitamin D are now, however, commonly added to margarine prepared from fats which lack these vitamins.

(6) Cod-liver oil.
(7) Egg yolk.
(8) Certain green vegetables, e.g. cabbage, spinach (in winter); lettuce, watercress.[1]
(9) Carrots, fruits and tomatoes.[1]

Vitamins of Class B.

Vitamin B_1 (anti-neuritic).
Found in: (1) Yeast and in Marmite, an extract of yeast.[2]
(2) Husks and germ of wheat; rice-polishings.
(3) Peas and beans.
(4) Eggs (yolk).

Vitamin B_2 (or F) (anti-pellagric).
Found in: (1) Most vegetables and milk.
(2) Many other common foodstuffs, e.g. in yeast, liver, meat, egg-yolk.

Vitamins of Class C (anti-scorbutic).
Found in: (1) Fresh green vegetables, e.g. cabbage, sprouts.
(2) Green salad materials, e.g. watercress, mustard and cress.
(3) Parsley.
(4) Roots and tubers (swedes and potatoes).
(5) Fresh citrous fruits (lemons, oranges, grape fruit).
(6) Black currant juice, rose-hip juice.
(7) Tomatoes.

Vitamins of Class D (anti-rachitic).
(*a*) Natural sources.
Found in: (1) Animal fats (including lard).
(2) Oily fish, e.g. salmon, herrings, kippers, bloaters, sardines and eels.
(3) Cod-liver oil.
(4) Milk and milk products, e.g. butter, cheese.
(5) Liver.
(6) Egg yolk.
(7) Green vegetables (summer varieties).
(*b*) Artificial sources: produced by the action of ultra-violet rays on ergosterol.

[1] Vegetables contain carotene, which is the precursor of vitamin A.
[2] The yeast preparation Marmite is one of the most concentrated sources of vitamin B_1 known. The commercial extracts of yeast used instead of meat in the preparation of soup cubes are found to retain the original vitamin value of yeast.

Before going on to consider the effect of cooking on vitamins one or two facts regarding the sources of *vitamins A and D* are of importance. It is well to remember that milk is a valuable source of these vitamins. The use in cases of tuberculosis and malnutrition of *cream*, *butter*, *cod-liver oil*, i.e. the fats of animals or fish in preference to *lard* and *vegetable fats and oils*, has been shown by research to be justified. Again, the *liver fats of the sheep*, *calf and ox* are valuable sources of vitamin A. For example, these liver fats have ten times as much vitamin A as cod-liver oil, hitherto considered the richest source, and from 200 to 1,000 times more than a good average sample of butter. These fats are free from unpleasant flavour and are otherwise suitable for incorporating with other foods.

Effects of Cooking on Vitamins. It now remains briefly to consider how vitamins are affected by the usual methods of cooking or otherwise preparing for eating such foods as are not usually eaten raw. Obviously, the more restricted the diet the more carefully must the cooking be considered.

The factors which affect vitamins appear to be:

(*a*) The degree of heat employed.

(*b*) The length of time for which the food is heated.

(c) The presence or absence of air during heating.

Vitamins of Class A (anti-infective). (1) In the presence of air, exposure to heat ultimately destroys the vitamin. (This presence or absence of air is of importance in the preservation of foods by tinning.)

(2) In the absence of air, a temperature of 120° C. (248° F.), i.e. a temperature well over boiling point, can be used with impunity.

Oxidation thus appears to be the main factor. For example, when milk is heated or is cooked in a milk pudding, vitamin A is probably not destroyed to any great extent because the bulk of the milk is not exposed to air. Again, the vitamin A of suet cooked in a suet pudding is probably little harmed, but that in butter, spread over small particles, and therefore exposed largely to air as it is in pastry, is probably largely destroyed.

Vitamins of Class B_1 (anti-neuritic). (1) Withstand drying for long stretches of time. As we have seen, dried foods form the chief sources of vitamins of this class.

(2) Are not affected by exposure to air.

(3) Can be exposed to a temperature of 100° C. (212° F.) for a long time, being destroyed only slowly: at a higher temperature, e.g. 120° C. (248° F.) destruction is more rapid.

Vitamin B_2 (or F) (anti-pellagric). Unlike B_1, B_2 is not readily susceptible to heat and neither ordinary cooking nor tinning destroys it.

Ordinary cooking does not, therefore, destroy these vitamins to any harmful extent. For example, when a loaf of bread is baked, the temperature of the interior does not rise above 100° C. (212° F.), and there is probably no great loss of the vitamin. But when foods are tinned, a temperature much above 100° C. (212° F.) is used and certain foods therefore contain little or no B vitamin. There are, however, some which do, e.g. tinned tomatoes and various forms of condensed milk.

Vitamins of Class C (anti-scorbutic). (1) Readily destroyed by drying at a temperature of 80° C. (176° F.); by heating to 100° C. (212° F.) for one hour, 90 per cent of the vitamin is destroyed.

(2) Highly sensitive to air, especially when combined with heat. The rate of destruction depends upon the temperature and on the duration of heating. At a temperature of 80° C. (176° F.) to 100° C. (212° F.) i.e. at a temperature between simmering and boiling, about 90 per cent of the vitamin is destroyed in one hour. High temperatures for shorter periods appear to be less harmful than longer heating at lower temperatures.

(3) Readily affected even at moderate temperatures by alkalies, e.g. soda, which rapidly destroy them.

Since drying and cooking readily destroy vitamin C, fresh raw vegetables and fruits (the main source of the vitamin) are, weight for weight, much more valuable than dried or cooked vegetables and fruits, and it is desirable to include regularly fresh uncooked vegetables and fruit in the diet, especially during the winter when the supply of vitamin C is most likely to be overlooked. When, however, cooking is desirable or necessary (as it often is in the case of vegetables) it is important to choose methods which shall harm the vitamin as little as possible. Firstly, though it helps to retain the original green colour of the vegetables, soda destroys their vitamin C. Secondly, short and rapid cooking is to be preferred to long and slow cooking. Hence, when such vegetables as onions, potatoes, carrots and swedes are stewed slowly with meat, their vitamin C value is lessened. Similarly, cooking in home-made hay boxes is not a sound plan for foods containing vitamin C, useful and economical as it may be for other purposes.

Vitamins of Class D (anti-rachitic). These, like those of Class A, are destroyed by heat in the presence of air, but are the more resistant of the two groups.

When considering the effect of cooking on vitamins as a whole it will be seen that only vitamin C is much affected. Hence it is well to include in a diet uncooked oranges, lemons, etc., and green salad stuffs, foods which can be obtained all the year round.

Water is contained often in large quantities in all foods, and forms the chief part of most fluids. It is needed for a variety of purposes, including that of replacing the water lost continually from the body, for example, in perspiration and in the breath. The amount of fluid required daily is usually estimated as at least three pints; care should be taken that not less than this amount is taken each day.

Dehydrated Foods. In recent years much research has been done on the preservation of foods by drying. It has been necessary to find artificial ways of dehydrating vegetables and such liquid foods as eggs and milk. Dehydration is the drying of foods by hot air, the temperature and the circulation of which are controlled. The process of blanching or scalding foods in boiling water before dehydration destroys the active enzymes responsible for deterioration of the colour, flavour and food value.

Vegetables are scalded and shredded, then placed on trays in cabinet dryers, through which hot air is fanned. The vegetables are stored in sealed containers, sometimes with an inert gas, usually nitrogen.

Eggs and Milk are dried by being sprayed into heated rooms where the moisture is evaporated and the powder drops into a moving conveyor.

Meat and Fish. These two foods are usually minced and cooked before being dehydrated. The use of these foods is limited, but they make excellent réchauffé dishes.

Tinned Foods. The preservation of food by tinning has reached a high standard of perfection and it is very rare to find deterioration of the contents of a tin which has been kept under suitable conditions. The loss of food-value as a whole by tinning is negligible but it is sometimes thought that the vitamin content of fruit and vegetables is largely lost. The process of gathering, preparing, packing and sealing the contents of the tins is done under such ideal conditions that there is very little loss of nutrients by oxidation. Tinned foods give variety to the diet, particularly when the foods tinned are out of season.

The tins should be examined every six months and turned upside down. A dented tin should be opened at an early date as this fault may cause a weakness in the sealing of the tin. The bulging of a tin at one or both ends indicates fermentation of the contents; the tin should be opened immediately and the contents destroyed.

Meat and fish will keep from two to five years, fruits and vegetables from one to two years, according to the type of food.

Study of Foods and Foodstuffs. Foods can be tested to determine of what substances they are constituted, and their constituents in their turn can be tested to determine of what elements, e.g. carbon, hydrogen, oxygen, nitrogen, they are composed. Flour, for example, can be shown by means of iodine solution to contain starch. Starch, a carbohydrate foodstuff, gives off water vapour when it is heated, denoting the presence of hydrogen and oxygen; if the heating is continued further, the starch becomes charred and blackened, indicating carbon. Further tests will show that in addition to starch, flour contains two proteins which, when mixed with water, form the substance known as gluten. Gluten in its turn can be shown to contain not only hydrogen, oxygen and carbon, but also nitrogen and other elements.

Again, if the protein albumen, contained in the white of an egg, be tested, it can be shown to be made of the same elements as gluten, though further tests will show that the two differ as to their properties.

For successful cooking it is thus desirable to have some knowledge of (1) the source of the food, (2) its constituents, (3) the properties of these constituents. Further, it is desirable to take into account the varying *structure* of foods, since this also influences cooking. Animal substance, as we shall see, differs considerably from plant substance, and there are marked differences within each group. For example, the structure of meat muscle or flesh differs from that of the internal organs, e.g. liver and kidneys, of the animal used as food, and these differ from each other. Again, the structure of meat muscle differs from that of fish. We shall see as a result of this difference that while it is possible to keep at boiling point for the first 5 minutes the water in which meat is being 'boiled', it is not practicable to do so in 'boiling' fish since the less dense and more fragile structure of fish muscle makes it break easily. We find also that while all plant substance consists of many-sided cells, with coverings of cellulose this is denser in some vegetable foods than in others. A short experience of cooking vegetables, fruits and cereals makes such differences clear. For instance, the flower of a cauliflower is less compact in structure than the leaves and stalk and therefore breaks more easily in cooking. The stalk of a cabbage is very dense in structure and resists the action of boiling water so sturdily that the thick coarse parts are often cut away from the interior before cooking. Again, the age and condition, whether young or old, fresh or dried, of plant substance is a factor to be considered in cooking it. Young carrots take less cooking than old, dried peas and dried apples more than fresh. The group of plants known as cereals exhibit similar differences. Fats also show variations. Some, e.g. fat of meat, are in their natural state, a mass of globules enclosed in connective tissues, others, e.g. lard, dripping, have been extracted from this tissue, while others, cream, for example, are in the form of an emulsion.

As regards the *properties* of the constituents of foods as they concern the cook, one constituent generally predominates. In cooking eggs, meat and fish, for example, it is the effect of cooking on the proteins these foods contain which has chiefly to be borne in mind. In cooking vegetables and cereals the effects of the processes on cellulose and starch and mineral salts have to be considered. Finally, since vitamins are so widely distributed among foods, the effects on them of temperature, length of cooking and oxidation need to be taken into account.

The illustrative tests given in the following chapters are intended to show those properties of the foodstuffs which have a distinct bearing on the cooking of the foods of which they form a part.

CHAPTER VIII

THE COOKING OF PROTEIN FOODS: EGGS

Shell Eggs.

The *white* of an egg is a colourless, sticky fluid, only divisible with difficulty. It consists of water and almost pure albumen the name given to this particular form of protein.

The *yolk* of egg, in addition to protein and phosphorus, contains much fat, and, unlike the white, is a rich source of vitamins A, B_1, B_2 and D.

Cooking would appear to have no effect on vitamins B_1 and B_2 nor, when the eggs are cooked in their shells, on A and D. It seems probable that other methods of cooking affect A and D only slightly; for example, when a custard is baked only the small portion which is in contact with air is presumably affected. The preservation of these vitamins in a fried egg would seem to be questionable, since the fat does not usually cover the egg (as does water when an egg is poached), and the temperature of the fat is well above 100° C. (212° Fahr.). It is worth noting that vitamins have been found unimpaired in dried eggs.

Before going on to illustrate the properties of egg-albumen it may be well to point out that '*custard-powders*' are practically innocent of egg-substance and consist of starch and soluble colouring-matter, which respectively thicken and colour the custard. Similarly, *egg-powders* used for cakes and puddings contain chiefly starch with baking-powder, which 'lightens' the mixture.

Properties of Egg-Albumen. The following tests illustrate these properties of egg-albumen which directly influence the treatment and cooking of eggs.

Test	*Result*
(1) *Action of cold water.* Put white of egg in a test-tube; add cold water and shake.	Egg dissolves in the water.[1]
(2) *Action of boiling water.* Drop a little white of egg into boiling water.	Egg immediately sets or coagulates into a firm white solid.

[1] If the egg is quite fresh, the liquid is often cloudy.

Test	*Result*		
(3) *Stages of coagulation.* Put white of egg in a test-tube and place in a pan of cold water. Put a thermometer in the egg and another in the pan. Heat the water slowly and stir the egg so that it is heated evenly. Notice the changes in the egg and the temperatures registered by the thermometers when the changes occur.	Temp. of Water.[1]	Temp. of Eggs,[1]	Appearance of Egg,
	63° C.—145° F.	56° C.—133° F.	Clouded.
	73° C.—163° F.	63° C.—145° F.	Opaque.
	90° C.—194° F.	82° C.—180° F.	White and lightly set.
	100° C.—212° F.	91° C.—196° F.	White and firmly set.
	After 2 minutes at 100° C.—212° F.	96° C.—205° F.	White and so firmly set that thermometer is held upright in it.
(4) *Action of Weak Acids.* Put white of egg in a test-tube and add lemon juice. Repeat the experiment using vinegar.	Slight coagulation results, causing the egg to become cloudy.		
(5) *Action of Beating or Whisking.* Put white of egg on a plate, add a pinch of salt and beat with an egg-whip or knife.	Egg loses its tenacity and becomes a light, frothy substance with air-bubbles entangled in it.		

Note. To 'beat the white of an egg stiffly' is to continue the beating until the egg is so stiff that it will keep its shape when dropped from the beater. Over-beating destroys the smoothness and makes the egg dry and flaky by over-stretching the bubbles so that they collapse in much the same way as soap bubbles which have been blown too far. The egg should be beaten immediately before use; the froth subsides quite soon.

The yolk also holds air when beaten, though not to the same extent as the white.

Dried Eggs. Dried eggs may, if necessary, be used instead of shell eggs for most purposes, but obviously not where it is

[1] The temperatures given are an average of the results obtained from a series of tests. They are found to vary slightly with the freshness of the egg.

required to separate the white from the yolk of the egg. In using dried eggs care must be taken in measuring and mixing to ensure success.

General Directions for the Use of Dried Eggs.

(1) Allow one level tablespoonful of dried egg and two tablespoonfuls cold water for each shell egg required.

(2) (*a*) For such *flour mixtures* as batter, pudding mixtures, buns, plain cakes, etc., sift the egg with the flour and add the required amount of water with the rest of the liquid.

(*b*) For *pound cake mixtures* (pp. 248, 249) sift the dried egg into the creamed fat and sugar, beating well and add at this stage half the measured water. Beat till smooth then stir in the rest of the water, mixing well.

(3) *For all other purposes* reconstitute the egg with the measured water shortly before use. Crush the egg powder or, if very lumpy, put it through a fine sieve. Mix to a thick paste with part of the measured water and beat till smooth. Then stir in the rest of the water and mix well.

METHODS OF COOKING EGGS
(Shell or Dried)

Whole Shell Eggs. *A. In Shell.* (1) Boiled (soft or hard).
B. Without Shell. (1) Steamed (in moulds).
(2) Poached.
(3) Fried.

Beaten Eggs. (*Shell or Dried*) *A. Cooked in medium of heated margarine or butter.*
(1) 'Buttered' or Scrambled Eggs, Tomato Toast, etc.
(2) Lemon Cheese, Orange Cheese.
B. Cooked in medium of heated milk.
(1) Plain Custards.
(2) 'Cabinet' Custard-Puddings.

Beaten Eggs are also used:

(*a*) As a means of introducing air into mixtures, e.g. sponge cakes, light puddings.

For this purpose shell eggs give better results than dried eggs.

(*b*) To bind together mixtures of meat, fish, etc., as in réchauffés or of sugar and ground almonds as in Macaroons.

(*c*) To form a protective casing for foods which are to be fried.

In all cooking of eggs the results of the tests should be borne in mind, and only just sufficient heat used to bring them to the right degree of firmness or thickness.

Boiled Eggs. *Soft-boiled Eggs.*

Test 1. Put an egg in a small saucepan containing sufficient boiling water to cover it. Put on the lid and place the pan for 6–8 minutes where the water will keep hot but will not boil. Allow 1–2 minutes extra for each additional egg.

Test 2. Put an egg in a small saucepan and cover with cold water; heat the water gently to boiling point and boil 1 minute. Serve the egg at once.

Test 3. Put an egg in a small saucepan of boiling water and boil 3½ minutes.

In Test 1 the temperature of the boiling water falls to about 77° Cent. (170° Fahr.). When the egg is opened, the white is seen to be a soft, tender jelly and the yolk lightly and evenly set. In Test 2 the egg is in a similar condition. In Test 3, though the white of the egg is firmly set, the yolk is set on the outside only; this is because the cooking has been too rapid to allow the heat to reach the centre of the yolk, which is still semi-liquid.

Hard-boiled Eggs.

Eggs which are firmly set are sometimes required for use in salads or sauces or for other purposes.

Method. Put the eggs into boiling water and boil gently for 10–15 minutes; if the eggs are to be stuffed, allow the longer time. Cover with cold water, then remove shells and skins.

[Dried eggs, reconstituted as already directed and steamed as described in the recipe for Savoury Eggs (page 71) can be used instead of hard-boiled shell eggs in salads, sauces, egg patties, etc.]

Stuffed Eggs: Cress, Anchovy, or Sardine Eggs.

Ingredients.		
3 hard-boiled eggs 1 teaspoonful margarine Salt, pepper, cayenne.	*plus*	1 tablespoonful finely chopped cress or watercress. *Or,* 1 teaspoonful anchovy essence. *Or,* 3 sardines, boned and skinned. ½ teaspoonful finely chopped parsley.

Garnish of cress, watercress or other salad.

Method. (1) Remove the shells and skins from the eggs and cut them in half across the width; remove the yolks. Cut a small slice from the bottom of each piece of white of egg so that it will stand firmly.

(2) Wash, dry, and chop the cress and mix it, or the anchovy essence or sardines and parsley as the case may be, with the yolks, margarine and seasonings. Work the mixture into a smooth paste, rubbing it through a sieve or strainer if necessary.

(3) Fill the egg-cases with the mixture, piling it high. Arrange them in a dish and garnish with the salad, carefully washed, picked and dried.

Steamed Eggs in Moulds.

Savoury Eggs.

Ingredients.

For each egg:
- 2 teaspoonfuls fine white bread-crumbs.
- 2 teaspoonfuls finely chopped parsley.
- Salt and pepper.
- 1 small square 'buttered' toast.

Method. (1) Grease a dariole mould or a cup and press two-thirds of the bread-crumb mixture on to the bottom and sides. Break the egg whole into the mould and sprinkle the rest of the mixture on top. Cover with greased paper.

(2) Put in the bottom of a saucepan a plate or saucer upside down, or two or three folds of kitchen paper. Place the mould on this, putting it on the side of the pan away from the fire or gas-light, and pour in hot water to come rather more than half-way up the sides of the mould. Cover the pan and let the water simmer gently until the egg is set just sufficiently to turn out without breaking. Time, 10–15 minutes.

(3) Turn the egg on to the 'buttered' toast, garnish with tiny pieces of parsley and serve on a hot dish.

Note. When the hot water comes into contact with the cold mould its heat is at once reduced, so that the egg is cooked at a low temperature. The placing of the moulds on a plate or paper helps to prevent over-cooking. If the egg rises or is pierced with small holes, the heat has been too great. The rising is due to expansion of air imprisoned in the mould when the egg was put in. The holes are caused by water in the egg being changed into steam and forcing a way out.

Poached Eggs.

(1) Prepare 'buttered' toast on which to serve the eggs and put it on a warm dish where it will keep hot.

(2) Put in a frying-pan enough water to cover the eggs. Bring it to the boil, add ½ teaspoonful salt and ½ teaspoonful lemon-juice or vinegar.

(3) Break the eggs, one at a time, into a saucer or cup, taking care not to pierce the skins of the yolks. Slip them carefully into the boiling water and at once reduce the heat so that the water simmers. Baste the eggs with water if necessary; cook until the whites are just set and until a white skin forms over the yolks. Time, 2½–4½ minutes.

(4) Lift out eggs, one by one, on a drainer, hold over a clean towel for a moment to dry them, then trim the edges, place on the toast, garnish with parsley and serve at once.

Note. Since the egg is neither in its shell nor in a mould the water at first must be boiling to set it. Lemon juice or vinegar is added for the same purpose. Undue hardening of the egg is avoided by reducing the heat of the water at once.

A method of serving poached eggs with spinach is described on p. 166.

Fried Eggs with Bacon or Ham.

Method. (1) Cut away the rinds and trim the edges of the bacon or ham. Warm the frying-pan and cook the bacon or ham slowly, turning it occasionally, until it is cooked through and is crisp and lightly browned. Put on a hot dish and keep warm.

(2) Heat the dripping until it gives off a faint blue vapour. Slip in the eggs, one at a time, from a saucer or cup and at once reduce the heat; baste with the dripping. When the eggs are set lightly, lift them out, place on the bacon or ham and serve at once.

Note. The heat of fat at frying-point is considerably greater than that of boiling water; the eggs therefore cook more rapidly than when they are poached.

Curried Eggs.

Ingredients

4 eggs, ¾ pint curry sauce, 3 oz. rice.

Method. (1) Boil eggs hard (p. 70), cut in half lengthwise.

(2) Make curry sauce (pp. 104–5) and heat eggs gently in it for 10–15 minutes.

(3) Boil rice (p. 142) and serve in border round eggs and sauce.

Beaten Eggs (*Shell or Dried*) cooked in a Medium of Heated Margarine.

Example 1. **'Buttered' Eggs, Tomato Toast, etc.**

'Buttered' Eggs	*Scrambled Eggs*	*Tomato Toast*	*Tongue or Ham Toast*
1 oz. margarine. 1 teaspoonful thyme (optional).	1 oz. margarine. 1 teaspoonful chopped parsley.	1 oz. margarine. 2 medium-sized tomatoes, skinned and sliced.[1]	1 oz. margarine. 2 oz. lean cooked ham or tongue, chopped finely.
	½ teaspoonful chopped shallot.	½ teaspoonful chopped shallot.	1 teaspoonful chopped parsley. Pinch of sweet herbs.
Salt, pepper, cayenne. 2 eggs. 1 tablespoonful milk.	Salt, pepper, cayenne. 2 eggs. 1 tablespoonful milk.	Salt, pepper, cayenne. 2 eggs.	Salt, pepper, cayenne. 2 eggs.

For all.—4 small squares of 'buttered' toast.

Method. (1) Make toast, spread with margarine and keep hot.

(2) Melt 1 oz. of margarine in a pan, add milk if used, seasonings, herbs and solid ingredients and heat until they are thoroughly warm or cooked, as the case requires.

(3) Beat the eggs until they run freely from the beater, and, add them to the other ingredients.

(4) Stir over a gentle heat until the eggs are lightly set and the consistency of soft porridge; they stiffen slightly as they cool. If the eggs are over-cooked they will be dry and tough.

(5) Arrange the egg mixture on the toast, garnish with parsley and serve at once.

Note. In dishes of this kind, the margarine in which the eggs are cooked, unlike the fat used in frying whole eggs, becomes part of the dish. If eggs cooked in this fashion are to be served with bacon, bacon fat may be substituted for the margarine.

[1] To facilitate the removal of the skin put the tomatoes in boiling water for a minute or two, then into cold water.

Example 2. **Lemon Cheese; Orange Cheese.**

Ingredients

Lemon Cheese	*Orange Cheese*
2 oz. butter or margarine.	2 oz. butter or margarine.
2 oz. lump sugar.	2 oz. lump sugar.
6 oz. castor sugar.	6 oz. castor sugar.
Rind and juice of 2 lemons.	Rind and juice of 2 oranges.
	Juice of ½ lemon.
3 eggs.	4 eggs.

Method. (1) Choose fresh and clear-skinned lemons and oranges. Wipe the rinds and rub them with lumps of sugar to remove the oily flavouring. Continue until the rinds are quite smooth; the rubbing must not remove any of the white skin under the rind or the cheese will have a bitter flavour.

(2) Put the butter or margarine, lump and castor sugar and the strained fruit-juice into the inner vessel of a double saucepan and pour boiling water round. Stir the mixture and heat until the sugar is completely dissolved and the mixture hot, but not so hot as to curdle the egg.

(3) Beat the eggs well and add a little cautiously to the butter or margarine in the pan. If there is no sign of curdling, that is, of tiny hardened pieces of egg, add the remainder, stirring well.

(4) Continue to stir the egg methodically and heat until the mixture forms a thin coating over the back of the spoon and clings to the tip. Then pour at once into jars and cover with parchment paper.

Lemon and Orange Cheese are frequently substituted for jam as the filling for sponge sandwiches or for afternoon tea sandwiches of white or brown bread.

Beaten Eggs (*Shell or Dried*) cooked in Medium of Heated Milk.

1. **Plain Custards.** These are mixtures of eggs and sweetened, flavoured milk. When a semi-liquid or so-called 'boiled' custard is made, the mixture is stirred constantly and is heated until the setting or thickening of the egg gives it the consistency of fairly thick cream. A solid custard is left undisturbed and is cooked until the eggs have set sufficiently to give it the consistency of jelly. The degree of thickness or firmness to which a custard will attain depends on the number of eggs used in proportion to the milk.

Proportion of Eggs to Milk.

Solid Custards			*Semi-Liquid Custards*[1] (*'Boiled' Custards*)
Custards to be served in a Dish or Mould.	*Custards to be turned out.* *Small Moulds*	*Large Moulds*	
1 large egg to ½ pint of milk *or* 1 small egg to ⅜ pint of milk.	2 eggs to ½ pint of milk.	3 eggs to ½ pint of milk.	2 eggs to ½ pint of milk. *or* 3–4 eggs to 1 pint of milk.

Additions for All—1–2 teaspoonfuls sugar to ½ pint of milk.
Pinch of salt.
Vanilla or almond essence, etc.

The quantity of eggs may always be increased but **not** decreased, and two yolks may be substituted for a whole egg.

Making of Solid Custards.

Preparation. Break eggs, remove 'specks' and beat well. Add the required amount of milk, pinch of salt, sugar and vanilla or almond essence; mix well.

If dried eggs are used, the milk should be fairly hot when mixed with the reconstituted eggs to allow of the more rapid cooking necessary for good results.

Cooking. (1) **Baked Custards.**

Pour the custard into a greased pie-dish and grate a little nutmeg on top. Put the dish in a baking tin, with hot water round to act as a water-jacket; bake in a moderate oven.[2] The water must simmer gently; if it becomes too hot add a little cold water. *Time*: 1 pint custard, 35-45 minutes.

(2) **Steamed Custards.** Pour the prepared custard into greased darioles or moulds and cover with greased paper. Prepare the saucepan as directed on p. 71 for steaming eggs in moulds or stand the mould on a cutter, allowing the simmering water to come to the top of the cutter. Put the custard to one side of the pan so that the heat does not come directly under the custard. The water must simmer very gently; on no account must it boil. *Time*: ¼-pint moulds, 20 to 30 minutes; 1 pint mould, ¾ to 1 hour.

[1] A more economical custard can be made by using 1 teaspoonful of cornflour to thicken each ½ pint of milk, when 1 egg will suffice. See recipe on p. 146.

[2] When an electric oven is used this water-jacket is best omitted.

If a regulation steamer is used, the water in the boiler must boil only gently.

Tests for Cooking. Baked and steamed custards are sufficiently cooked when they are lightly set in the centre and when a clean cut can be made in them with a knife.

If the cooking has been successful, the custard will be tender and perfectly smooth, not tough and sponge-like. If it has risen and is full of holes, the cooking has been too rapid. As in the case of eggs cooked in moulds, the rising is due to expansion of enclosed air and the holes to the conversion of some of the water into steam. Wateriness of the custard is also due to over-cooking. A custard cooked with the right degree of heat is a soft solid in which a considerable amount of liquid is still distributed. If too much heat is used, the solid parts set still more firmly and cause the liquid to separate out, so that the custard 'breaks' and becomes watery.

Making of Semi-Liquid Custards or 'Boiled' Custards.

(For ingredients see p. 75.)

The risk of curdling is diminished if these are prepared in a double saucepan or in a jug placed inside a saucepan.

Method. (1) Put the milk in the inner vessel and pour boiling water round it. Make the milk thoroughly hot and add sugar.

(2) Add a small portion of the beaten egg to the heated milk; if there is no sign of curdling add the remainder, stirring carefully. Reduce the heat so that the water surrounding the custard simmers gently.

(3) Cook the custard, stirring all the time, until it is thick enough to coat the back of the spoon. It will become thicker as it cools and should then be the consistency of thick cream. The first sign of thickening is the ease with which the spoon moves on the bottom of the pan, due to the setting of the custard there.

(4) Add the vanilla or almond essence and serve.

Signs of Over-cooking. Slight over-cooking causes curdling of the custard; if the heating is continued still further the custard thickens so much that it resembles thin 'buttered' egg. At the first suspicion of over-cooking plunge the vessel containing the custard into a bowl of cold water or pour custard into a large basin and whisk.

2. Cabinet Custard Puddings.

These consist of custard with a basis of bread, cake, etc. The custard is poured over the bread or cake, and when a sufficient quantity has been absorbed, the pudding is steamed or baked until the egg sets just sufficiently to make the parts of the pudding cohere and form a solid mass. The same care is necessary to avoid over-heating as in cooking plain custards, though the solid bread or cake perhaps makes the custard rather less liable to become over-cooked.

The ingredients found in puddings of this type are:

Basis. (*a*) Bread-crumbs, or dice of stale bread or light-coloured crusts, or slices of bread and butter, or tea-cakes.

Or (*b*) Stale cake, sponge-cake or sponge-biscuit with a few macaroons or ratafias.

Custard. 1-3 eggs to every ½ pint of milk required, pinch of salt, sugar and flavouring.

Additions. (*a*) Sultanas or raisins or currants; candied peel.

Or (*b*) Glacé cherries and angelica.

Or (*c*) Jam.

There must be just enough custard to cover the solid part of the pudding. For a baked pudding, the dish should be almost full, but the mould for a steamed pudding should be filled only three-quarters of the way up.

Method. Cut the bread or cake into small dice, crumble biscuits or macaroons. Warm the milk, especially when the bread or cake is very dry; warm milk is absorbed more readily than cold milk, but it must not be so hot as to cook the eggs. Beat the eggs, and add them with the sugar, salt and flavourings to the milk. Pour the custard over the bread or cake, cover the mixture and let it stand for ½ hour or longer, until the bread, etc., is soft and swollen and the custard almost completely absorbed. When bread-crumbs are used a shorter steeping suffices.

Grease a mould or pie-dish and if the pudding is to be turned out, put a round of greased paper at the bottom of the mould to facilitate this, then decorate with fruit. Put in the pudding mixture lightly, adding any fruit not used in decoration and bake or steam as for plain custards until the pudding is lightly set in the centre.

If jam is used it is put in the bottom of the mould or pie-dish.

Illustrative recipes are appended: see pp. 78–81.

Miscellaneous Uses.

In later chapters will be found examples of the use of beaten eggs as a means of introducing air into various gelatine, cereal,

[Continued on p. 80

Pudding	Basis	Custard	
		Eggs and Milk	Flavourings
BREAD AND BUTTER PUDDING	3 thin pieces of bread and 'butter', cut into neat squares, with crusts removed.	1 egg and ½ pint milk. (For 1½ pints of milk for a larger pudding 2 eggs will suffice.)	Pinch of salt. ½ oz. sugar. Essence of vanilla almonds *or* pinch grated lemon rin
TEACAKE, SPONGE-CAKE OR CAKE PUDDING	1 stale tea cake. *Or* 2 sponge- cakes. *Or* the equivalent of the above in plain cake.	1 egg. ½ pint milk.	Pinch of salt. ½ oz. sugar. Essence of vanilla, pinch of grated lemon rind.
PLAIN CABINET PUDDING	¼ lb. stale bread in ¼ inch dice.	1 egg. ½ pint milk.	Pinch of salt. 1 oz. sugar. Essence of vanilla almonds *or* pinch grated lemon rin
VIENNOISE PUDDING	¼ lb. stale bread in ¼ inch dice.	2–3 eggs. ½ pint milk.	Pinch of salt. Grated rind of 1 sm lemon. 1 oz. sugar, 1 teaspoonful water } Fo car me
CABINET PUDDINGS	2 oz. plain cake *or* 2 oz. sponge-cake *or* sponge biscuit, with crumbs of macaroons or ratafias.	1 large *or* 2 small eggs. ½ pint milk.	Pinch of salt. ½ oz. sugar. Essence of vanilla almonds *or* pinch grated lemon ri
LEMON PUDDING	½ pint fine white bread-crumbs. *Note.* If a stiffer pudding than this quantity of crumbs makes is liked, increase the proportion. Cf. Recipe on pp. 80, 81.	Yolks of 2 eggs. 1 pint of milk.	Pinch of salt. 2 oz. sugar. Juice and grated ri of 1 lemon.

[1] When an electric oven is u

Additions	*Additional Directions for Preparing and Cooking Puddings.*
oz. currants or sultanas. oz. candied peel.	Put the slices of 'buttered' bread into a greased pie-dish with fruit and peel between each layer, keeping a little fruit for the top. Add flavoured and sweetened custard and allow bread to steep for 1 hour, or longer if possible. Put the dish in a baking tin and pour boiling or warm water round.[1] Bake in a moderate oven for ¾–1 hour, until the pudding is set.
tablespoonfuls jam.	Split the tea cake or sponge cake, spread with jam, put two halves together and cut into thin strips. Treat cake in similar fashion. Put the cake into a pie-dish, add the custard and steep ½ hour or longer. Put the dish in a baking tin surrounded with boiling or warm water, and bake in a moderate oven ½–¾ hour, or until the pudding is set.[1]
oz. Valencia raisins, stoned and split in two. r 2 tablespoonfuls jam.	Decorate a greased mould or small cups or darioles with the raisins, placing the cut sides to the mould, or put the jam in the bottom of the mould. Steep bread in prepared custard and put into moulds. Steam slowly 1–1¼ hours, or, if in cups or darioles, 20–30 minutes. Prepare ½ pint custard (pp. 76 or 146) or jam sauce (p. 186), and pour it *round*, not over the pudding.
oz. sultanas. oz. candied peel, in dice. oz. castor sugar.	To make the caramel, put the sugar and water in a small iron pan and heat strongly; stir continually and heat until the caramel is a deep brown, but not black colour. Cool slightly, then add the milk. When the milk is a deep coffee colour, add beaten eggs and pour this custard over the bread, raisins, peel, sugar, salt and grated lemon rind. Steam 1½–1¾ hours, or, if in small cups, 25–35 minutes. Serve with ½ pint custard (pp.76 or 146).
8 preserved cherries. oz. angelica *or* citron *or* Valencia raisins.	Grease darioles or small cups and decorate them with halves of cherries and strips of angelica or citron. Break up the cake, etc., and pour the prepared custard over. Let the cake soak for ½ hour, then put into darioles and steam for 15–30 minutes. Serve with ½ pint jam sauce (p. 186) or ½ pint custard (pp. 76 or 146) poured round.
hites of 2 eggs. 2 oz. sugar. } For Meringue.	Boil the milk and pour it over the crumbs. Add to the steeped crumbs salt, 2 oz. sugar, lemon rind and juice, and beaten yolks of eggs. Put the mixture in a greased pie-dish and bake in a moderate oven till set, 20–30 minutes. Prepare the meringue (p. 80) and pile it on top of the pudding. Sift sugar over and bake in a cool oven for ¾ hour or longer till the meringue is crisp and lightly browned.

s water-jacket is best omitted.

Pudding	*Basis*	*Custard*	
		Eggs and Milk	*Flavourings*
QUEEN PUDDING	½ pint fine white bread-crumbs.	Yolks of 1–2 eggs. ½ pint milk.	Pinch of salt. 2 oz. sugar. Grated rind of lemon.

Miscellaneous Uses. (*Continued.*)
cake and batter mixtures, in order to make them light. Below are given other typical examples of such use:

Apple Snow.

Ingredients
3 lbs. apples, ¼ lb. sugar, whites of 3 eggs.
Rind of 1 lemon (optional).

Method. (1) Wipe and prick apples, bake in oven till soft, then remove skin and rub the apple through a sieve. Add sugar, grated lemon rind (if used) and cool.

(2) Put a pinch of salt with the whites and whip till stiff. Fold them carefully into the apple mixture and continue to whisk slowly until the mixture is very stiff. Pile up neatly in a dish. Decorate, if liked, with 'hundreds and thousands' or finely chopped glacé cherries sprinkled on top.

Whites of eggs and sugar form the meringue mixture put on the top of certain puddings and sweet pastries. Whites of eggs are also used to bind together sugar and desiccated cocoanut or ground almonds to form sweet cakes.

Meringue for Tarts, Puddings, etc. Beat the whites of eggs very stiffly. Then add for each white used ½-2 oz. of sifted castor sugar, folding it in lightly but thoroughly. Put the meringue in heaped spoonfuls on the top of the pudding or pastry. Sift castor or icing sugar over and put the dish in a very cool oven for ¾ hour or longer, till the meringue is faintly browned and crisp on the outside. If the egg is beaten too little or too much, or if the meringue is put into too hot an oven, its texture will be leathery.

Additions	*Additional Directions for Preparing and Cooking Puddings.*
z. margarine (optional). 3 tablespoonfuls am. hites of 2 eggs. z. sugar. } For Meringue. *Or* ite of 1 egg.	Boil the milk and pour it over the bread-crumbs. Add salt, 2 oz. sugar, lemon rind, the margarine (if used) and the beaten yolks of eggs. Put the mixture in a greased pie-dish and bake in a moderate oven till set, 20–30 minutes. Spread the jam on top of the pudding, and cover it with the meringue, prepared according to directions on p. 80. Sift sugar over, and bake the pudding in a cool oven for ¾ hour or longer till the meringue is crisp. If the white of *one* egg only is used, pile it on top of the pudding, merely sifting a little sugar over, and serve without further cooking.

If a less rich meringue is desired, the white of egg may be beaten stiffly as before and merely have a little sugar sifted over it. In this case it is best served as it is without cooking.

Cocoanut Cones.

Ingredients

3 oz. desiccated cocoanut. White of 1 egg.
3 oz. castor sugar. Few glacé cherries.

Method. Mix the cocoanut and sifted sugar together. Beat the egg slightly, and fold in the cocoanut and sugar. There should be sufficient egg to hold the sugar and cocoanut together, without making the mixture at all moist or soft. A little milk may be added if necessary. Put the mixture in tiny cone shapes on a baking tray covered with rice paper or greased with margarine; put a small piece of cherry on the top of each, sift sugar over and bake in a cool oven for about ½ hour, till the mixture is set and the cakes very faintly browned.

CHAPTER IX

THE COOKING OF PROTEIN FOODS: MILK AND CHEESE

Cow's Milk is used fresh, or is dried, or evaporated or condensed.

Fresh cow's milk consists of water, caseinogen, fat, lactose (milk sugar) and mineral salts with vitamins A and D, B and C.

The amount of vitamins A and D is very good, but that of vitamin B is small. The carbohydrate, starch, is not present in milk, hence milk is frequently combined with cereals in milk puddings, milk moulds and so forth.

The soluble protein, caseinogen, clots or coagulates when acted upon by the enzyme rennin and this is the preliminary stage in the digestion of milk. When junket is made, the milk is brought to blood-heat and rennet (prepared from the rennin of the calf's stomach) is added. The enzyme precipitates or clots the caseinogen, forming a solid mass. It is important to keep the junket in a warm place until the action of the enzyme is complete and the junket has set.

Dried milk is obtainable in two forms :

(*a*) Full-cream dried milk.
(*b*) Skimmed dried milk.

The nutritive value of dried milk is high as it contains protein and calcium salts. It should be used in addition to, *not as a substitute for* fresh milk, particularly when catering for children.

It may be reconstituted with water or used in powder form.

Directions for Using Dried Milk.

(1) Mix with water, as and when required, according to the directions given on the container. When re-constituted thus, dried milk keeps for approximately the same time as fresh cow's milk.

(2) In making scones, cakes, batter puddings, etc., sift the correct amount of milk powder with the dry ingredients and use the measured water in moistening the ingredients.

(3) When dried milk is used in soups and sauces or in making puddings or moulds with cereals, using a saucepan, it is very liable to burn. To avoid this, make the soup or sauce, the pudding or mould with the *measured water*, keeping back enough to mix the milk powder to a smooth paste. Add this paste at the end of the cooking.

Evaporated milk has had some of the water removed; use as directed on the container.

Condensed milk is evaporated milk to which sugar has been added. The sugar not only sweetens the milk but also preserves it; hence, the milk can be kept two or three days after the tin has been opened. The top of the tin should be removed entirely and the tin be covered with a piece of fine muslin and kept in the coolest place available. If treated thus, the milk remains good for four or five days. In the *unopened* tin the milk remains perfectly good and wholesome almost indefinitely provided it is kept in a cool, dry place. It will, however, thicken with keeping and will darken slightly in colour; this is due to the sugar and these changes have no harmful effect on the product.

Milk is much used in cooking, in the making of sauces and soups, in mixing batter, scone, bun and cake mixtures, and in making puddings and moulds with cereals, as well as in the preparation of various beverages and of patent foods. Fresh cow's milk, dried milk, evaporated milk and sweetened condensed milk can all be used, with a strong preference in favour of fresh milk. Sweetened condensed milk supplies sugar to dishes which require it but obviously cannot be used for savoury dishes or soups nor for sauces for meat, fish and vegetables.

In addition to the various examples of the uses of milk which will be found in subsequent chapters some recipes are given here.

Junket.

Ingredients

1 pint cow's milk (fresh).
½ to 1 oz. sugar.
Pinch of cinnamon.
Grated nutmeg.
Rennet as directed on the bottle.

Method. Warm the milk slightly until it is at blood-heat or lukewarm: add sugar, rennet and pinch of cinnamon, if liked. Stir well and pour at once into individual dishes or into a glass dish which will take the full quantity. Grate nutmeg on top. Leave the dish or dishes undisturbed in a warm place until the junket is set.

Milk Jelly.

Ingredients

½ pt. milk (fresh)
Strip of lemon rind.
½ oz. sugar.
½ oz. gelatine.
1 tablespoonful water.
1 tablespoonful cream.

Method. (1) Wipe a lemon with a clean cloth and cut a thin strip off the rind. Put rind with the milk into a pan and simmer gently for 10 minutes. Remove rind, stir in the sugar until it is dissolved, then put to cool.

(2) Dissolve the gelatine in the water over a gentle heat, stirring well and put this also to cool.

(3) When both milk and gelatine are cool, mix them together, stir in the cream and put into a mould, previously rinsed with cold water. Turn out when set.

If the dissolved gelatine is too hot the milk may curdle; if, on the other hand, the milk is too cool the jelly may be made lumpy.

Egg Flip.

Ingredients

1 egg. ½ pint milk (fresh). Sugar to taste.
Few drops of vanilla.

Method. Break egg into a basin, remove speck, add sugar. Beat until very light and frothy, then pour on the heated milk, taking care not to curdle the egg. Stir well, add vanilla, strain into a glass and serve at once with a biscuit.

Cup of Arrowroot.

Ingredients

2 teaspoonfuls arrowroot.
½ pint milk.
Pinch of salt.
1 teaspoonful sugar.

Method. Mix the arrowroot to a very smooth paste with a little of the cold milk. Bring the remainder of the milk to the boil and pour it on to the arrowroot paste, stirring it rapidly. Return to the pan, bring to boil and boil for three minutes, stirring continually. Add salt and sugar. Serve in a breakfast cup with a biscuit or with toast cut in strips.

Chocolate Cakes.

Ingredients

1 tablespoonful golden syrup.
1 tablespoonful powdered chocolate or cocoa.
1 oz. margarine.
1 tablespoonful dried milk.
Few drops vanilla essence.
Wheat kernels *or* rolled oats, flaked oats, e.g. Quaker Oats, Provost Oats, etc.

Method. (1) Put syrup, chocolate or cocoa with margarine into a pan and heat till melted. Add the dried milk and stir till the mixture is uniformly coloured and smooth. Add vanilla essence.

(2) Add sufficient wheat kernels or oats to take up all the syrup, cocoa and margarine mixture; the kernels, etc. must all be completely coated.

(3) Put small heaps of the mixture on a greased baking tray and put in the larder till cold.

Cottage Cream Cheese.

Fresh cow's milk which has inadvertently turned sour may be converted into cream cheese.[1]

Allow the sour milk to stand until it becomes quite thick. Then put it into a piece of muslin, forming the muslin into a bag, suspend the bag over a basin and leave it to drain for two or three days, until it no longer drips. Season carefully with salt, form into a flat cake and press between two plates.

Cheese.

Cheese is made by the clotting of milk by the enzyme rennin. Its nutritive value is high, consisting as it does of one-third protein, one-third fat and one-third water together with a high concentration of calcium salts, phosphorus and vitamin A. It is an excellent substitute for meat as the percentage of protein is high. It is, however, difficult to digest because the fat surrounds the protein and the gastric juices cannot act until the fat is broken down.

To facilitate digestion:

(1) Grate raw cheese and serve with some form of carbohydrate, e.g. bread, biscuits, or oatmeal bannocks.

(2) Cook cheese correctly in order to avoid 'oiling' of the fat and toughening of the protein.

(*a*) Grate finely or shred finely and chop before using.

(*b*) Add cheese to sauces after they have been well cooked and allowed to cool slightly. (See recipes on p. 112 (No. 2); Macaroni Cheese, pp. 144–5; Cheese Cauliflower, p. 166.)

(*c*) In making Rarebit, Toasted Cheese (p. 46) and similar dishes, melt the cheese over a very gentle heat.

(*d*) When browning cheese under the griller use great heat to prevent a greasy appearance round the edge of the dish.

(*e*) Cook cheese pastry slowly; the starch grains in the flour will absorb the fat and the pastry will be light and crisp.

Uses of Raw Cheese.

(1) Use as a sandwich filling combining it with watercress, mustard and cress, or shredded lettuce or chopped parsley or slices of tomato if liked, and seasoning it carefully with pepper.

(2) Serve grated with vegetable salads.

(3) Serve grated with vegetable soups.

[1] Small amounts of sour milk, too small for conversion into Cream Cheese can be used in making scones, etc. See p. 227 and pp. 230–231.

Cooked Cheese Dishes.

Toasted Cheese.

Ingredients

1¼ oz. flour.
1¼ oz. margarine.
½ pint milk.
3 oz. grated cheese.
Pepper, cayenne and mixed mustard to taste.
2 slices of bread (preferably wholemeal).

Method. (1) Grate the cheese or cut it into very thin shreds and chop lightly.

(2) Make ½ pt. of savoury white sauce with the margarine, flour and milk (see pp. 151–2). Boil gently for 2 or 3 minutes, then cool slightly.

(3) Add the grated cheese and heat gently till the cheese has melted. Add seasonings.

(4) While the cheese melts toast the slices of bread, cut each slice into four and place in a fireproof dish. 'Butter' toast first.

(5) Pour the cheese mixture on to the 'buttered' toast and brown quickly under the griller. Serve at once.

Buck Rarebit.

Ingredients

2 eggs.
4 oz. cheese.
1 tablespoonful milk.
1 oz. margarine.
¼–½ teaspoonful made mustard.
Pepper and cayenne.
Paprika pepper.
2 slices of bread (preferably wholemeal).

Method. (1) Grate cheese finely and make preparations for poaching eggs. (See p. 72.)

(2) Melt margarine in a pan, draw pan to one side and add milk, grated cheese and seasonings. Stir over a very low heat until the cheese has melted and the mixture is thick and creamy.

(3) Toast bread, 'butter' it, place in a fireproof dish. Pour the cheese mixture over and brown quickly under the griller.

(4) Meanwhile, begin poaching the eggs (see p. 72); put one on each slice of bread and sprinkle a little paprika pepper on top.

Cheese and Tomatoes.

Ingredients

4 good-sized tomatoes.
4 slices bread.
3 oz. grated cheese.
Salt, pepper, cayenne.

Method. (1) Cut tomatoes into slices and put a pinch of salt on each.

(2) Grate cheese finely.

(3) Toast slices of bread on one side only and put in a greased fireproof dish with the *untoasted* side uppermost.

(4) Arrange tomato on bread, sprinkle cheese over, season with pepper and cayenne and heat quickly under griller to brown cheese.

(5) Serve very hot.

Semolina and Cheese Pudding.

Ingredients

1 pt. milk.	2 oz. cheese.
1½ oz. semolina.	Salt, pepper and made mustard.
1–2 eggs.	

Method. (1) Mix semolina to a smooth paste with a little of the milk.

(2) Bring the rest of the milk to the boil, add it to the paste, mix smoothly and boil gently, stirring frequently, for ten minutes.

(3) Cool slightly, then add the eggs, well beaten, seasonings and grated cheese.

(4) Pour into a greased pie-dish and bake in a moderate oven for about ¾ hour until the pudding is set and a golden-brown colour.

Cheese Soufflé.

Ingredients

1 oz. fine flour.	3 oz. Parmesan or other cheese (dry).
1 oz. margarine.	Salt, cayenne.
¼ pt. milk *or* tomato pulp.	Lemon juice (if milk be used).
Yolks and whites of 3 eggs.	

Method. (1) Prepare a moderately hot oven. Grease fireproof dish or dishes thickly.

(2) Melt margarine in a pan, add sifted flour, and mix thoroughly over a gentle heat. Add milk gradually, stirring all the time and keeping the mixture very smooth. Boil 2 minutes.

(3) Add finely grated cheese, seasonings, and when slightly cool, the yolks of eggs, one at a time, beating each in well.

(4) Add pinch of salt to whites of eggs, beat stiffly and fold gently but thoroughly into the mixture until it is uniform in colour and consistency.

(5) Put mixture into dish and bake for about 30 minutes in a moderate oven keeping the oven door shut for the first half of the time. Serve immediately, covering the dish while taking it to the table.

Potatoes Stuffed with Cheese.

Ingredients

4 large potatoes.
3–4 oz. grated cheese.
1½–2 oz. margarine.
Milk for mashing potato-mixture.
Salt and pepper.

Method. (1) Bake potatoes in their skins, until soft (see p. 162).

(2) Split potatoes lengthwise along one side, scoop out the contents, put in a pan and mash with margarine and hot milk. Season and beat till the mixture has a smooth texture.

(3) Finally, add the grated cheese, mix well and heat gently, then pile the mixture into the potato jackets and serve hot.

CHAPTER X

THE COOKING OF PROTEIN FOODS: MEAT

The lean part of meat consists of bundles of muscle held together by connective tissues. Each bundle consists of a number of fibres. If, by means of two needles, some fibres are separated out, soaked in salt water, and examined under the microscope, they are seen to resemble hollow tubes.

The fat of meat is contained in cells which are massed together in large numbers or are distributed among the fibres and tissues.[1]

Meat Albumen. The 'juices' of meat contained in and clinging to the fibres consist of water holding certain substances in solution. One of these substances is meat-albumen, whose properties resemble those of egg-albumen.

Properties of Meat Proteins.

Test	*Result*
1 *Action of Cold Water.* Shred 1–2 oz. lean steak, scraping it across the grain. Put into a tumbler, cover with cold water, and leave 10–20 minutes, stirring occasionally.	Substances dissolve out which make the water first a faint yellow, then a red colour. As the colour of the water deepens, the meat becomes paler.
Filter some of the extract.	A clear red liquid is obtained.

[1] These facts may conveniently be demonstrated by examining the hind leg of a rabbit and a section of the muscle of an ox, e.g. shoulder steak.

<table>
<tr><th>Test</th><th colspan="3">Result</th></tr>
<tr><td>2. Stages of Coagulation of Extract.
(a) Put in a test tube a thermometer and sufficient filtered extract to cover the bulb. Put the test tube in a beaker or pan of cold water with a second thermometer. Heat slowly and note the temperatures at which changes occur.</td><td>Temperature of Water.
61° C.—142° F.
68° C.—154° F.
80° C.—176° F.</td><td>Temperature of Extract.
53° C.—128° F.
57° C.—135° F.
72° C.—161° F.</td><td>Appearance of Extract.[1]
Cloudy.
Opaque.
Small pieces of semi-solid, light brown substance are seen in the liquid.</td></tr>
<tr><td>(b) Filter half the contents of the test tube, examine the residue and filtrate.</td><td colspan="3">The residue is a soft jelly-like substance, resembling soft-boiled white of egg in consistency. It is albumen extracted from the meat. The filtrate is a clear transparent liquid.</td></tr>
<tr><td>(c) Continue to heat the remainder of the extract.</td><td colspan="3">Dark-brown, gritty pieces of albumen float in a clear watery liquid.</td></tr>
<tr><td>3. Action of Weak Acids on Extract.
Put some filtered extract in a test tube and add a little lemon juice or vinegar.</td><td colspan="3">Extract becomes clouded, showing slight coagulation; colour changes to deep orange.</td></tr>
<tr><td>4. Action of Boiling Water.
Put a small piece of meat (1–2 oz.) into a pan of boiling water and boil for a moment or two. Cut open and examine the meat.</td><td colspan="3">A rind or case about the thickness of a sixpence has formed on the outside of the meat; the interior is still raw and red. The water is a faint yellow colour, showing that the hardening of the meat on the surface has allowed of only a slight loss of the soluble substance.</td></tr>
</table>

When meat is tested after the soluble albumen has been extracted, it is found that it still contains an abundance of protein matter, mainly the substance known as myosin. Myosin resembles meat-albumen in that, as we have seen, it is hardened by heat, but differs from it in being insoluble in water, though it *is* soluble in a salt solution of the strength of $\frac{1}{2}$ per cent, a fact to be borne in mind in connection with the pickling of meat.

Meat is thus a valuable if somewhat expensive source of 'first-class' protein and of fats with the accompanying vitamins A and D, meat from grass-fed animals being richer in vitamins

[1] The temperatures given are an average of the results obtained in a series of tests. They vary slightly owing to the difficulty of distinguishing *precisely* when each change occurs.

than that of animals whose diet has lacked plant materials. Liver is rich not only in vitamins A and D, but in B also.

COOKING OF MEAT

The processes vary according as it is required:

(1) To *extract* all the soluble substances of the meat, as in making beef-tea, meat-stock and soups, etc.

(2) To *retain* all the soluble substances, as in roasting, grilling, baking, steaming, boiling and frying meat.

(3) The *process of stewing* is a compromise between these two aims. Meat chosen for stewing is usually somewhat tough, and the making of it tender involves partial extraction of the soluble substances.

I. The Making of Meat Extracts: Beef-Tea, Invalid Mutton Broth, etc.

Ingredients

Beef-Tea	*Invalid Mutton Broth*
½ lb. lean, juicy beef of good quality, from rump or round.	½ lb. lean, juicy mutton from upper end or middle of leg.
½ pint of water.	½ pint of water.
Pinch of salt.	Pinch of salt.

The *method* of preparing the extracts, based on the results of the experiments just described, is as follows:

(1) Remove fat and gristle from the meat and shred it finely to expose a large surface; if time is short, chop or mince it.

(2) Put meat, water and salt into a bowl, cover, and steep ½ hour or longer, stirring occasionally.

(3) Put the extract into a double saucepan, with cold water in the outer pan. Heat slowly, till the water-jacket simmers gently. Cook carefully thus for 40–50 minutes; from time to time stir the extract and press the meat against the sides of the pan.

(4) When the extract has just lost its reddish colour, press it through a coarse strainer or through butter muslin. Add cayenne and celery salt (if seasonings are allowable) and remove all traces of fat by drawing strips of kitchen paper across the surface. Serve in a warmed cup or basin.

Meat extracts do not keep good long and should be made in quantities sufficient for one day only. To re-heat them, put them in a jar in a pan of boiling water and leave till hot.

Food Value of Meat Extracts. If beef-tea or mutton broth stands undisturbed for a short time it separates into two layers

The upper layer of clear fluid consists of water holding in solution the mineral salts of meat and certain substances known as 'extractives' which give meat its characteristic flavour and have valuable stimulating properties. The lower layer consists of soft flake-like particles of lightly-set albumen, the only genuinely nutritious material in the extract. If the meat used is of poor quality or if it is heated to too high a temperature, the extract is practically worthless as food. Indeed, it is the general opinion that however carefully they are made, extracts can only contain a small percentage of the nutriment of the meat. They should be regarded not as food, but rather as tonics or medicines, which by virtue of their stimulating properties give the body temporary energy. They are easily digested and absorbed and are valuable in cases of exhaustion or of weak digestion, but they cannot re-build the tissues wasted by illness, though they help to prevent further loss.

As we have seen, the meat used for extracts, though flavourless, is not without value, and in small quantities can be used in réchauffés (*e.g.* Rissoles, Shepherd's Pie), or failing these, in the making of stock.

II. Boiling, Steaming, Baking, Roasting, Grilling and Frying Meat.

Choice of Cookery Processes. It is necessary to consider (1) the quality, (2) the weight, (3) the thickness of the meat.

Quality. For baking, roasting, grilling and frying, meat should be of good quality, well-hung and tender. Meat of less good quality should be steamed, boiled or stewed to soften and gelatinise the connective tissues. In baking, roasting and grilling, the only moisture available is that in the meat itself, and this is insufficient when tough tissues are plentiful.

Boiling, steaming and stewing are not suited to meat which has much fat; such meat, provided it is otherwise suitable, should be baked or roasted when the fat will supply dripping.

Weight and Thickness. Baking and roasting are suitable for thick pieces of meat, weighing four pounds and upwards, grilling and frying for smaller, thinner pieces of the same quality. Boiling also is adapted to large, thick pieces of meat; smaller, thinner pieces, of rather less good quality, should be steamed or stewed, the latter being advisable for meat which is both tough and flavourless. Steaming is suitable for both small and large pieces of meat, but the apparatus required and the length of the cooking often limit its use to the former.

Principle involved in Boiling, Steaming, Baking, Roasting, Grilling and Frying Meat.

In cooking meat by these methods the purpose is (1) to retain all the soluble albumen, salts and extractives, (2) to develop the flavours, (3) to set the proteins and soften the connective tissues and by so doing to make the meat tender and palatable.

Whichever method is chosen, the first step, as we have seen, is to apply sufficient heat to harden the surface of the meat and thus to prevent as far as possible the loss of the soluble substances. Inside the casing thus formed the meat cooks in its own juices. This subsequent cooking is carried on more slowly to allow the heat to reach the centre of the meat, which, like all foods, is a bad conductor of heat.

If the high temperature required for the first few minutes of the cooking were maintained, the outer layers of the meat would be over-cooked and dry, while the interior was still raw and tough.

As regards the vitamins A and D present in meat fat, it would seem probable that as these vitamins can resist a considerable degree of heat in the absence of air only those of the outermost layers are affected by cooking.

Roasting Meat. In household cooking this process is now very seldom used, either baking or 'pot-roasting' taking its place.

Pot-Roasting. This is a useful and economical way of cooking pieces of meat or birds too small to bake satisfactorily in the oven and too big to grill. Prepare the meat as for baking (see p. 96). Heat in a strong unlined pan sufficient dripping to make a layer about 1½ inches deep, and when a faint blue smoke rises (cf. pp. 190 and 191) put in the meat and brown the surface all over. Cover the pan closely and cook the meat at a moderate temperature, turning it from time to time. Allow the same time as for baking. Serve and make the gravy as for baked meat (pp. 96, 97).

Meat cooked in its own Juices.

A very useful process of cooking meat in a pan with little liquid other than its own juices may conveniently be described here.

Veal Cooked in its own Juices.[1]

Ingredients

Piece of veal (fillet or shoulder) about 3 lbs.
2–3 oz. margarine or bacon dripping or both.
Salt, pepper, small bayleaf.
White stock or water.

Method. (1) Wash the veal and tie with string into as compact a shape as possible.

(2) Put fat in a saucepan and heat carefully, *so that it does not smoke*. Put in the veal and cook *slowly* over a gentle heat until all the surface is a delicate brown colour. Cover the pan.

(3) Add a little salt and pepper and the bayleaf and not more than one tablespoonful stock or water. Cover the pan with a well-fitting lid and cook over a *very gentle heat* for two to three hours, according to the weight and thickness of the piece of meat. The meat should *not* require additional stock or water, if the cooking is done sufficiently slowly.

(4) Remove string from the meat, place on a hot dish and keep hot.

(5) Skim fat off the gravy and add three to four tablespoonfuls stock or water, scraping from the sides and bottom of the pan all the coagulated meat juices. Bring to the boil, season if necessary, strain into a tureen and serve with the meat.

The success of this method of cooking depends on (1) slow browning of the meat followed by (2) slow cooking.

Grilling, Frying.

Grilling. For grilling, meat must be of good quality, with only a little fat, and should be in pieces not less than 1 inch and not more than 1½ inches thick. Rump steak, loin chops and fillets from the thick end of a leg of mutton are all suitable.

In grilling, the outside of the meat is hardened at once as in roasting, and the cooking is then continued more slowly, but the thinness of the pieces necessitates even the slower cooking being fairly rapid. In grilling, as in frying, the time of cooking is regulated by the thickness of the meat and not, as in cooking joints, mainly by the weight.

[1] *Lean Beef* can be successfully cooked on the same lines, a piece of topside, weighing 3 lbs., taking 4–5 hours. In this case, when browning is completed, ½ pint of water, a 'bouquet garni', i.e. a sprig of parsley, a blade of mace, one bayleaf and, if possible, a sprig each of thyme, marjoram and rosemary, all tied in a piece of muslin, are added as well as 2 peeled onions, each with a clove stuck in it and 6 small carrots sliced thinly. The carrots are served with the meat as a garnish.

Method and Time	*Preparation of Meat*	*Apparatus*	*Hardening of Surface Albume*
BOILING FRESH MEAT. *Time*[1] 20 minutes per lb. and 20 minutes over, calculated from the time boiling begins.	Wash the meat and trim it, cutting off superfluous fat. See that the meat is properly jointed, and, if necessary, tie it with string into a compact shape.	Choose a pan just large enough to hold the joint and to contain enough boiling water or stock to cover the meat completely. Add 2 teaspoonfuls of salt to each ½ gallon of water or stock. If the meat is cooked in stock its flavour is improved.	Put the meat i the boiling wa or stock, bring quickly to the b and boil 5 minu Skim well.
BOILING SALT AND PICKLED MEAT. *Time*[1] 25 minutes per pound and 25 minutes over, calculated from the time boiling begins.	Wash meat in cold water. If very salt, steep 1–2 hours in cold water. Soak hams which have been dried as well as salted for 12 hours, scrape well, remove any rancid fat and saw off knuckle bone.	Choose a pan of suitable size and fill with unsalted tepid water. If the meat is very salt and has been dried as well as salted, use cold water. *Note.* The use of tepid or cold water extracts some of the salt and softens the hardened fibres.	Put the meat i the cold or te water and br slowly to the b Boil 5 minu Skim well. *Note.* The s heating preve further harder of the fibres.
STEAMING FRESH MEAT. *Time*[1] 35 minutes per pound and 35 minutes over. Steaks, etc., ¾–1 in. thick, 1 hour; ½–¾ in. thick, ¾ hr.	Wash meat and fasten into shape.	Have a good supply of water in the boiler and see that the lid of the steamer fits tightly. If necessary, wedge it with a piece of twisted paper.	Put the meat i the steamer an the water boil for the first minutes.

[1] In cooking very large or very small jc

Subsequent Cooking	Serving
Check boiling by adding a little cold water, d simmer carefully at a temperature not above ° Cent. (180° Fahr.) for the rest of the time, eping the pan covered closely. When all the um has been removed, add flavourings, etc. *Flavourings.* 1 onion, 2 or 3 cloves, 1 tea-oonful peppercorns, 2 or 3 bay leaves, sprig of rsley, and bunch of herbs. Put the cloves into onion and tie the rest of the flavourings in a ce of muslin. *Vegetables.* Pare and cut into large pieces. the vegetables are used merely for flavouring, arrot and 1 turnip will suffice and should be t into the pan with the onion and herbs, etc. r serving with the meat, any of the following y be added, allowing the times given: 2 or carrots (2–2½ hours); 2 or 3 turnips (1–1½ urs); 10 potatoes (½–¾ hour); 1 lb. Brussels outs (15–20 minutes). These quantities are table for a joint weighing 8–10 lbs.	Put the meat on a hot dish, garnish with vegetables and serve with some of the liquid or with sauce made in part with the liquid in which the meat has cooked. For mutton, white, caper, nasturtium, onion and parsley sauces are all suitable; for veal, parsley sauce (see pp. 151–153). Allow 1 pint sauce for a joint 8–10 lbs. in weight. Coat the meat with part of the sauce and serve the rest in a tureen. Keep the liquid for boiling a second piece of meat or for stock or gravy.
Check boiling by adding a little cold water d simmer very slowly for the rest of the time. he meat is so salt that the water tastes strongly it, or if the water is wanted for stock, change t the end of an hour and cover the meat with sh water at the same temperature. When nmering begins, add flavourings (onion, ves, etc.) as for fresh meat, and if the meat is be served hot, add vegetables also. Suet mplings as well as vegetables may be served h hot meat. If the water has to be changed, se additions must not be made until this has en done. *Dumplings.* 4 oz. flour, 1 tablespoonful ead-crumbs, pinch of salt, 2 oz. suet, finely opped, ¼ teaspoonful baking-powder, ⅛ pint d water. Mix the dry ingredients together; mediately before cooking, moisten with water d form the dough into 8 balls. Put into the pan our before the cooking of the meat is complete.	*Meat to be served hot.* Serve in the same way as fresh meat, garnished with vegetables and dumplings and coated with sauce, if this is served. For pickled beef, prepare white or caper sauce (see pp. 151–153). *Meat to be served cold.* Put the meat in a bowl, pour over it the water in which it has been cooked and let it go cold. When quite cold take out and serve according to the kind of meat, viz.: *Beef, Tongue.* Brush with melted glaze. *Ham.* Remove skin and sift raspings over. Put a frill round the knuckle.
Let the water boil steadily at the normal rate. vourings and vegetables may be cooked with meat, if desired. Allow for the vegetables f as long again as the times reckoned for boil-. Old carrots and turnips which require long oking may be boiled in the water-boiler of the amer.	Serve as for boiled meat. If sauce is to be served, use the liquid (condensed steam with meat juice) which collects on the floor of the steamer. Milk may be added if required to make the desired quantity of liquid.

se times must be modified (see p. 99).

Frying. Full directions for frying meat are given in Chapter XVI. Meat which is suitable for grilling is also suitable for frying.

Made Meat Dishes, e.g. galantines, meat rolls, are boiled,

COMPARATIVE DIRECTIONS FC

Method and Time	*Preparation of Meat*	*Apparatus*	*Hardening of Surface Albume of Meat.*
BAKING. *Time.*[1] *Beef and Mutton.* 20 minutes per pound and 20 minutes over. *Lamb and Veal.* 25 minutes per pound and 25 minutes over. *Pork.* 30 minutes per pound and 30 minutes over.	Wash the meat, see that it is properly jointed, and cut off any superfluous fat. If necessary tie the joint into shape with string.	(*a*) Have oven clean, well ventilated and set at correct control. Gas: Regulo No. 6; Electric 375–400 degrees.[2] (*b*) Put meat on a grid in a baking-tin, placing uppermost the side which will be uppermost when served.	Put the meat the centre of oven for the fi 10 to 15 minutes the cooking.
GRILLING. *Time.* For meat 1½ inch thick, 18–15 mins. For meat 1¼ inch thick, 15–12 mins. For meat 1 inch thick, 10–8 mins. For mutton cut-	Remove all but a narrow rim of fat, beat with a damp rolling pin to bruise the fibres and trim neatly. Sprinkle with salt and pepper, and if	(*a*) Have a clear, red-hot fire high in the grate *or* a red-hot gas or electric grill. (*b*) For fire-grilling, heat a double broiler or a gridiron and grease with suet or	For *fire-grilli* Place the meat position and h the broiler or gr iron from inches above glowing coals. For *gas or elec* grilling place

[1] In baking very large or very small joi

[2] Meat albumen coagulates at a temperature of 160° Fahr. Too strong h tough. Basting with hot fat is to be avoided as this causes undue hardening

steamed and baked on exactly the same principle as joints of meat, that is to say, they are cooked rapidly for the first few minutes, then rather more slowly for the remainder of the time.

ꓭAKING AND GRILLING MEAT

Subsequent Cooking	*Serving*
Cook the meat at a slightly lower temperature or the rest of the time. When the meat is half-ooked, turn it over. *Tests for Cooking.* If the dripping makes a entle sizzling sound and the surface of the meat ends out slight spurts of steam every now and hen, the cooking is as it should be. If there is no novement either of the dripping or the meat, the emperature is too low and the juices will soften he hardened surface and escape. If the dripping mokes and splutters vigorously, the tempera-ure is too high, and the meat will be dry and harred. The tests given below for grilling may be ap-lied to the thick fleshy part of the meat to deter-nine if it is sufficiently cooked. At the end of the aking the surface of the meat should be brown nd crisp, and the interior tender, evenly cooked, till slightly red, and full of juices.	Put the meat on a hot dish and keep it hot while the gravy is made. *To make gravy.* Pour dripping from the tin, keeping back the brown, semi-solid substances (meat juices) on the bottom of the tin. Add to these ½–¾ pint stock or water and mix well. Bring to boil, season and strain. The gravy should be clear and perfectly free from fat. If the colour is pale, add a *few* drops of caramel or gravy-browning. *Thickened gravy for veal, pork and richer meats.* Pour off fat, add to brown sediment 1 teaspoonful flour to every ½ pint of gravy required. Mix and cook, stirring till the flour browns; add stock gradually, boil, season and strain. Colour with caramel if necessary. Pour a little gravy round the dish and serve the rest in a tureen.
Hold the meat rather further away from the re or griller for the rest of the cooking. Turn very 2 minutes to cook the meat evenly and to revent the escape of juices which tend to flow way from the heat. The drops of melted fat hich occasionally cause a flame improve rather han spoil the flavour of the meat. As the meat ooks, the conversion of some of its moisture nto steam makes it plump and puffy.	Serve at once on a very hot dish. Pour over the meat a little melted butter or margarine or put on it small pats of Maître d'Hôtel Butter made beforehand. *Maître d'Hôtel Butter.* *Ingredients.* ½ oz. butter or margarine.

nese times must be modified (see p. 99).
ries and cracks the surface, the juices escape and the meat shrinks and becomes ne surface protein.

Method and Time	*Preparation of Meat*	*Apparatus*	*Hardening of Surface Albumen of Meat*
GRILLING—*cont.* lets, ½ inch thick, 8–6 minutes.	very lean, brush with melted margarine.	fat the part on which the meat will rest. For gas or electric grilling, place the wire stand in the griller pan.	meat on the wi stand and put tl griller pan in pos tion under tl heated plates. In each case tu the meat at the er of one minute a harden the secor side in the san way for one mi ute. If a gridiron used, turn the me either with ste tongs or with tw spoons to avo pricking it wi consequent loss juices.

Times for Cooking Joints of Meat

We have seen that the times allowed for cooking joints of meat are as follows:

Baking and Roasting.	Beef and Mutton	20	mins. per lb. and	20	mins. over.
	Lamb and Veal -	25	,, ,,	25	,,
	Pork - - -	30	,, ,,	30	,,
Boiling.	Fresh Meat -	20	,, ,,	20	,,
	Salt and Pickled Meat - -	25	,, ,,	25	,,
Steaming.	Fresh Meat -	35	,, ,,	35	,,

The two factors which decide these times are (1) the amount of heat used; (2) the kind of meat.

(1) *Amount of Heat Used.* It will be noted that the time required for steaming meat is greater than the time needed for boiling, since, though the heating value of steam, as we have seen, is great, the quantity of steam used is small, making the process of steaming a slow one.

(2) *Kind of Meat.* The fibres of the muscle of young animals, *e.g.* lamb, veal, are finer and more closely packed together than those of adult animals, and heat consequently takes longer to

Subsequent Cooking	*Serving*
Tests for Cooking. Press the meat lightly with knife. (1) If the meat yields readily to pressure ut does not regain its shape, or only very slowly, t is still underdone. (2) If it is still puffy and ields readily to pressure but regains its shape lmost at once, it is sufficiently cooked for average astes, that is to say, it is slightly red inside and eddish juices run from it. (3) If the puffiness as subsided owing to the drying up of the juices, nd the meat does not yield to pressure, it is vercooked and dry. The surface of grilled meat hould be crisp and a rich brown colour. If the olour is not good, it indicates lack of sufficient eat in the initial stages of the cooking.	1 teaspoonful parsley, finely chopped. Salt and pepper. Few drops of lemon juice. *Method*. Put on a plate, mix together with a knife and form into small balls, using butter pats or two knives.

penetrate them. This, and the fact that veal and lamb are not palatable when underdone, account for their being cooked for a slightly longer time than beef and mutton.

Pork is most unwholesome if underdone and for this reason is given a good allowance of time.

The fibres of pickled and salted meat are hardened by the salt; such meat is therefore cooked for a longer time than would be given to the same meat if it were fresh.

When a joint *weighs less or more than the average*, the times given in the table are found by experience to require modification. It is a safe rule to allow 5 minutes *more* per pound than the time given for joints weighing under 4 pounds, and 5 minutes *less* per pound for joints weighing over 10 pounds.

One knows that it takes nearly as long to boil 1 pint of water as to boil $1\frac{1}{4}$ or $1\frac{1}{2}$ pints, using exactly similar pans and exactly the same amount of heat: this is because the pan itself has to be heated by conduction before the convection currents which heat the water can be set up. Similarly, in cooking meat a certain time is required to bring the whole joint to the temperature at which cooking begins, and it takes almost as long to raise a 3 pound joint to the required temperature as one weighing 5 pounds. Once this has been done, very little extra time is needed to cook 2 or 3 pounds more, so that for large joints the time per pound is decreased rather than increased.

COMPARATIVE RECIPES

Name of Stew	*Meat*	*Vegetables, Herbs, Seasonings*
1. IRISH STEW.	2 lbs. middle neck, scrag, or breast of mutton, divided by cutting between the bones.	2 lbs. potatoes. 1 large or 2 small onions. 1 large or 2 small turnip (optional). 1 tablespoonful chopped parsley 2 teaspoonfuls salt. 1 teaspoonful pepper.
2. HOT POT.	2 lbs. mutton as for Irish Stew *or* 2 lbs. shoulder steak.	As for Irish Stew, omittin turnips and parsley.
3. LAMB STEW.	1½ lbs. scrag end of neck of lamb, divided by cutting between the bones.	1 teaspoonful chopped onion. 1 pint shelled green peas. 1 tablespoonful chopped mint. 1½ teaspoonfuls salt. ¾ teaspoonful pepper.
4. STEWED RABBIT.	1 rabbit, in joints. ¼ lb. fat bacon (in slices) for bacon rolls.	1 small onion (whole). 2–3 slices of carrot. Blade of mace. 1 bay leaf. 1 sprig of parsley. 1 teaspoonful salt. 8 peppercorns.

[1] See also general direction

Finally, all reckonings by weight must be checked by a consideration of the shape and thickness of the joint. For example, it takes longer for heat to travel to the centre of a sirloin of beef,

[Continued on p. 104

OR STEWS: METHOD I.

Gravy	*Additional Directions*[1]
pint of cold stock or water.	Cut onion into thin rings, turnip into slices, potatoes into quarters or halves according to size. Arrange meat and vegetables in a pan in layers, beginning with meat and ending with potatoes; season each layer. Add stock or water and simmer for 2 hours. Shake the pan occasionally so that the stew does not stick to it and burn. Serve on a hot dish and sprinkle the finely chopped parsley over.
old stock or water to come half-way up the dish.	Peel potatoes thinly, put into cold salted water and bring to the boil. Drain and cut into quarters or halves, according to size. Prepare the remaining ingredients as for Irish Stew, and cook the stew in a greased 'hot-pot' or other fire-proof dish, covering with greased paper. Stew in a moderate oven for 2–2½ hours. When the potatoes are soft take off the paper, so that the top layer becomes brown.
pint warm stock or water. oz. flour.	Put meat, onion and seasonings into the stock and simmer ½ hour. Shell the peas, add them with the mint to the stew and simmer 1–1¼ hours longer. Before serving, mix the flour to a smooth paste with a little cold water or stock, and add to the stew; stir thoroughly and cook for 10 minutes.
pints warm white stock or water. *uce*. 1 oz. margarine. oz. flour. pint milk. pint liquid strained from rabbit. tablespoonful finely chopped parsley. lt and pepper.	Cut the rabbit into neat joints suitable for serving and wash them. Steep for a short time in cold salted water any part on which blood has coagulated and blanch if necessary. Put the rabbit, vegetables, herbs and seasonings in the stock or water and simmer for 1½–2 hours. *Sauce*. Make white sauce (pp. 151–152), bring to the boil, boil 2 or 3 minutes, add seasonings and chopped parsley. *Bacon Rolls*. Remove rinds from the bacon, cut into short lengths, roll up, thread on a skewer, put into a dripping tin and cook in the oven or under the gas griller for 5–10 minutes till the rolls are crisp and brown. *To serve*. Arrange the rabbit neatly on the dish, coat the pieces with the sauce and garnish with the bacon rolls.

ı pp. 105, 106.

Name of Stew	Meat	Vegetables, Herbs, Seasoning[s]
5. Fricassee of Chicken.	1 chicken, skinned and divided into joints, viz.: 2 wings. 2 legs (4 pieces). 2 breast pieces. 1 merry-thought.	2–3 slices onion. 1 carrot (sliced). 1 blade of mace. 1 small bay leaf. 1 sprig of parsley. 1 good teaspoonful of salt. 8 peppercorns.

COMPARATIVE RECIP[ES]

Name of Stew	Meat	Ingredients for Gravy
Haricot Mutton.	1 lb. middle neck of mutton, divided by cutting between the bones.	1 oz. dripping. ½ oz. flour. ½ pint stock or water. 1 teaspoonful salt. ½ teaspoonful pepper.
Stewed Veal.	1 lb. fillet of veal. ¼ lb. fat bacon.	Dripping from bacon. ½ oz. flour. ½ pint stock or water. 1 teaspoonful salt. ½ teaspoonful pepper.
Stewed Veal with Macaroni and Tomatoes.	1 lb. fillet of veal. ¼ lb. fat bacon.	Dripping from bacon. ½ oz. flour. ½pint stock or water. 1 teaspoonful of salt. ½ teaspoonful of pepper.

[1] See also general directi[ons]

Gravy	Additional Directions
Sufficient warm white stock or water to cover the chicken. *Sauce.* 1½ oz. margarine. 1½ oz. flour. ¾ pint liquid strained from chicken. Yolks of 2–3 eggs. Juice of ½ lemon. Salt and pepper.	Put the chicken with the vegetables, etc., into a pan, cover with stock or water, bring to the boil, skim and reduce the heat till the stew simmers gently. Cook for ¾–1 hour, then arrange the joints in a heap in the middle of a hot dish. *Sauce.* Make sauce (Method 2, p. 152), taking care that the flour and margarine do not become discoloured. When the sauce has boiled, cool slightly, and add first the lemon-juice, then the beaten yolks of egg. Stir constantly till the egg thickens, taking care it does not curdle. Season and pour carefully over the chicken. *Note.* 1 The chicken carcase should be broken up, and with the giblets, be cooked either with the meat to enrich the gravy or separately for stock. 2. Rabbit may be cooked in the same way.

FOR STEWS: METHOD II.

Vegetables, Herbs, Seasonings, etc.	*Additional Directions*[1]
small onion cut into rings. carrot, small turnip } cut into dice.	Coat the meat with flour, salt and pepper and fry it in the heated dripping. Make gravy with the remainder of seasoned flour, browning it before adding the stock. Bring to the boil, cool slightly, add meat, onions, carrot and turnip. Stew 2–2½ hours.
small onion, whole. carrot, sliced.	Cut the bacon into dice, fry it and put it on a hot plate. Heat the dripping and fry the pieces of veal in it. Then brown the flour in the remainder of the fat, add the stock, bring the gravy to the boil and season it. Return the bacon and veal to the pan, add the carrot and onion. Stew 2–2½ hours. Remove the onion before serving.
small onion, cut into rings. carrot, sliced. blade of mace, bay-leaf, sprig of parsley. *Garnish.* lb. tomatoes. oz. macaroni.	Stew the veal as above, but fry the sliced onion after browning the veal and before browning the flour. Stew for 2–2½ hours. Remove mace, bay-leaf, and parsley before serving the stew. *Garnish.—Tomatoes.* Grease a baking tin and sprinkle with a little water or stock. Cut the tomatoes in halves, season, and put a tiny bit of margarine on each. Put in the tin and cover closely with greased paper. Bake in a moderate oven 10–15 minutes till the tomatoes are tender, but still smooth and unwrinkled. *Macaroni.* Cook according to directions on p. 144. *To serve.* Put the stew on a hot dish, pile the macaroni at each end and garnish with the tomatoes.

[1] ...n pp. 105, 106.

Name of Stew	*Meat*	*Vegetables, Herbs, Seasonings*
STEWED STEAK WITH SAVOURY DUMPLINGS.	1 lb. steak from shoulder or round, *or* 1 lb. gravy beef.	1½ oz. dripping. ¾ oz. flour. 1½ pints stock or water. 1 teaspoonful of salt. ½ teaspoonful of pepper.
BEEF OR VEAL ROLLS.	1¼ lbs. lean steak from the round, *or* fillet of veal, ½ inch thick. ¼ lb. bacon, sliced.	1½ oz. dripping. ¾ oz. flour. ¾ pint stock or water. 1 teaspoonful of salt. ½ teaspoonful of pepper.
CURRIED VEAL OR MUTTON.	1½ lbs. fillet of veal. ¼ lb. fat bacon } *Or*, 1½ lbs. middle neck or leg of mutton, freed from superfluous fat.	Dripping from bacon (for veal). 1½ oz. margarine or dripping (fo mutton). ¾ oz. flour. 1 teaspoonful curry paste. 1 tablespoonful curry powder. Juice of ½ lemon. ¾ pint stock or water. Salt.

which is boned and rolled, than to the centre of the same joint cooked in its natural shape, though the weight of the rolled joint is actually less, owing to the removal of the bone. In the same way stuffed joints, *e.g.* fillet of veal, require a rather longer allowance of time than is necessary for the same joint without stuffing. Again, the time for cooking such thin joints as breast of veal, neck of mutton, cannot be regulated wholly by weight, since the thickness does not increase with the weight.

Vegetables, Herbs, Seasonings, etc.	*Additional Directions*
onion, cut into rings. *Dumplings.* ¼ lb. flour. oz. chopped suet. teaspoonful chopped onion. teaspoonfuls chopped parsley. easpoonful herbs. easpoonful salt. easpoonful pepper. teaspoonful baking powder. pint cold water.	Stew the meat as for Haricot Mutton, allowing 2–2½ hours for steak from the shoulder or round, 3–4 hours for gravy beef. *Dumplings.* Mix all the dry ingredients together; immediately before cooking, moisten with the cold water and mix to a fairly stiff paste. Form into 10–12 small balls and roll in flour. Cook with the stew for the last ¾ hour. *To serve.* Put the meat on a hot dish and garnish with the dumplings.
small onion, finely minced. teaspoonful lemon rind, finely chopped. teaspoonful capers, (optional). ablespoonful red currant jelly.	Cut the meat into 8 squares, put a piece of bacon on each, dredge with the flour, salt and pepper, roll up and tie loosely with thread. Heat dripping and fry in it first the meat rolls, then the onion. Brown the remainder of flour and continue to make the gravy in the usual way. Put back the meat and onion, add the lemon rind and capers and stew 2–2½ hours. Just before serving, add the red currant jelly. Remove the thread from the rolls, arrange neatly on a dish and strain the gravy over.
mall onions } finely our apple. } minced. omato sliced *or* ablespoonful tomato pulp or sauce. easpoonful chutney. z. Patna rice.	Fry the bacon, if used, and put it on a hot plate. Heat the dripping and fry the onion. Take out the onion, re-heat the fat and brown the pieces of meat. Return the bacon and onion to the pan. Mix together the flour, curry paste and curry powder and sprinkle them with the lemon juice over the meat. Cover the pan and cook the curry *very gently* for 10 minutes to develop the flavours. Shake the pan from time to time to keep the meat from burning. Add the stock gradually, mixing it smoothly. Put in the apple, tomato, chutney and salt, and simmer gently 2–2½ hours, covering the pan closely. Shortly before the curry is to be dished, boil the rice (see p. 142) and arrange in a border round the curry or serve in a separate dish.

Stewing.

Preparation of Ingredients for Stews. (1) Cut away superfluous fat and divide the meat into pieces about 1 inch thick and 2 inches across, or less, if it is very tough, to expose an increased surface to the softening action of the heated stock. If rump steak, chops and other cuts of meat of good quality are stewed, they should be cooked whole.

(2) Clean and pare the vegetables and cut them up neatly.

Cut onions into rings or chop them, unless they are not to be served, when they should be left whole.

(3) Tie peppercorns, herbs, etc., in a small piece of muslin.

(4) Remove fat from stock to be used.

Cooking of Stews. Method I.

Arrange meat and vegetables in alternate layers in a pan or stew-jar, seasoning each layer well. Add herbs, etc., and cold or lukewarm stock or water. Cover the pan closely and heat slowly till the stew simmers. Simmer very gently at about 71° Cent. (160° Fahr.) from 2–4 hours, according to the quality of the meat.

Method II (suitable only for meat of fairly good quality).

1. *Browning of Meat and Preparation of Gravy.* Coat the pieces of meat (if desired) with flour seasoned with salt and pepper. If the meat is very lean and bacon is used, cut the latter into small slices or dice, put it in a warmed pan and fry till it is crisp and brown; take it out, and put it on a hot plate. Heat the bacon dripping, or whatever fat is used, until a pale blue vapour rises from it; put in the pieces of meat, brown them quickly and lightly and put them on the hot plate. This preparatory cooking should not harden the surface of the meat to any extent, and red juices should still run from it.

Re-heat the fat, fry the onion till it is a golden-brown colour and put it with the meat. Or, omit the frying and add the onion with the rest of the vegetables after the gravy is made.

To make the gravy, add the seasoned flour, or what remains of it, to the dripping, stir it constantly and cook it till it is a bright coffee colour. Cool the pan for a moment, then add the stock gradually and mix it smoothly, cooking the gravy slightly between each addition. Finally, boil the gravy for 2–3 minutes.

2. *Stewing of Meat.* Cool the gravy slightly, put in the bacon (if any), the meat and the juices which have run from it, and the fried onions; add the remainder of the vegetables and the seasonings. Cover the pan closely and let the stew simmer gently but steadily for the required time, 2–4 hours, according to the quality of the meat.

It will be seen from what has been said that stewing results neither in complete extraction nor in complete retention of the juices. If the meat were put straightway into boiling liquid so as to harden the surface at once, not only would the softening of the tough tissues be hindered but the meat would not absorb the flavours of the vegetables and herbs so readily. But though the escape of some of the juices of the meat is thus unavoidable, they are not wasted since they form part of the gravy in which the meat is stewed, and which, being small in quantity, is served with the meat and vegetables as part of the dish.[1]

The maintenance of a low, steady temperature is most essential to the success of a stew. If a stew boils or even simmers rapidly for any length of time, the connective tissues of the meat are softened and gelatinised so completely that the fibres fall apart; as a consequence, the meat *looks* tender, but in reality is dry, tough and difficult to masticate.

While long, slow cooking is essential to make the meat of a stew tender and well-flavoured, it has not, as we have seen, a good effect on the vitamin C of the vegetables cooked with it. Where stews occur only occasionally in a plentiful and varied diet which includes fresh vegetables and fruit this need cause no great concern. When, however, stewing is used frequently, as it is liable to be when cooking is done on a large scale, as in army camps, schools, hospitals and other institutions, it is wise either to cook the vegetables separately and rapidly, adding them to the stew a short time before serving, or, if it is possible (since the flavour of the stew cooked thus suffers), to be at pains to see that vitamin C is supplied by other means.[2]

CHAPTER XI

THE COOKING OF PROTEIN FOODS: FISH

Like meat, fish contains proteins, fats, salts and water, with vitamins A and D associated with animal fats. The proportion of water is greater in fish than in meat, and fish is therefore a less concentrated food. It is also more digestible,

[1] When meat which is known to be tender and well-flavoured is stewed, it is advisable to boil it for a few moments to prevent too great a loss of juices.

[2] In this connection a report on an investigation into an outbreak of 82 cases of scurvy in a camp in Scotland is of interest. "At the time potatoes were scarce, but the ration contained a fair proportion of fresh meat, and 2 oz. of swedes were available daily. These . . . are among the most potent anti-scorbutic vegetables we possess, and if cooked satisfactorily should have afforded considerable protection. The causes of the outbreak were investigated by Prof. L. Hill, who discovered that the meat was always served as a stew, the vegetables added and the whole cooked for about 5 hours. This circumstance was considered by Prof. Hill to be a sufficient explanation of the outbreak."

though it has not the stimulating properties which characterise meat.

It is usual to classify the different kinds of fish according as they are:

(1) *Oily Fish, e.g.* salmon, mackerel, herring. These have a large amount of fat distributed throughout the somewhat dark-coloured flesh.

(2) *White Fish, e.g.* plaice, cod, halibut, whiting. In these most of the fat is in the liver, and the amount is much less than in oily fish.

Since their flesh lacks both fats and the vitamins associated with them white fish are the less nourishing, though also the more digestible of the two groups. Oily fish, provided they can be digested, are in many cases cheap sources of fats and vitamins, and it seems probable that their vitamin value, like that of meat, is not seriously diminished by cooking.

(3) *Shell-fish.* These belong to two groups (*a*) *Crustacea, e.g.* lobster, crab, cray-fish, prawns, shrimps, (*b*) *Molluscs, e.g.* oysters, mussels. Shell-fish do not make any substantial contribution to a diet, though glycogen, the animal carbohydrate (see p. 57) is found in small proportions in lobsters, crabs, and oysters. Eaten to make a change in a diet or to stimulate appetite, shell-fish have their uses, but should be eaten only when in season and very fresh, since they decompose rapidly. There are the further drawbacks that crustacea are in general foul feeders and that molluscs may convey typhoid infection, having become themselves infected by sewage poured into the sea near their breeding places.

Shell-fish are for the most part indigestible; lobsters and crabs, for example, have very long and coarse muscle fibres. Oysters are more digestible raw than cooked. In most shell-fish there is some inedible part, *e.g.* the beard of oysters, gills of lobsters and crabs.

Recipes illustrating the use of shell-fish will be found on pp. 119–20.

Examination of Fish Flesh.

Examine a piece of cod and compare its appearance and structure with those of meat. Notice that (1) the flesh is more watery and less dense, and (2) the connective tissues hold the fibres together less firmly and are themselves finer than those of meat.

This greater delicacy of structure has to be taken into account in cooking fish. Since the flesh is less firm and compact than that of meat, heat can penetrate more easily and a shorter cooking suffices. Further, the flesh breaks very easily, and care is necessary both in cooking and handling.

Properties of Fish Proteins.

Test	*Result*
1. *Action of Cold Water.* Pound a little cod or fresh haddock in a mortar, cover with cold water and leave 10–15 minutes, stirring occasionally; filter the extract.	Substances are dissolved out which give the water a faint yellow colour and a strong smell of fish.
2. *Stages of Coagulation of Extract.* Determine these in the manner already described for meat. (Test 2, p. 89.)	
3 *Action of Weak Acids on Extract.* Test as in Experiment 3 for meat, p. 89.	
4. *Action of Boiling Water.* Put a small piece of cod or haddock into boiling water and cook two or three minutes.	The fish becomes white and set. A soft white jelly, somewhat resembling white of egg, lightly set, can often be seen between the flakes.[1] The water smells of fish, showing that the coagulation of the flesh has not wholly prevented loss of substance.

Preparation of Fish for Cooking.

All fish require careful cleansing and trimming before cooking. Wash them very thoroughly in cold water, and rub with salt to remove any blood near the backbone and any dark-coloured membranes. The fish must not soak in water, but must be dried at once with a towel. If the fish is to be fried or baked, rub it with a little flour to complete the drying.

Bones, trimmings and pieces of skin should be washed and made into fish-stock (see p. 124). This can be substituted for milk in stewing fish or in making sauce to be served with the fish.

[1] Coagulated fish albumen can readily be seen between the large flakes near the bone in a piece of cooked cod or halibut, or on the surface of steamed fillets of fish.

COOKING OF FISH

The principles observed in cooking fish are the same as those which underlie the cooking of meat and have already been demonstrated by the tests. They may be summarised thus: (1) When all the substance of the flesh is to be *extracted*, as in making a fish soup (see recipe on p. 132), cut up the fish, put it into cold liquid, heat it slowly and let it simmer.

(2) When all the substance is to be *retained* use sufficient heat to set the flesh on the surface, then cook rather more slowly to allow the heat to reach the interior.

(3) When fish is *stewed*, the milk (or whatever liquid is used), into which the fish is first put may be lukewarm or even cold, since any soluble substance lost from the fish becomes part of the sauce into which the milk is afterwards converted.

Methods of Cooking Fish.

I. Boiling Fish. Boiling is best suited for the cooking of whole fish of a fair size or for large pieces of fish. Since the flesh breaks easily and since some loss of substance and flavour is unavoidable, boiling is not well adapted for cooking such small fish as whiting or haddock, or for small cuts of fish weighing less than 2–3 pounds.

If the directions given below are compared with those already given for boiling meat, it will be seen that the process is modified to suit the less dense and compact structure of fish.

To boil fish. (1) Weigh the fish, trim and wash it.

(2) Put into a pan just enough water to cover the fish and bring it to the boil. To every gallon of water add 2 oz. salt and 2 tablespoonfuls of vinegar or the juice of half a lemon; the acids hasten the setting of the albumen.

(3) Lay the fish on the drainer of the fish-kettle. If an ordinary saucepan is used, put the fish on a plate or large saucer which will fit into the pan, put the plate on a piece of loosely woven muslin and tie the opposite corners of the muslin so that the fish can be lifted out of the pan without breaking.

(4) When the water boils, draw the pan to one side and put in the fish when the water is just *below* boiling point. Simmer very gently for the rest of the cooking.

If the water were actually boiling when the fish was put in, it would cause the skin to contract and break. The subsequent cooking must be watched very carefully; if the water becomes too hot, its movements will break the flesh and cause much loss of substance.

Exceptions. Salmon. Put into boiling water and boil two or three minutes to soften the tough skin and to keep the flesh a good colour. Then simmer gently for the rest of the cooking. *Mackerel.* Put into lukewarm water so that the very thin skin is not broken, and simmer carefully.

Time for Boiling. 6 minutes to the pound for small cod, hake, etc., and medium-sized pieces of fish; 10 minutes to the pound for large whole cod, halibut, salmon, etc., or large pieces of fish. For small fish allow 6–10 minutes.

Tests. When the cooking is complete, a skewer put into the thickest part of the flesh near the bone will pierce it easily. A cut of fish is sufficiently cooked when the flesh *just begins* to come away from the bone.

(5) Drain the fish well and put on a drainer on a hot dish. Garnish with parsley and thin slices of lemon. Serve sauce in a tureen; white, parsley, anchovy, shrimp and egg sauces are all suitable (see pp. 152–153).

II. Steaming. Steamed fish has not quite the same woolly texture as boiled fish, and its substance and flavour are much better preserved. Such substance as *does* escape mixes with the condensed steam which can be served with the fish, either as it is or as part of a sauce. Steaming is well adapted for cooking small whole fish, or pieces of fish, or cutlets and fillets for which boiling would be totally unsuitable. Whenever it is practicable, steaming should be used in preference to boiling for large pieces of fish also. The delicate taste and absence of fat or other substances which would cause it to be rich and indigestible make steamed fish suitable for invalids or for people with weak digestions.

To steam fish. (1) Weigh the fish, trim and wash it. Rub with a cut lemon or squeeze lemon juice over it and season with salt and pepper; a little very finely chopped parsley may also be sprinkled over it. The fish may be prepared thus some time beforehand to allow the flavour of the seasonings to be absorbed.

(2) Put the fish on a saucer or small plate so that it can be lifted out easily, and put it in the steamer.

If a steamer is not available, flat thin pieces of fish, *e.g.* fillets, cutlets, may be steamed between two greased plates or saucers placed over a pan of boiling water (see Process 2, p. 53).

[Continued on p. 114

COMPARATIVE RECIPES T

Type	*Ingredients*	*Preparation of Fish*
No. 1. Adapted to fillets of fish.	1 plaice or sole, filleted. *Fish Stock*. Bones, trimmings, and skin of fish, ¼ pint of milk, ¼ pint water, blade of mace, bay-leaf, parsley, 3 or 4 peppercorns, salt. *Sauce*. 1 oz. margarine, ¾ oz. flour, ½ pint strained fish stock, lemon juice, salt, pepper.	Skin fillets, wash, roll u skin side inwards, and loosely with string. Wa bones, trimmings, etc.
No. 2. Adapted to small cuts of cod, hake, halibut, etc.; whole plaice, lemon soles or whitings (skinned), which do not provide bones, skin, etc., for stock.	6 cutlets of cod, *or* 2 or 3 steaks of halibut, etc. ½ pint milk, salt, pepper. *Sauce*. 1 oz. margarine, 1 oz. flour, ¼ pint fresh milk, ½ pint of milk used to cook fish, salt, pepper, lemon juice, 1 tablespoonful grated Parmesan cheese (optional).	Wash fish, dry, a sprinkle with salt and pe per. Grease a baking thickly, put fish in and pc the milk round, not over i
No. 3. Adapted to same kind of fish as No. 2. Fish is cooked in dish in which it is served.	2–3 whitings (skinned), *or* similar quantity of other fish. 2 teaspoonfuls flour, a very little nutmeg, salt, pepper, 1 oz. of margarine, ¾ pint milk, 1–2 teaspoonfuls finely chopped parsley.	Wash and dry fish. M together flour, salt, pep and nutmeg and coat t with them. Grease firepr dish thickly. Put in fi sprinkle parsley over a pour milk round.
No. 4. Adapted to smoked and dried fish, e.g. smoked filleted fish.	1 lb. smoked filleted fish. 3 or 4 eggs. *Sauce*. 1 oz. margarine, 1 oz. flour, ½ pint of milk, ¼ pint water used to cook fish.	Put fish in boiling wate covered pan and heat ge for 5 minutes.
No. 5. Adapted to smoked and dried fish, e.g. Finnan haddock or smoked filleted fish.	1 Finnan haddock. *Maître d'Hôtel Butter*. ½ oz. margarine, 1 teaspoonful finely chopped parsley, salt, pepper, little lemon juice.	Put fish in boiling wa for 5 minutes, then rem the skin. The fish may cut into pieces of a suita size for serving.

[1] For general directi

.LUSTRATE THE STEWING OF FISH[1]

Stewing	Serving
Put ingredients for fish stock in enamel-lined ın, heat slowly and boil very gently ½ hour, then ·ain and return to the pan. Put fillets in pan ıd simmer for about 10 minutes till they are ıder but not at all broken. Take out, remove ·ing and keep hot. Make white sauce according directions on pp. 151, 152. *Note.* For a rather small fish ¼ pint of sauce ffices.	Put fillets on a hot dish and coat with sauce. Garnish each fillet with a little very finely chopped parsley, or with coralline pepper.
Cover the fish closely with a greased paper or ıte, stew gently in a moderately hot oven for out 30 minutes, till fish is tender. Make white cheese sauce (see pp. 151 and 115) adding first fresh milk, then that strained from the fish. If eese is used, add it at the last.	Put fish on a hot dish, and if white sauce is used pour part over the fish and serve the rest in a tureen. Garnish fish with parsley and very thin slices of lemon. If cheese sauce is made, pour it all over the fish and put the dish in the oven or under the griller for about 10 minutes to brown.
Cover fish closely with greased paper or plate, t in the oven and simmer gently for 20–30 nutes, according to thickness of fish. *Note.* In this method, the flour thickens the lk as the fish cooks, and the fat used to grease dish becomes part of the sauce thus made.	Garnish with parsley and serve at once.
Make white sauce (see pp. 151, 152). Cut fillets o 3 or 4 pieces of suitable size for serving, put m in the sauce, and let sauce simmer *very* ıtly 15–20 minutes till fish is thoroughly hot. ach the eggs (see p. 72).	Arrange fish on a hot dish, pour sauce round and put a poached egg on top of each piece of fish.
ut the fish into a frying pan, pour on hot ter till it is almost covered, put plate over pan l let water simmer *very* gently 10–15 minutes. *Maître d'Hôtel Butter*. Mix margarine, parsley, ., pepper and lemon juice to a paste and form o small balls.	Drain fish, put on a hot dish and distribute the balls of Maître d'Hôtel Butter over it.

p. 114.

Type	*Ingredients*	*Preparation of Fish*
No. 6. Adapted to fresh herrings.	4 large herrings. ½ small teaspoonful salt. ⅛ teaspoonful pepper. ⅛ teaspoonful mustard. Pinch of nutmeg. 2 bay leaves. ¼ pint of vinegar. Cold water.	Wash herrings, remov scales, heads and tails. Spli and take out bones. Mi together the seasonings, sal pepper, etc., and sprinkl a little on each fillet. Ro up the fillets skin side in wards and pack tightly in pie dish Bruise the roes, mi with them a little seasonin and vinegar, and pour ove fish; add enough water t cover the fish, and put in th bay leaves

(3) Allow from one-third to one-half as long again as for boiling, *i.e.* 8–9 minutes per pound for small pieces, 13–15 minutes for large pieces of fish; doubled fillets, 15–20 minutes; cutlets or steaks, 1 inch thick, 30–40 minutes.

(4) Serve on a hot dish with the liquid, or cover with sauce to which the liquid has been added. Garnish with parsley and lemon.

III. Stewing. Like steaming, stewing is well adapted to the cooking of small whole fish and cuts of fish. There is no waste of flavour or substance since the fish stock or milk in which it is stewed is almost invariably served with the fish, either as it is or in the form of sauce.[1]

The maintenance of a low, steady temperature is, if possible, even more important in stewing fish than in stewing meat, since the fibres of fish fall apart much more readily than those of meat. As in stewing meat, the pan or dish must be covered closely to retain all the flavours.

The recipes on pages 112–113 show typical methods of stewing fish.

IV. Baking.

Most fish can be baked, and the process is well adapted for cut pieces of fish or for whole fish too small to boil. Baking does not make the fish watery and does not involve any loss of the flavour or substance of the fish; any 'juices' which escape can

[1] Recipe No. 1 on page 112 is a good example of the utilisation of all the nutriment and flavour to be got from the fish.

Stewing	*Serving*
Cover the dish with a greased paper and let the fish stew gently in a slow oven for 1¼–1½ hours.	Take out the rolls of fish when they are cold, and serve on a dish, garnishing each roll with a small piece of parsley.

be served with the fish, either as they are or as part of a sauce. Baked fish usually have an attractive exterior and are more savoury than fish cooked by other methods, especially when the fish are stuffed.

Methods of Baking Fish

1. Fish without Stuffing.

Method 1. This method is suitable for (*a*) skinned whitings; (*b*) soles, plaice, etc., from which the dark skin has been removed; (*c*) fillets of sole, plaice, fresh haddock; (*d*) cutlets and steaks of cod, hake, etc.

Wash and dry the fish and season with salt, pepper and lemon juice. Fillets of fish may be laid one on top of the other or doubled in half, or rolled up and tied loosely with cotton which must be removed before serving. In each case put the skinned side innermost.

Put the fish in a greased tin or fire-proof dish, covering it closely with a greased paper, or put it between two greased plates. Bake in a moderate oven, allowing 10–15 minutes for fillets, 20–30 minutes for cutlets, steaks, and such flat and rounded fish as plaice and fresh haddocks.

To Serve. (*a*) Put the fish on a hot dish and mask with sauce.[1] If Cheese Sauce (*i.e.* savoury white sauce (pp. 151, 152) with the

[1] When *fillets* are baked, fish stock should be made from the bones and trimmings (p. 124) and used for the sauce. Any juices which come from the fish should be added to it.

[Continued on p. 118

Fish, etc.	*Ingredients for Stuffing*	*Preparation of Fish*
No. 1. 2 lbs. of cod or hake, middle cut. 1½ oz. margarine or dripping. Salt, pepper, lemon juice. Beaten egg.	3 tablespoonfuls fine bread-crumbs. 1 teaspoonful finely chopped parsley. ½ teaspoonful mixed herbs. Grated rind of ½ lemon. Salt, pepper.	Wash fish, dry with a tow and rub with flour. Sprink over lemon juice, salt ar pepper and brush with eg Mix together the ingredien for the stuffing and roll the fis in it.
No. 2. 1 small fresh haddock. Beaten egg. } (optional). Browned crumbs. } 1½ oz. margarine or dripping. Parsley and lemon for garnish. ½ pint anchovy or parsley sauce (p. 153).	2 tablespoonfuls fine bread-crumbs. ½ tablespoonful finely chopped parsley. Pinch of dried herbs, salt and pepper. 1 oz. margarine *or* dripping *or* suet, finely chopped. Egg or milk to moisten above.	Remove eyes, scrape scale wash and dry well. Pack th stuffing into the cavity of th fish, sew it up with a need and thread, leaving room f the stuffing to swell. Wi fine string and a trussin needle, fasten the fish into t shape of an 'S'. Brush wi egg and sift browned crum over; the egg and crumbs m be omitted if desired.
No. 3. 1 large plaice or sole. Salt, pepper and lemon juice. ½ pint stock or water. 1 oz. margarine or dripping. Browned crumbs. Parsley for garnish.	1 tablespoonful fine bread-crumbs. Pinch of mixed herbs. 1 tablespoonful finely chopped parsley. Few shrimps or bits of red lobster (optional). Juice and grated rind of ½ lemon. Salt, pepper, cayenne. Beaten egg to moisten the above.	Remove the black skin fro the fish, trim and wash Make a cut down the cen line of the skinned side, or, the black skin is left on, as may be, on the white side. C each side of the cut, lift up t flesh with the knife for a lit way, as though filleting t fish. Into the cavities th made press the stuffing, givi the fish a rounded shape a bringing the edges fairly cl together. Season with sa pepper and lemon juice.
No. 4. 1 plaice or sole, whole or filleted. 1 oz. margarine.	3–4 tablespoonfuls white bread-crumbs. 2 or 3 mushrooms, peeled and chopped. 1 tablespoonful finely chopped parsley. Salt and pepper.	Remove the dark skin fro the fish if desired, trim a wash it. Mix together the gredients for the stuffi Grease a fireproof dish thic and cover the bottom of it w half the stuffing; lay the fish it, the skinned side or wh skin uppermost, and sprin the rest of the stuffing on top.

[1] Note carefully the precautions tak

Cooking[1]	*Serving*
Put the fish in a greased baking tin with ırgarine or dripping. Bake in a mod- ıtely hot oven 30–40 minutes, basting quently, to brown fish.	Put fish on a hot dish. Add a little stock or water to the juices in the tin, bring to the boil, season and strain round the fish. Garnish with parsley.
Grease a tin with 1½ oz. margarine or pping, put in the fish and bake in a rly quick oven for 20–30 minutes, sting frequently.	Put the fish on a hot dish and re- move the string carefully. Garnish with parsley and slices of lemon, arranged alternately down the back of the fish. Serve the sauce in a tureen.
Put the fish in a greased tin with small ces of margarine or dripping, and pour ck round. Bake in a moderate oven for minutes, or rather longer for a very ck fish. If the fish becomes at all dry, ver it with a greased paper.	Lift the fish very carefully on to a hot dish and sift browned crumbs over. Strain the stock round the fish, and garnish with small pieces of pars- ley arranged down the centre to mark the division.
Cover the fish with a greased paper and e in a moderate oven for 15–20 ıutes, according to the thickness of fish.	Serve the fish at once in the dish in which it was baked.

revent the fish from becoming dry

Fish, etc.	*Ingredients for Stuffing*	*Preparation of Fish*
No. 5. 2 mackerel. 1 oz. margarine or dripping. 1 oz. bread-crumbs. Parsley for garnish. ½ pint anchovy sauce (p. 153) *or* ¼ pint mustard sauce (p. 153).	Roes of 2 mackerel. 2 oz. fine bread-crumbs. 2 teaspoonfuls finely chopped parsley. ½ teaspoonful lemon thyme. Grated rind of ½ lemon. Salt and pepper. Yolk of 1 egg.	Clean the mackerel, rem the head and fins. Split o down the back and remove bones. Bruise the roes, with the dry ingredients of stuffing, season and moi with beaten yolk of egg. Spr the stuffing on the inside of fish and lay the second fish top, skin side outermost.
No. 6. 2 steaks of cod or hake. 2 slices of lean ham or bacon. Margarine or dripping. ½ pint anchovy sauce (p. 153).	3 tablespoonfuls fine bread-crumbs. 3 tablespoonfuls finely chopped parsley. Pinch of herbs. Juice and grated rind of ½ lemon. Salt and pepper. Beaten egg or milk to moisten above.	Wash and dry the Spread stuffing on each p and cover with bacon or h

addition of 1 tablespoonful grated Parmesan or other cheese to each ½ pint sauce) is used, put the dish in a hot oven or under the griller to brown.

Or (*b*) put the fish on a hot dish, with small pats of Maître d'Hôtel Butter (Recipe 5, p. 113) on it. Garnish with parsley.

Or (*c*) sift fine bread-crumbs, freshly browned, over the fish and pour the fish juices round it. Garnish with parsley and lemon.

Method 2. This is suitable for the same fish as Method 1 Season the fish with salt, pepper and lemon juice, brush with beaten egg and coat with fine bread-crumbs, freshly browned Bake as in Method 1 and serve on a hot dish, garnished with parsley and lemon. Pour the fish juices round the fish and serve sauce in a tureen.

Method 3. This is suitable for (*a*) unskinned plaice, soles haddocks; (*b*) cuts of cod, hake, etc., with the skin still in position.

Put the fish in a greased tin, putting the white side of flat fish uppermost. Place pieces of margarine or dripping in the tin for basting, or pour melted margarine or dripping over the fish and strew fine white bread-crumbs over it. Bake in a fairly quick oven, allowing 20–30 minutes for plaice, soles and

Cooking	*Serving*
Grease a baking tin with half the mar- ;ine or dripping and put in the fish; .lt the rest of the margarine or dripping d pour it over. Sprinkle 1 oz. of bread- ımbs on top and bake 20–25 minutes a moderate oven.	Lift the fish carefully on to a hot dish and garnish with parsley. Serve the sauce in a tureen.
Put the fish in a greased baking tin or h. Cover with a greased paper and ke in a moderate oven 20–35 minutes. move the greased paper for the last few nutes.	Serve on a hot dish and pour the anchovy sauce round.

haddocks, and the same time for cuts of fish about 2 pounds in weight.

Serve the fish on a hot dish, garnished with parsley and lemon.

2. Stuffed Fish.

There are several ways of stuffing fish, instances of which are given in the recipes on pages 116–119.

V. Frying. The frying of fish is described fully in Chapter XVI.

Recipes for Use of Shell Fish

Potted Lobster or Salmon.

Ingredients

¾ lb. tinned lobster or salmon.
3 oz. margarine.
Pepper, cayenne, powdered mace.
Clarified margarine for covering.

Method. Chop the lobster or salmon finely, first removing any bones, etc. Melt 3 oz. margarine in a pan, add seasonings, then the fish, with further seasoning, if desirable. Heat the mixture well, pressing the parts together. While it is still warm, press it into pots, making the surface level.

Melt some margarine in a pan, remove the curd, then cover the fish with it.

Lobster or Crab Soufflé.

Ingredients. As for Cheese Soufflé (see p. 87) substituting ¼ lb. lobster or crab purée (*i.e.* lobster or crab meat, rubbed through a sieve) for cheese. *Method.* As for Cheese Soufflé.

Shrimp Paste. For sandwich filling.

Ingredients

2 oz. margarine.
½ gill picked shrimps.
Pepper and cayenne.
Little lemon juice.

Method. Chop shrimps very finely. Beat margarine to a cream, add shrimps, seasoning and lemon juice. Blend well together.

CHAPTER XII

THE COOKING OF PROTEIN FOODS: BONES, GRISTLE, ETC.

We now come to the consideration of gelatin, a protein obtained from the connective tissues, gristle and bones of animals, whose properties differ greatly from those of the proteins we have already examined.

Extraction and Properties of Gelatin.

Test	*Result*
(1) Take some fresh bones, remove fat and marrow, put in a pan and barely cover with cold water. Put the lid on the pan and let the water boil gently 5–6 hours, adding more water if required. Strain into a bowl.	A greyish coloured liquid is obtained.
(2) Cool the liquid.	Liquid sets to a jelly as it cools.
(3) Heat a little of the jelly.	Jelly melts.
(4) Heat melted jelly to boiling point. (5) Add lemon juice or vinegar to melted jelly.	No coagulation, such as occurs with egg-albumen, meat-albumen.

The liquid thus obtained is a solution of gelatin extracted from the bones by prolonged boiling in water. Gelatin can be extracted in the same manner from gristle and all connective tissues of meat, as well as from the bones, skin and tissues of fish. (Cf. (1) the jellying of an extract prepared from meat rich in connective tissues, *e.g.* beef-tea prepared from shin beef; (2) the preparation of jellies from calves' feet which are used because of their gristly nature; (3) the thin film of jelly often found on a dish on which a piece of boiled fish has cooled.)

Commercial Extraction of Gelatin.

The bones and tissues of animals are heated by steam under pressure. The first product extracted is made into size or glue; after further purification, the substance obtained is dried and sold as gelatine.

Kitchen Extraction of Gelatin.

This may take two forms: (1) the preparation of the stock so constantly in request in all good cooking for soups, stews, gravies, sauces and other purposes; (2) the preparation of jellies.

STOCK MAKING

Though we have thus far spoken only of bones and gristle in this connection, meat also is used, and by the term 'stock' is meant either an extract of gelatin, or an extract of the soluble substances of meat, or both, according as the stock is made of bones and gristle only, of fresh meat only, or of bones, gristle and meat combined.

In the ordinary household the cost of stock need only be slight if, during the daily inspection of the larder, all such things as are suitable are set on one side for the stock-pot. It should not, as a rule, be necessary to buy meat or bones for the purpose.

The following should be utilised in stock making:

Foundation Materials. (1) Bones and gristle of meat, poultry or game, raw or cooked. (2) Trimmings of raw or cooked meat, not suitable for other purposes, *e.g.* scraps from joints, meat from beef-tea. (3) Necks, hearts and gizzards of poultry or game.

Flavouring Materials. (1) Rinds and trimmings of tongue, ham or bacon. (2) Small pieces of raw carrot, turnip, onion, leaves and outer sticks of celery, or leeks, also vegetables of these kinds which have already been used for flavouring.[1] (3) Herbs and seasonings.

[1] A selection only of these may be used, if so desired, or they may be omitted completely. See p. 124.

Liquid. (1) Water in which meat or poultry has been cooked. (2) Small portions of unthickened gravy not required for other purposes. (3) Cooking water from such cereals as rice, macaroni, or such legumes as haricot beans, lentils, or such vegetables as celery, asparagus, etc. In default of these water is used.

The stock-pot is *not* intended to be a useful institution for the reception of odds and ends of food of every description. Care must be taken that the suitable materials are perfectly clean and free from all taint, and that the following *unsuitable* substances are not used:

(1) Pieces of fat which would make the stock greasy.

(2) Pieces of potato or cabbage. (3) Pieces of bread or toast. (4) Pieces of cheese. (5) Remains of thick sauce or gravy. (6) Remains of sauce containing milk.	These would either thicken the stock or would cause it quickly to become sour.

(7) Cooking water from cabbage, sprouts, etc.

Fish bones and trimmings should be kept if fish stock is required for fish soup or sauces; they must be cooked separately, according to the directions given on p. 124.

Preparation of Materials for Meat and Bone Stock.

The cooking of stock should be begun each forenoon so that it can be strained and cooled in the evening and be ready for use the next day. The fat can be removed much more easily when the stock is cold than when it is warm.

Meat: cut into small pieces, removing fat. *Bones*: break up into small pieces and remove fat and marrow. *Necks of poultry and game*: steep in salt water to remove any blood. *Vegetables*: clean, pare and cut into large pieces. *Herbs*: tie fresh herbs in a bunch; tie dried herbs and peppercorns, etc., in a small piece of muslin. Allow to 3–5 pounds of meat or meat and bones, 1 onion, 1 carrot, 1 turnip, 1 stick celery, 1 sprig parsley, 1 blade mace, 8 peppercorns, 2 teaspoonfuls salt.

Temperatures for Stock Making.

We have seen already that (1) to extract the soluble substances of meat it must be cut up finely, steeped in cold salted water, heated slowly and simmered gently; (2) to extract gelatin from bone, gristle and connective tissues the water into which they are put must boil continuously.

A. Stock of Raw Meat or of Raw Meat and Bones.

When fresh meat alone is used, it is treated as described in (1) above. When both fresh meat and bones, *e.g.* shin beef, are used, a double cooking is necessary, the first at a low temperature, to extract the soluble substances from the meat, and the second at boiling point, to extract the gelatin from the bones, gristle and connective tissues. In the first cooking the tissues are gelatinised and partly dissolved, but boiling is necessary to extract the gelatin completely.

B. Stock of Cooked Meat and Bones.

When stock is made of meat and bones which have been used once already for stock, or from the small pieces of cooked meat and bones which collect in the larder, the water must boil all the time. The soluble substances have already been extracted from or coagulated in the meat, so that the high temperature required to extract the gelatin from the tissues and bones can no longer be harmful.

C. Stock of Raw or Cooked Bones and Gristle only.

When bones only are used the treatment is the same as that already described for stock made of cooked meat and bones.

Stock made chiefly from fresh meat naturally bears a strong resemblance to beef tea and mutton broth. If bones are used, or if the proportion of bones is great, the stock, as it cools, will stiffen, if it does not actually set to a jelly.

Cooking of Stock.

1. *Raw meat or raw meat and bones.*	2. *Cooked meat and bones, or bones (raw or cooked) only.*
(1) Cut up meat and put with the bones and salt into pan. Add for every pound of meat or meat and bones from 1½–2 pints cold water.	(1) Put pieces of meat and bones with salt into pan and cover with cold water.
(2) Let meat steep in water for 1 hour or longer, stirring occasionally, then heat slowly till the stock simmers.	(2) Bring to boil and skim well.
(3) Add vegetables and herbs and continue to simmer slowly for from 4–5 hours.	(3) Add vegetables and herbs and boil gently but continuously 5–6 hours.

(4) Keep pan covered closely to prevent loss by evaporation.

(5) When cooking is finished, strain the stock into an earthenware or enamel bowl and leave it to become cold. Put the meat and bones into a second bowl, removing the vegetables and herbs which are now useless.

(6) If it is necessary to use stock while it is still hot, skim off as much fat as possible and remove what remains by drawing strips of absorbent kitchen paper across the surface. Remove the cake of fat from cold stock before using it.

(7) Use the meat and bones a second time, cooking according to the directions given in the opposite column; add fresh vegetables, herbs and seasonings.

(7) The bones may be cooked a second time, and will give a weak stock. When they become porous they are useless and must be burnt.

Kinds of Meat Stock.

First Stock is the product of the first cooking of the stock materials and is prepared from raw meat or bones or both. For stock of good quality, the upper part of shin of beef or knuckle of veal is used; for stock of a rather less good quality, the lower cuts of the same piece, with less meat in proportion to bone, are suitable. Stock of a still less good quality is made from bones only or from bones with such small trimmings of raw meat as may be at hand.

Second Stock is made from cooked meat or bones or both.

Brown Stock is made from bones and meat of beef.

White Stock is generally prepared from knuckle of veal; the addition of the bones and trimmings of ham, poultry and game improves the flavour.

Flavoured Stock is prepared with vegetables and herbs. This is the best for general purposes, but in hot weather it is wise to make *unflavoured* stock, or else to use only small quantities of vegetables, omitting turnip completely. The vegetables hasten the 'souring' of the stock.

Fish Stock. This is made from bones, trimmings and skin of fish.

Method. Break up the bones and wash them, also the skin and trimmings; put them into a pan and cover with equal parts of milk and water. Bring slowly to the boil, skim and add flavourings, *i.e.* small pieces of carrot and onion, with a sprig of parsley, a bay leaf, a blade of mace, 3–4 peppercorns and salt. Boil very gently 20–30 minutes, then strain.

The flavour of fish bones is much stronger and their substance more easily extracted than that of meat; the cooking is thus much shorter.

When a good quality of fish stock is wanted, the flesh of fish is used in addition to the bones and trimmings. (Cf. Fish Soup, p. 132.)

SOUP MAKING

Soup is an economical, stimulating and in some cases, genuinely nourishing form of food: economical, because the stock is inexpensively prepared from small quantities of food which in many cases could not otherwise be used; stimulating, because by its warmth, and in the case of soups made with meat stock, by its 'extractives', it assists digestion in the same way as beef-tea and other concentrated meat extracts; nourishing, because it often contains such substances as milk, haricot beans, lentils, in addition to stock.

As part of a meal soup may serve either as (1) an introductory course intended chiefly to stimulate appetite, and so digestion; or as (2) a substantial course, substituted wholly or partially for meat or fish, and intended to satisfy hunger. The character of the soup determines which of these two functions it fulfils.

Kinds of Soup. Soups lend themselves to almost greater variety than any other preparations of food, but all may be classified as belonging to one of three distinct types: (1) broths, (2) thickened soups, (3) purées.

Broths. A broth consists of stock with a 'garnish' or addition of a small quantity of vegetables, cut in neat pieces, or of barley, vermicelli, etc., or of combinations of these.

Thickened Soups. These are practically broths, with the addition of sufficient starch or egg to give the soup the consistency of thick cream.

Purées. These also are thickened soups, but the thickening is due to the solid materials—vegetables or cereals—which are rubbed through a sieve to form a pulp. To give the soup a smooth texture, by preventing the pulp from separating from the liquid, some binding material, *e.g.* flour, egg, is often used.

The *liquid part of soups* may be first or second stock, milk, water, or any of the liquids already mentioned as serving for stock, or combinations of these. The amount of nutriment afforded by the stock or other liquid must be considered in deciding the kind of soup into which it can best be converted. A good quality of stock is necessary when the only addition to the soup is a few spoonfuls of rice or vegetables. But if there is a fair proportion of genuinely nourishing material, as is often the case in purées, second stock, or water in which meat has been boiled, or even water alone, with or without milk, will suffice. For white soups white stock, or milk, or both form the liquid.

Broths. The recipes given below show the typical methods of preparing broths.

Method 1.

Vegetable Soup No. 1.

Ingredients

1 quart good stock.
½ oz. vermicelli *or* rice.
½ small carrot, ½ small turnip, 1 stick of celery.
Salt and pepper.

Method. Wash rice or vermicelli and steep in little cold stock for ½ hour. Clean and peel vegetables and cut into fancy shapes or small dice. Bring stock to the boil, add vegetables and rice or vermicelli and simmer gently till tender, about 1 hour. Season and serve very hot. Grated cheese can be served with the soup.

Method 2.

Vegetable Soup No. 2.

Ingredients

2–3 young carrots.
½ pint of shelled peas.
6 kidney beans.
2 oz. cucumber.
1 small lettuce.
1 oz. margarine.
1 small teaspoonful salt.
¼ teaspoonful pepper.
1 small teaspoonful castor sugar.
1 quart good stock.

Method. (1) Scrape carrots, wash, and cook in boiling salted water for 10 minutes, then cut into dice. Wash, string and cut up kidney beans. Peel cucumber and cut into pieces rather larger than the carrot. Wash lettuce well, dry the leaves gently and cut into fine shreds.

(2) Melt margarine in a white-lined pan, put in vegetables, salt, pepper and sugar; cover the pan and cook the vegetables for 5–10 minutes, shaking the pan so that they do not stick to the bottom. This preliminary cooking in margarine develops the flavours of the vegetables.

(3) Bring the stock to the boil, add it to the vegetables and

boil gently 20–30 minutes till the vegetables are quite tender. Serve very hot. Grated cheese can be served with the soup.

Cabbage Soup.

Ingredients

1 white cabbage.
2 oz. margarine or dripping.
3 pints stock (white or light coloured), *or* water.
½ pint milk.
Pepper and salt.
Bread.

Method. (1) Wash the cabbage thoroughly and soak in salted water for ½ hour. Then shred finely and 'blanch' in boiling water for 5 minutes. Strain off the water.

(2) Melt the margarine in a pan, put in the cabbage, cover the pan and cook for 5–10 minutes, shaking the pan from time to time.

(3) Bring the stock or water to the boil and pour it on to the cabbage; boil the soup gently for 1 hour, skimming if necessary. Add ½ pint of milk, bring to boil and season.

(4) While the soup cooks, cut some stale bread into dice, dry them in a cool oven and put them in the soup tureen. Pour the soup on to the bread and serve at once.

Method 3.

Scotch Broth.

Ingredients

½ oz. pearl barley.
¾ lb. scrag of mutton.
2 quarts stock or meat-water.
1 small turnip.
1 small carrot.
½ small onion.
1 leek.
1 stick celery.
Salt.
Pepper.
2 teaspoonfuls finely chopped parsley.

Method. (1) Wash barley and soak in the cold stock 10 to 15 minutes.

(2) Remove fat from meat and divide the meat into pieces by cutting between the bones.

(3) Put meat, barley and stock into pan, heat slowly to boiling point, then simmer gently 1 hour. Skim off any fat.

(4) Prepare the vegetables, cutting them into neat dice; add them to the soup at the end of 1 hour and let soup simmer another 2 hours.

(5) Take out meat, remove lean from bones and cut it into small pieces. Return to soup, re-heat, season, add finely chopped parsley and serve very hot.

Thickened Soups.

Except for the thickening, these are prepared in much the same way as the broths. If the soup is to be thickened with starch, the usual plan is to mix the flour or cornflour to a smooth paste with a little stock or water or milk. When the vegetable or other garnish is tender, the paste is added gradually to the soup, which is boiled 5–10 minutes to cook the starch grains thoroughly.

If eggs are used, they are beaten and put in the soup tureen, and the soup, hot, but not boiling, is poured on to them and stirred well.

COMPARATIVE RECIPE

Kind	*Basis*	*Flavourings and Seasonings*	*Fat*	*Liquid*
1. POTATO SOUP. (*Method* 1.)	1 lb. potatoes. 1 onion. 3 sticks white celery.	1 sprig parsley. 1 bay leaf. 1 blade of mace. 6 pepper-corns. 2 cloves. } Tie in mus-lin. Salt.	1 oz. margarine *or* dripping	1 quart ligh coloured sto *or* meat-wat *or* water, milk *or* mi tures of thes
2. CARROT SOUP. (*Method* 1.)	3 large carrots. 2 slices onion. 1½ oz. ham or bacon.	1 sprig parsley. 6 peppercorns. Salt.	½–1 oz. margarine.	1 quart stock.
3. LENTIL SOUP. (*Method* 2.)	½ lb. Egyptian (red) lentils. 1 stick celery. 1 small onion.	2 sprigs parsley. 1 small blade mace. 1 bay leaf. 8 pepper-corns. } Tie in mus-lin. Salt.	1½ oz. margarine *or* dripping.	3 pints wat *or* meat-wate preferab that in whi ham has be boiled.

* S

Thickened Vegetable Soup.

Ingredients

1 oz. margarine.
1 turnip, 1 carrot, 1 small onion, 2 potatoes.
1½ pints stock (preferably white stock).
½ oz. flour *or* cornflour.
¼ pint milk.
Salt, pepper, nutmeg.

Method. (1) Prepare the vegetables and cut them into very thin strips or shred them, using a coarse grater. Cook in the margarine for 5–10 minutes, covering the pan and shaking it frequently. [Continued on p. 132

FOR PURÉE SOUPS [1]

Binding	*Method*
1 oz. crushed tapioca *or* small sago. ½ pint milk.	Melt margarine or dripping in enamel-lined pan, add potatoes and onion, thinly sliced, the celery, cut into small pieces, and the flavourings. Put lid on pan and cook gently 5–10 minutes, shaking pan frequently; this develops the flavours of the vegetables, etc. Add boiling liquid and simmer till tender, about 1½ hours. Remove herbs, rub soup through wire sieve with a wooden spoon, return to the pan and bring to boil. Add the tapioca or sago and boil gently till perfectly transparent, 10–15 minutes. Stir occasionally, and be careful the soup does not burn. Add milk, bring to boil, season and serve very hot.
1 oz. flour *or* ½ oz. cornflour. ½ pint milk.	Clean carrots and grate them. Cut ham or bacon into small dice. Melt margarine, cook carrots, onion and ham in it for 5–10 minutes, covering the pan and shaking it occasionally. Add boiling stock, parsley and peppercorns, and boil gently 1 hour. Remove parsley and peppercorns and rub soup through sieve. Re-heat, mix flour and milk to smooth paste, add to boiling soup and boil 10 minutes.
1 oz. flour. ½ pint milk.	Wash lentils in several waters, put in a pan with water, bring to boil and skim well. Cut onions into rings, and celery into small pieces; add to the boiling soup with herbs and salt. Simmer till tender, about ¾ hour; remove herbs and rub soup through wire sieve. To bind the solid and liquid parts of the soup together, melt fat in a pan, add flour, cook 3–4 minutes without browning; add soup gradually, mixing smoothly, then add milk and seasoning. Bring to boil, being careful soup does not burn.

. 132.

Kind	*Basis*	*Flavourings and Seasonings*	*Fat*	*Liquid*
4. TOMATO SOUP. (*Method* 2.)	1 lb. ripe tomatoes *or* ½ quart tin of tomatoes. 1 onion.	1 sprig parsley. 1 sprig of thyme. 1 blade mace. 6 peppercorns. } Tie in muslin. Salt. Cayenne. Sugar.	1 oz. margarine.	1½ pints stock.
5. ARTICHOKE SOUP. (*Method* 3.)	2 lbs. Jerusalem artichokes.	Pepper. Salt.	1½ oz. margarine.	1 quart whit[e] stock. ¾ pint milk.
5. RICE AND VEGETABLE SOUP. (*Method* 3.)	1 large carrot. 1 stick of celery. 1 oz. rice.	1 sprig of parsley. 1 bay leaf. 1 blade of mace. } Tie in muslin. Salt and pepper.		1 quart stock.
7. HARICOT BEAN SOUP. (*Method* 3.)	1 lb. haricot beans. 1–2 onions.	Few bacon rinds. Salt and pepper.	2 oz. margarine *or* 1½ oz. dripping (bacon).	2 quarts water.
8. CHESTNUT SOUP. (*Method* 3.)	½ lb. chestnuts. 1 small onion.	Salt, pepper.	1 oz. margarine.	1 pint whit[e] stock *or* wate[r] ½ pint milk.

N.B.—Croûtons are usually served with or in soups. They are prepared b[y] cutting stale bread into dice and either drying them in a cool oven till they ar[e]

Binding	*Method*
1 oz. flour *or* ½ oz. cornflour. ¼ pint milk.	Chop onion finely and put with stock, herbs, tomatoes, etc., into an enamel-lined pan. Boil very gently till the tomatoes and onion are tender, ½–¾ hour. Rub through wire sieve, first removing bunch of herbs. Prepare binding as for Lentil Soup, adding first soup, then milk, to the cooked fat and flour. Bring to boil, season with cayenne, salt and sugar, and serve very hot.
	Peel artichokes, cut up, and put at once into cold water containing a little vinegar or lemon juice so that they do not discolour. Melt margarine in enamel-lined pan, cook artichokes in it for 5–10 minutes, covering the pan and shaking it occasionally. Add the boiling stock to the artichokes and boil gently 30–40 minutes, or until tender. Put through fine sieve and re-heat, adding milk, pepper and salt. Serve very hot.
	Wash vegetables, cut carrot into thin slices and celery into small pieces. Put with rice and herbs into the stock and simmer slowly about 1 hour, or until vegetables and rice are quite tender. Remove herbs and rub soup through wire sieve; re-heat and season.
	Wash beans and steep overnight in a good supply of cold water, covering the bowl. Put the beans into a pan with the bacon rinds and 2 quarts of the steeping water, and cook gently till perfectly tender, from 2½–4 hours, according to the size and condition of the beans. Remove rinds and rub beans through a sieve, leaving only the skins behind. Put the margarine or dripping in the saucepan with the onions, finely chopped, and cook 15 minutes, covering the pan. Then add the purée, boil gently 30 minutes, season and serve very hot.
	Prick the chestnuts and boil till tender, ¾–1 hour, according to size. While still hot, cut the chestnuts in half, scoop out the meal, leaving the shells and brown skins behind. Chop the onion finely, put it with the chestnut meal, stock and milk into a pan, and boil gently ½–¾ hour. Then rub the soup through a sieve, return it to the pan and bring it to the boil. Add margarine, a small portion at a time, season and serve.

crisp and faintly browned or by frying them in a small quantity of fat and draining them on soft paper.

(2) Add boiling stock and simmer for about 1 hour, oı until the vegetables are tender. Skim well.

(3) Mix flour and milk to a smooth paste, add it to the soup and boil 10 minutes, stirring carefully. Season and serve very hot.

Fish Soup.

Ingredients

¾ lb. cod, hake or fresh haddock.
Or, cod's head *or* fish bones and trimmings (*e.g.* of plaice or sole)
1½ pints water *or* milk and water.

½ carrot, ½ onion (sliced).
1 small bay leaf, 1 small blade of mace.
1 sprig of parsley, 4 pepper corns, salt.

½ oz. margarine.
¾ oz. ground rice.
½ pint milk.

1–2 tablespoonfuls shelled peas
1–2 tablespoonfuls dice of carrot } garnish (optional).

Method. (1) Wash fish, cut it up and put with the bones, etc., into an enamel-lined or earthenware pan; add carrot and onion, herbs, etc., the latter tied in muslin, 1½ pints water or water and milk. Heat slowly and simmer gently ¾ hour, then strain the stock, putting on one side a small portion of the fish. If fish bones and trimmings only are used, boil gently ½ hour, then strain.

(2) Melt margarine in a pan, add ground rice, cook without colouring for 3–4 minutes. Add gradually the prepared fish stock and the ½ pint of milk, mixing smoothly; bring to the boil, boil 2–3 minutes and season. Put back a small quantity of white fish in the pan and when it is hot, serve the soup.

Garnish. Cut the dice of carrot from the red part and use the trimmings to flavour the fish stock. Boil the dice of carrot and the peas separately in boiling salted water till tender, strain and add them to the soup just before serving.

Purées. If the recipes on pp. 128–131 for purée soups are examined, it will be noticed that the vegetables, meat, etc., which form the basis, bear a larger proportion to the liquid than is the case in broths or thickened soups, and that there are three ways of treating them.

GELATINE AND JELLY MAKING

When gelatin is to be extracted from bones to make jelly, as is done, for example, in making calf's-foot jelly, the bones are put into cold water and boiled for several hours. The solution of gelatin thus obtained is then flavoured and subjected to a process which removes from it all substances which would cloud it, so that a clear sparkling jelly results.

Nowadays jellies are much more commonly prepared from the manufactured gelatine, and we will therefore treat of its properties and use at greater length.

Properties of Gelatine.

Experiment	*Test*
(1) Cover a little leaf gelatine with cold water and leave 15–30 minutes.	Gelatine becomes soft, swollen and semi-transparent, but does not melt.
(2) Heat the softened gelatine.	Gelatine melts gradually, forming a sticky fluid.
(3) Put some of the fluid gelatine on a saucer and let it cool.	Fluid stiffens and finally sets to a jelly.
(4) Heat the jelly.	Jelly again melts.
(5) Heat the melted jelly to boiling point. (6) Add lemon juice or vinegar to the melted jelly.	No coagulation, such as would occur with true proteins.

It will be noticed that the properties of manufactured gelatine are precisely the same as those of the gelatin extracted in the process of making stock from bones.

Kinds of Gelatine.

There are four varieties of gelatine:

(1) *Leaf gelatine, i.e.* gelatine in thin sheets. This, when torn into pieces and steeped, is readily softened and melted and is therefore convenient to use. It is inexpensive, but its flavour, especially in the cheaper makes, is occasionally too reminiscent of glue to be attractive.

(2) '*Packet*' *gelatine, i.e.* gelatine in small pieces or shreds, usually sold in packets. Before melting this requires soaking in cold liquid from ½–1 hour, according to the make.

(3) *Granulated Gelatine*, as its name implies, is gelatine in a finely powdered form; it does not require steeping.

(4) *Isinglass* is the purest and most expensive form of gelatine and is much used in invalid cooking. It requires only a short steeping.

When gelatine is heated it must not be allowed to reach boiling point as the great heat affects the 'setting' property of the gelatine.

The mould for jelly should be filled beforehand with cold water and the jelly should be cool, without being at all set, before it is poured into it. The mould should be put on a level surface in a cool place to set, a process which will take from 3–6 hours. If a more speedy setting is required, the mould may be packed with a mixture of three parts of crushed ice and one part of salt, or may be placed in a bowl of cold salted water.

If there is any difficulty in turning out a jelly, dip the mould overhead for a few seconds only in water rather hotter than the hand can comfortably bear. Dry the surface at once with a clean towel and invert the jelly on to the dish on which it is to be served. If a vigorous shake does not suffice to loosen it, repeat the dipping in hot water.

Orange Jelly.

Ingredients

3 oranges.
1 lemon.
3 oz. sugar.
½ oz. gelatine.
½ pint water.

Method. (1) Wipe rinds of the oranges and lemon, and peel very thinly so as not to remove any of the bitter white part under the rind. Put with ½ pint water into the pan and simmer 5 minutes to extract flavour.

(2) Strain juice from the fruit and soak gelatine in it.

(3) When the gelatine is soft, add sugar and strained water from rinds, heat until gelatine is dissolved.

(4) Strain, and when nearly cold, pour into small moulds or darioles.

Lemon Cream.

Ingredients

½ oz. gelatine.
½ pint water.
Rind and juice of 2 small lemons.
2 oz. lump sugar.
6 oz. castor sugar.
½ pint milk.
2 eggs.

Method. (1) Soak the gelatine in the water.

(2) Wipe the lemons and rub the lumps of sugar on them until all the rind is removed, leaving the skin quite smooth.

(3) Put the lump sugar, castor sugar and milk into a pan and bring to the boil, then pour into a bowl and put to cool. When cold add the beaten eggs.

(4) Heat softened gelatine until dissolved, add strained lemon

juice, cool slightly, then add it to the milk and eggs, mixing all together thoroughly.

(5) When nearly cold, pour into moulds.

Prune Mould.

Ingredients

½ lb. prunes.	Rind and juice of ½ lemon.
1¼ pints water.	½ inch of cinnamon stick.
¼ lb. sugar.	½ oz. gelatine.

1 tablespoonful raspberry jam (optional).

Method. (1) Wash the prunes and soak for 12 hours in ¾ pint of water, covering the bowl.

(2) Peel the lemon rind thinly and put with the sugar, cinnamon stick, prunes and steeping water into the pan; cook gently until the prunes are tender (15–20 minutes), then take out the stones and cut up the prunes.

(3) Steep the gelatine in ½ pint of water, heat until dissolved, add the jam, lemon juice and water in which the prunes were cooked.

(4) Strain into a bowl, add prunes and when nearly cold put into the mould.

The stones may be cracked and the kernels blanched and used to decorate the mould.

Pineapple Sponge.

Ingredients

1 small tin pineapple.	White of 3 eggs.
½ oz. gelatine.	1½ oz. castor sugar.

Method. (1) Cut pineapple into small pieces, keeping a few larger pieces for decoration.

(2) Make up syrup to ½ pint with water and steep gelatine in it. When soft, heat until dissolved and put to cool, stirring occasionally.

(3) When gelatine is nearly cool, whip whites of eggs to a stiff froth, and put into a bowl. Add gradually the cooled gelatine fluid and whisk until it begins to set, then add sugar and small pieces of pineapple.

(4) Continue whisking for a moment or two, until the gelatine is just sufficiently stiff to hold the pineapple in position Then pile up at once in smooth masses in a dish and decorate.

Food Value of Gelatin. We know that proteins are not all of equal value to the body. Gelatin is a protein whose 'biological value' is extremely low. It lacks three of the amino-acids required for the building of human tissues, and is therefore useless, by itself, for this purpose, though it can usefully be added to other good proteins. Gelatin acts as a 'protein-sparer', a substance which economises the use of the more valuable proteins, though it cannot replace them entirely and cannot perform their work of building up the tissues. For the purpose of nourishment, therefore, gelatin is less valuable than is generally supposed. It is, however, easily digested, and is a convenient and attractive medium for the serving of eggs, milk, fruit juice, etc.

CHAPTER XIII

THE COOKING OF CARBOHYDRATE FOODS: CEREALS

The group of foods known as cereals includes most of the grains or plant seeds which provide materials for bread, cakes, puddings and a variety of other dishes. Cereals supply starch more abundantly than any other foods; they also contain proteins (not, however, first-class proteins), small amounts of minerals, and in some cases fat also, with 'roughage' and vitamin B. As a general rule, the vitamin B is not distributed evenly in the grains, but is chiefly in the germ and in the bran, especially in the germ. Highly milled cereals thus lack roughage and vitamin B.

In cooking cereals it is the starch grains with their indigestible cellulose which have chiefly to be considered, for vitamin B can resist heat well.

Among the more important and widely used cereals are:

(1) Wheat. Wheat contains not only a large quantity of starch, but also two insoluble proteins which, when wheat flour is mixed with water, form the substance known as gluten. Gluten may be examined by making a small quantity of stiff dough, wrapping it in muslin and kneading or squeezing it in cold running water until the water ceases to be milky. By this means the starch is washed out, leaving the yellow, sticky, elastic gluten.

Wheat-gluten is unlike the proteins of all other cereals except that of rye in this elastic, tenacious property, and it is this property which enables flour prepared from wheat and rye to be made into bread.

In the structure of a wheat grain several points are noticeable:

(*a*) The external covering or husk of the grain is formed of two coats, the inner consisting of a layer of bran cells, underneath which are cells which contain mineral salts.

(*b*) The interior of the grain is made of tiny, closely packed cells containing starch and proteins. In the outer, browner cells, the cellulose walls are harder, and the cells contain rather more protein in proportion to starch than do the central whiter cells.

Wholemeal flour is prepared from the whole grain from which only the husk has been removed and contains the browner, outer parts as well as the white interior. *Brown flour* contains bran in addition. Both these, brown flour especially, are less digestible than white flour, though the indigestible cellulose has a certain use in cases of constipation, its very indigestibility making it of value in exercising the muscles of the alimentary canal. The best quality of *white household flour* is made from the interior of the grains and contains the greater proportion of the starch and most of the protein, though the proportion of the latter is not quite so great as in wholemeal and brown flour. Since in the milling as much as possible of the bran and germ is removed the finished flour is proportionately lacking in vitamin B and also in roughage. *Pastry or Austrian flour* is a very white flour consisting chiefly of starch.

Macaroni, Vermicelli and Italian Paste, all nutritious cereals, are prepared from wheat which contains a large proportion of protein. Genoa macaroni (curled), Naples macaroni (coarse and straight), spaghetti (fine and thin) are different varieties of macaroni. *Semolina* is a granular preparation of wheat consisting of small fragments of the interior of the grain; it is often prepared from wheat rich in protein.

(2) **Oats** contain a large quantity of fat and protein. The amount of cellulose is also large, hence oats require very thorough cooking.

Oats in the husk are not used as human food, but from oats are derived:

(*a*) *Groats*, oat grains with the outer coats or husks removed, leaving the nutritious part of the grain.

(*b*) *Quaker Oats, Provost Oats*, etc., prepared from crushed groats.

(*c*) *Oatmeal*, groats ground into fine or medium or coarse meal.

(3) **Barley** resembles wheat in composition, but has rather less starch and protein and more fat and cellulose. Barley with the husk removed and roughly ground is known as *Scotch barley*; when the grains are ground still further *pearl barley* results. The first is the more nourishing of the two, as the protein is contained in the outer rather than in the inner cells.

(4) **Rice** is deficient in almost everything but starch and is the least nourishing of the cereals; on the other hand, there is very little cellulose, and the starch is therefore very digestible.

Carolina and *Patna rice* are most generally used. Carolina rice, which absorbs liquid most readily, is used for puddings, moulds, etc., and Patna rice, a longer and more pointed grain, for serving with curry and mince, or as a substitute for vegetables.

(5) **Maize or Indian Corn** is not much used in this country except in the prepared form of *cornflour*, which contains only the starch of maize.

Though they are not cereals, we may include here certain substances which provide starch and are used for the same purposes as cereals. Among these are:

Arrowroot and Tapioca. These are almost pure starch derived from the roots of plants.

Sago. This is extracted from the pith of the stems of certain palms.

Nature and Properties of Starch.

Starch is stored up as a reserve food supply by the plants from which it is derived. It is in the form of microscopic grains, enclosed in walls or bags of cellulose and packed very tightly together. A so-called 'grain' of rice consists of an enormous number of such tightly packed starch grains.

Examination of Starch Grains. Examine the following starch grains under the microscope, noticing that they differ in size, shape and formation.

Potato Starch. Though not derived from a cereal, potato starch may be examined first with advantage because the grains are unusually large and show the formation very clearly.

Cut a potato, moisten the cut surfaces with water and rub them together. Examine the starch thus obtained under the microscope. Notice the central point or hilum and the concentric markings, showing the arrangement of starch granulose (the starch proper) and starch cellulose.

Sago Starch. Steep a little sago for several hours in water, crush finely and mount a tiny portion in water. Notice the size of the grains and the irregular shape.

Maize Starch or Cornflour. Mount in water. Notice that the grains are much smaller than those already examined; they are many-sided, and the hilum is star-shaped.

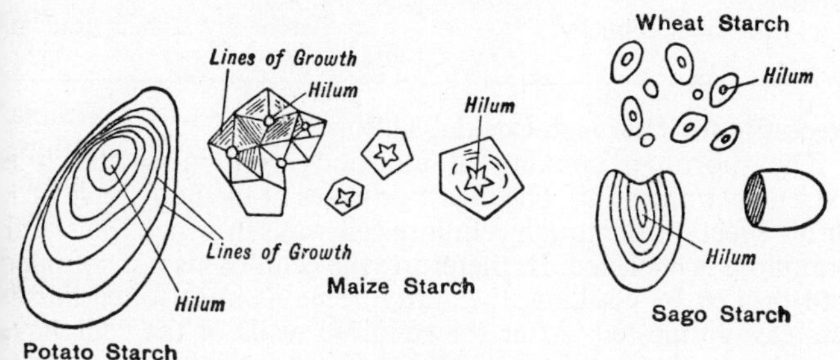

FIG. 10.

Wheat Starch. Tie a little flour in a piece of muslin, soak in vater for a few minutes, then squeeze a drop of the starch water on to the slide. Notice that the grains are very small and are in wo sizes, one larger than the other. The hilum is not very distinct.

Tests.

Test	*Result*
(1) Mix a little laundry rice starch o a cream with cold water, and add ne drop of very weak iodine solution.	Starch turns indigo blue colour.
(2) Mix a little cornflour to a ream with cold water and divide nto three portions, *A*, *B*, *C*. Test *A* ith iodine solution.	Cornflour gives blue coloration as in Experiment 1.
Filter *B* and test filtrate with odine solution. Let *C* stand undisturbed for a hort time.	The iodine shows no blue coloration. Starch is therefore insoluble in cold water, and if allowed to remain undisturbed sinks and forms a white sediment, leaving clear water on top.

Test	*Result*
(3) (*a*) Put ½ oz. cornflour in a bowl and add about ¼ pint boiling water, stirring well.	(*a*) Part of cornflour changes to semi-transparent jelly but the mass is lumpy. If the lumps are broken they are seen to contain dry, unchanged cornflour.
(*b*) Mix ½ oz. cornflour to a cream with 3 teaspoonfuls cold water. Add ¼ pint boiling water, stirring carefully.	(*b*) The cornflour is uniformly changed to a semi-transparent jelly-like solution, quite free from lumps.
(*c*) Cool the starch-jelly.	(*c*) Starch jelly stiffens gradually and finally gelatinises.

Necessity for Thorough Cooking of Starch.

The thorough cooking of all foods containing starch is extremely important. The digestive juices of the body have little or no effect on the tough cellulose cell-walls in which the starch granulose is enclosed. If, therefore, the cellulose is not softened and broken by cooking, the starch remains imprisoned and is less easily digested. After the cellulose walls of the cells have been burst, the starch, as we have seen, swells, takes up water and forms a gelatinous solution.

Group 3 of the tests just carried out demonstrates that the first stage in the cooking of the cornflour must be the separation of the tightly packed grains, so that they may be uniformly acted upon by heat and moisture. Without the preliminary separation only the more exposed grains are able to take up water and to become soft and jelly-like. These swollen grains cover up the less exposed ones which remain unchanged.

MAKING OF PUDDINGS, MOULDS AND BEVERAGES FROM CEREALS[1]

1. *Preparation.*

A preliminary moistening of the starch is desirable for cereals which are in the form of a powder or meal. The liquid separates the starch grains and so prevents the formation of lumps during the cooking. Whenever possible the cereal should be moistened with or soaked in the liquid in which it is to be cooked, so that no loss of substance, *e.g.* loose starch grains occurs.

[1] For the present purposes the term cereals may be taken as including such starchy foods as tapioca, arrowroot and sago.

(*a*) *Cornflour*, *Arrowroot*, etc. A few minutes before cooking mix to a smooth paste with a little of the milk or whatever liquid is to be used.

(*b*) *Ground Rice*, *Semolina*. Moisten with a little of the milk before cooking.

(*c*) *Rice*, *small Sago*, *or 'Grains' of similar size*. Wash well.

(*d*) *Macaroni*. Break into inch lengths if necessary.

(*e*) *Tapioca*. Crush it with a glass jar or china rolling-pin to expose a large surface.

2. *Cooking*.[1]

The methods of supplying the cereals with the heat and moisture necessary to make them tender and digestible may be summarised thus:

(1) Boiling in a fairly large quantity of water.

Examples. Preparation of macaroni, spaghetti, rice, as the foundation for such savoury dishes as Macaroni Cheese, or as substitutes for vegetables.

(2) Cooking rather more slowly in a smaller quantity of liquid, usually milk. The cooking is done either wholly over the fire, or is begun over the fire and completed in the oven.

Examples. (*a*) Cornflour and ground rice moulds. (*b*) Semolina pudding.

(3) A still slower cooking, also usually in milk. This method is used chiefly for whole grains.

Examples. Puddings of rice, sago, tapioca, which are baked in a moderate oven for at least 2 hours.

Before giving typical recipes for making puddings and moulds, the *proportion of cereals to milk* may be noted:

(*a*) For creamy milk puddings, 1 oz. rice, sago, etc., to 1 pt. milk.

(*b*) For thick milk puddings, 1½ oz. rice, sago, etc., to 1 pt. milk.

(*c*) For moulds to be turned out when cold, 2 oz. rice, sago, ground rice to 1 pint of milk.

(*d*) For moulds of cornflour, farola or similar preparations, 1½–2 oz. to 1 pint milk, according as a moderately stiff or decidedly stiff mould is required.

[1] *Prepared Cereals*. The long cooking necessary for many cereals has led to the introduction of Flaked Rice, Quaker Oats, etc., cereals which have already been cooked and need only a comparatively brief cooking to prepare them for use. As a rule, the directions given by the makers rather under-estimate the time required for the completion of the cooking.

Skim milk may be used for puddings and moulds, provided a little margarine or very finely chopped suet be added to replace the cream.

COMPARATIVE RECIPES FOR CERE

Name	*Foundation of Pudding, etc.*	*Additional Ingredients*	*Preparation*
RICE OR SAGO PUDDING.	1–1½ oz. rice, or small sago. 1 pint milk.	Pinch of salt. ½–1 oz. sugar. Nutmeg *or* cinnamon.	Wash the gr well.
CREAMED RICE.	2 oz. Carolina rice. 1 pint milk.	Pinch of salt. Strip lemon peel. 2 oz. sugar. ½–1 oz. glacé cherries. ½–1 oz. angelica.	Wash rice well.
COLD RICE MOULD.	2 oz. Carolina rice. 1 pint milk.	Pinch of salt. 2 oz. sugar. Vanilla or almond essence.	Wash rice well.
(1) CORNFLOUR (2) GROUND RICE. (3) CHOCOLATE MOULD.	(1) 1½–2 oz. cornflour. (2) 2 oz. ground rice. (3) 2 oz. (bare measure) ground rice and 1 oz. grated chocolate. For 1, 2 and 3, 1 pint milk.	Pinch of salt. 1½–2 oz. sugar. Vanilla essence.	Mix cornflour ground rice or gro rice and chocolate smooth paste wit little of the cold n Add salt.
BOILED RICE (For serving with curry, mince, etc.)	4–6 oz. Patna rice.		Wash rice in sev waters and steep cold water for ½ h This removes l starch, which w make the grains c together in a st mass. Pour off the wat

For hot puddings, moulds and dishes must be greased; for moulds to be turned out when cold, the mould or dish must be rinsed in cold water and left wet.

'DDINGS, MOULDS AND SAVOURIES

Cooking

ut cereal and milk in a greased pie-dish, add salt, sugar and stir together. ıte nutmeg or sprinkle cinnamon on top. Bake in a moderate oven for 2 hours.

dd salt, lemon peel and cook *very slowly*, stirring occasionally, till rice is thick soft. The cooking is most easily done in a double saucepan with boiling water ne outer vessel, and will take from 1½–2 hours. When rice is tender, take out , add sugar, and when almost cold, the chopped cherries and angelica, keeping k a small quantity of each for decoration. Serve rice unmoulded in a glass dish, orated with cherries, halved or quartered, and strips of angelica. The addition hese is optional. Stewed apples or pears (p. 180) or tinned or bottled fruit orated with cherries and angelica may be served with the rice, if desired.

Add salt and cook rice in milk as for Creamed Rice, until it is soft and tender has absorbed nearly all the milk. Time, 1½–2 hours. Add sugar and vanilla or ond essence, pour into wet mould and put aside to cool. Serve with jam or stewed, tinned or bottled fruit.

ıt rest of milk on to boil. When it boils, pour it on to the cereal-paste and mix othly. Return it to the pan, bring to boil and boil very gently 5–8 minutes or the cereal leaves sides of the saucepan clean. Stir continuously, taking care the mixture does not burn. When cooked add sugar and vanilla and pour a wet mould. Turn out when cold. Serve cornflour or ground rice mould jam or stewed or preserved fruit; serve chocolate mould with ½ pint boiled ard (pp. 76 or 146).

ave a large pan of boiling water, add 1 teaspoonful salt to each quart. Drop ice grains gradually into the water and stir till the water re-boils. Skim well boil quickly, keeping the pan uncovered, until the grains can *just* be crushed een the finger and thumb. Average time, 7–10 minutes. Drain the rice on a and pour over ½ pint cold water to separate the grains. Dry for a few minutes ont of the fire, if possible. Rice cooked thus should be light and dry with each separate.

ote.—The water in which rice is boiled should be used for stock.

Name	*Foundation of Pudding, etc.*	*Additional Ingredients*	*Preparation*
RICE SAVOURY.	4 oz. Patna rice.	1 oz. margarine. ½ pint tomato pulp. Salt, cayenne. 1 tablespoonful grated cheese.	As for Boiled R p.142.
BOILED MACARONI.	4 oz. Genoa *or* Naples macaroni.	½ oz. margarine.	Break macaroni 1 inch lengths.
MACARONI CHEESE.	4 oz. Genoa *or* Naples macaroni. 1 oz. margarine. ¾ oz. flour. ¼ pint milk. ¼ pint water in which macaroni has been boiled.	3 oz. grated cheese (preferably Gruyère). 1 small teaspoonful made mustard. Salt, cayenne, a few drops lemon juice. Browned crumbs.	As above.
MACARONI AND TOMATO.	4 oz. Genoa *or* Naples macaroni.	1 oz. margarine. 4 oz. cooked tongue or ham. ½ pint tomato pulp. Salt, cayenne pepper. Browned crumbs.	As above.

PORRIDGE AND BEVERAGES PREPARED FROM CEREALS

Oatmeal Porridge.

Ingredients

2 oz. medium oatmeal. ½ teaspoonful salt.
1 pint water.

Method. Heat the water, adding salt. When the water boils sprinkle the oatmeal into it, stirring all the time. Boil fairl rapidly for ½ hour; stir frequently so that the porridge neithe burns nor becomes lumpy.

The proportion of meal to water varies according to taste and varies also with the kind of meal—fine, medium or coarse The fineness or coarseness of the meal naturally also influence the length of cooking.

Cooking

Boil rice (p. 143) and drain when just tender. Melt margarine in pan, add rice cook gently without browning 3–4 minutes. Add tomato pulp and simmer wly till rice is soft and thick, and has absorbed all the tomato. Season well, pile high in a hot dish, and sprinkle grated cheese over. Serve very hot.

'ake macaroni, put into boiling salted water and boil gently till swollen and fectly soft. *Time*: Naples macaroni, 30–45 minutes; Genoa macaroni, 1½–2 rs. Pour off water, add the margarine. Serve very hot. *Note.*—The water uld be used for stock.

Boil macaroni as above till tender, then strain. Make white sauce with marga-, flour, milk and macaroni water (pp. 151, 152). Mix with the sauce the cooked caroni, three-quarters of the cheese and the seasonings and lemon juice. Put a greased dish and sprinkle the remainder of the cheese and a few browned mbs on top. Bake in a quick oven till thoroughly hot and delicately browned. ne, 10–15 minutes.

Boil macaroni as above till tender, drain off water. Melt margarine in a pan, add caroni, tomato pulp and the ham or tongue cut into thin pieces. Season well put in greased dish, sprinkle crumbs over. Bake in a hot oven 10–15 minutes, serve at once.

Oatmeal Gruel.

Ingredients

1 tablespoonful fine oatmeal.
Pinch of salt.
1 pint water *or* milk *or* equal parts of both.
Sugar and lemon juice to flavour.

Method. Moisten oatmeal with a little cold water; add salt. Bring the water or milk to the boil and when boiling stir in the oatmeal. Boil gently 20–30 mins., strain, add sugar and flavouring.

Barley Water.

Ingredients

1½ oz. pearl barley.
1 pint water.
Strip of lemon rind.
Juice of ½ lemon.
Sugar.

Method. Wash barley and steep 10–15 minutes in the water.

Put in pan with lemon rind, bring slowly to the boil and boil gently for ½ hour. Strain and add lemon juice and sugar to taste.

Cocoa.

Ingredients

2 teaspoonfuls cocoa.
2 teaspoonfuls sugar.
½ pt. milk or milk and water
or
½ pt. water with 2½ tablespoonfuls dried milk.

} For each cup required.

Method. (1) Mix cocoa, sugar and dried milk, if used, to a smooth paste with some of the cold milk or cold water.

(2) Bring the rest of the milk or water to the boil and pour it on to the cocoa mixture, stirring well. Return to the pan.

(3) Bring to the boil and boil for 2–3 minutes in order to cook the starch the cocoa contains.

COMPARATIVE RECIPES SHOWING COOKI

Name	*Foundation*	*Additions*	*Eggs*
CUSTARD.	1 teaspoonful cornflour. ½ pint milk.	1½ teaspoonfuls sugar. Vanilla or almond essence.	1 egg (whole).
LEMON MOULD.	2 oz. cornflour *or* 2 oz. ground rice. 1 pint water.	2 large lemons. 6 oz. sugar.	2 eggs (whole)
GROUND RICE AND ALMOND PUDDING.	2 oz. ground rice. Pinch of salt. 1 pint milk.	Strip of lemon rind. 2 oz. sugar. 1–2 oz. margarine. 1 oz. sweet almonds. 4 tablespoonfuls apricot jam.	1–2 eggs (who

Cooking of Cereals in Combination with Eggs.

Beaten eggs are often added to cereals, either to enrich them or to lighten them by enclosing air.

In combining cereals and eggs thus, it must be remembered that the thorough and often prolonged cooking required to make cereals digestible would make eggs extremely hard and :ough, egg-albumen, as we have seen, setting rapidly under the nfluence of a gentle heat. It follows, then, that before egg is ıdded, the cooking of the cereal must be so nearly finished that :he light cooking which is all that is needed for the egg will complete it. The cereal must be cooled slightly before the egg is ıdded to prevent curdling and in the subsequent cooking care nust be taken not to over-heat the egg. The eggs may be added vhole or the yolks and whites separately. Whites of eggs hould be folded into rather than mixed with the cereal, o as not to crush out the air. It is important that the egg and

[Continued on p. 148

CEREALS IN COMBINATION WITH EGGS

Preliminary Cooking of Cereal	*Addition of Eggs and Completion of Cooking*
ix cornflour to a smooth paste with a little ie cold milk. Bring remainder of milk to oil and add it to the cornflour paste, stir- carefully. Return to pan, boil for 3 minutes, ng all the time. Add sugar and cool tly.	Stir in the beaten egg and mix well. Heat the custard carefully, stirring it constantly, until the egg thickens. Take care the egg does not curdle. Add vanilla or almond essence.
ipe lemons and peel very thinly. Put rinds ater and boil for 5 minutes. Mix cornflour ce to a smooth paste with the strained of the lemons, adding a little water if the alone makes the paste at all stiff. Pour on to boiling water strained from the rinds, mix othly, return to pan and boil 3 minutes, stir- continually. Add sugar and cool slightly.	Add beaten eggs and stir over a gentle heat till the eggs thicken. Pour into a wet mould and turn out when cold.
ix rice to a smooth paste with a little of the milk and put the rest of milk with lemon on to boil. When the milk boils, take out mon rind and pour milk on to rice paste, ıg smoothly. Return to pan and boil y for about 10 minutes or until the rice s the sides of the saucepan clean. Add , margarine and almonds, finely chopped, nix well.	Add beaten eggs and put into greased pie-dish. Put dish into tin of hot water and bake in a moderate oven for $\frac{1}{2}$–$\frac{3}{4}$ hour or until pudding is set. Then spread jam on top and return to oven for 5 minutes.

Name	*Foundation*	*Additions*	*Eggs*
RICE BALLS.	3 oz. rice. Pinch of salt. 1 pint of milk.	Strip of lemon rind. ½ oz. margarine. 2 oz. sugar. Few crystallised fruits. } optional. — Egg and bread-crumbs for frying balls.	1 egg (whole).
TAPIOCA CREAM.	2 oz. tapioca. Pinch of salt. 1 pint milk.	1 oz. sugar. Vanilla or almond essence.	Yolks and w of 2 eggs.
SEMOLINA PUDDING.	1–1½ oz. semolina. Pinch of salt. 1 pint milk.	1 oz. sugar. Vanilla or almond essence.	1–2 eggs (wh or yolks whites separ.
GROUND RICE PUDDING.	1½ oz. ground rice. Pinch of salt. 1 pint milk.	Strip of lemon rind. 1 oz. sugar. 4 tablespoonfuls jam (optional).	Yolks of 2 egg Whites of 2 eg 2 oz. castor s
HOT RICE MOULD.	4 oz. rice. Pinch of salt. 1 pint milk.	1½ oz. sugar. Strip of lemon rind *or* vanilla or almond essence. 1 oz. stoned raisins *or* glacé cherries.	Yolks and w of 2 eggs.

cereal should be mixed thoroughly until the mixture is unifor in colour.

Recipes are given to illustrate the different ways of combinin cereals and eggs. (Pp. 146–149.)

Preliminary Cooking of Cereal	*Addition of Eggs and Completion of Cooking*
Vash rice well. Put in double saucepan with on rind and salt, and cook as for Creamed e (p. 142) from 1½–2 hours or until the rice ender and has absorbed all the milk. Add garine, sugar and chopped crystallised ts, if used; mix well and cool slightly.	Add beaten egg and cook gently 15–20 minutes. Remove lemon rind and spread mixture on a plate to cool. Flour the hands and form the mixture into small balls, coat with egg and bread-crumbs and fry in deep fat. (See Chap. XVI.) Drain on paper, sift sugar over and serve very hot.
rush tapioca, add milk and salt and l gently, stirring from time to time, until oca is thick and quite transparent. Add ar and cool slightly.	Add beaten yolks of eggs and cook till they thicken. Whip whites stiffly and fold them in carefully and thoroughly. Add vanilla or almond essence. Serve hot or cold.
loisten semolina with a little of the cold ., add salt. Add rest of the milk (heated), g to boil and boil 10 minutes, stirring well. l sugar and cool slightly.	Stir in beaten eggs or add beaten yolks first, then fold in the whites, previously beaten to a stiff froth. Put into a greased pie-dish and bake in a moderate oven 20–30 minutes.
ook rice as for Ground Rice and Almond ding (p. 146). Add sugar and cool slightly.	Add beaten yolks of eggs and put into a greased pie-dish. Bake in a *moderate* oven till set. Spread jam on top, pile over it the meringue of whites of eggs and sugar (p. 80), and cook in a cool oven for ¾ hour or longer till crisp and slightly browned.
repare a greased mould and decorate it the cherries or raisins cut in half. Cook as for Creamed Rice (p. 142). Then add r and cool slightly.	Add beaten yolks of eggs, then whip the whites stiffly and fold them in. Put in a greased mould and cover with greased paper. Steam for 1–1¼ hours. Serve with ½ pint custard (see p. 146, or p. 76) or jam sauce (p. 186) poured round the mould.

Dextrinisation of Starch.

So far we have only discussed the effects on starch of both noisture and heat. The following experiments show the changes vhich occur when *dry* starch is heated:

Experiment	*Result*
(1) Put 1 tablespoonful cornflour into a patty pan and heat it either in an oven or on the hot plate of a closed stove. Stir it occasionally so that it heats evenly.	Starch changes slowly, becoming first a yellow then a brown coffee colour, and acquires a smell rather like that of burnt sugar. The starch on the very bottom of the pan may become a dark brown colour.
Divide the baked cornflour into three portions *A*, *B*, *C*.	
(2) (*a*) Add to *A* cold water and to *B* hot water.	The starch dissolves slowly in cold water, more readily in hot water, forming with the latter a sticky gummy solution.
(*b*) Add a weak solution of iodine to the solutions obtained in (2) (*a*).	Iodine solution gives a reddish brown or port wine colour, showing that starch is no longer present.
(3) Put the portion *C* into a test tube and heat further.	Water forms on the sides of the test tube and the cornflour becomes a blackened mass.

The substance into which starch is changed when it is baked thus to a temperature of not less than 160° Cent. (320° Fahr.) is *dextrin*, familiar in the crust of well-baked bread. Part of the *dextrin* is further changed into caramel, which gives the brown coloration and the smell suggestive of burnt sugar. When starch is heated until it blackens, its oxygen and hydrogen pass off as water, leaving carbon behind.

The changes shown in these experiments occur in starch when cakes are baked and when bread is toasted. It is the conversion of some of the starch of bread into soluble dextrin which makes toast, when properly made, so much more digestible than bread.

THE MAKING OF STARCH-THICKENED SAUCES

A large number of sauces are thickened by means of substances consisting mainly or wholly of starch. Household flour is most used, but pastry flour, cornflour and potato flour are also employed when a very smooth sauce is desired.

Sauces are of many kinds, white and brown, sweet and savoury, plain and 'garnished'. We will take as a starting-point the making of plain white sauce which serves as a foundation for other sauces.

TABLE OF INGREDIENTS FOR FOUNDATION WHITE SAUCE

Sauce	*Margarine*	*Thickening*	*Liquid*	*Seasonings*
Savoury White Sauce (for Meat, Poultry or Vegetables).	½–1 oz.	1 oz. flour.	(*a*) ½ pint milk, *or* (*b*) ½ pint white stock, *or* (*c*) ¼ pint milk, plus ¼ pint white stock, *or* (*d*) ¼ pint milk, plus ¼ pint water from boiled or steamed meat or poultry, etc., *or* (*e*) ¼ pint milk, plus ¼ pint cold water.	Salt, pepper and cayenne. Lemon juice for fowls, rabbits and most vegetables.
Savoury White Sauce (for Fish).	½–1 oz.	1 oz. flour.	(*a*) ½ pint milk, *or* (*b*) ½ pint fish stock, *or* (*c*) ¼ pint milk, plus ¼ pint fish stock. *or* (*d*) ¼ pint milk, plus ¼ pint water (*i.e.* condensed steam and juices) from steamed fish. *or* (*e*) ¼ pint milk, plus ¼ pint cold water.	Salt, pepper and cayenne. Lemon juice.
Sweet White Sauce (for Puddings).	½–1 oz.	¾ oz. flour.	(*a*) ½ pint milk *or* (*b*) ¼ pint milk, plus ¼ pint water.	1–2 teaspoonfuls sugar. Vanilla or almond essence.
Melted Butter Sauce (Sweet or Savoury).	1½–2 oz.	1 oz. flour.	½ pint water.	*Sweet.* As above, plus a little lemon juice to modify the richness. *Savoury.* As above.

METHODS OF MAKING SAUCE

The flour used to thicken a sauce may be moistened in two ways to prepare the starch for cooking. The first method is advisable when the proportion of margarine or butter (if this is used) is small, ½ oz. margarine to 1 oz. flour and the second when the amount of margarine equals that of the flour. When a still larger proportion of fat is used, as in Melted Butter Sauce, the two methods are combined.

Method 1.

Mix the flour to a thin, smooth cream with a few tablespoonfuls of cold liquid. Heat the remainder of the liquid with a third of the margarine and when it boils, pour it on to the flour-cream, stirring it so that the sauce is perfectly smooth. Return the sauce to the pan, bring to the boil and boil 5 minutes, stirring all the time. Add seasoning or flavourings. Finally, add the remainder of the margarine, a small portion at a time, mixing each thoroughly before the next is added. After the margarine has been mixed in, the sauce must not boil.

Method 2.

Melt the margarine in the pan, add the flour and cook gently 3 or 4 minutes, without allowing it to colour. Add the liquid gradually, mixing it smoothly and cooking the sauce for a few minutes between each addition. Bring the sauce to the boil, boil 5 minutes, stirring all the time and taking care that it does not burn. Add seasonings or flavourings.

In making sauce by this method the addition of the liquid, particularly when it is hot, requires care to prevent the formation of lumps. At the first addition, the bursting of the starch grains causes the flour and fat to form a thick ball of paste, which becomes thinner as more liquid is added. Before each such addition of liquid the pan must be drawn back from the fire and must not be replaced till the sauce is perfectly smooth. If the sauce is cooked while it is lumpy, the further thickening of the starch will make it almost impossible to beat out the lumps and straining will be necessary.

Melted Butter Sauce. This is prepared by Method 2, but since the proportion of margarine is so large, only half is cooked with the flour, the remainder being added, a small portion at a time, after the final boiling, as in Method 1.

'Garnished' Sauces. These are made by adding a 'garnish' of distinctive ingredients, such as parsley, shrimps, to foundation white sauce. The garnish should be heated thoroughly in the sauce.

To ½ pint of foundation sauce prepared and flavoured according as it is required for meat or fish, add for:

Caper Sauce—1 small tablespoonful capers and 1 teaspoonful caper vinegar.

Nasturtium Sauce—1 tablespoonful nasturtium seeds.

Shrimp Sauce—1 oz. shelled shrimps.

Anchovy Sauce—Sufficient anchovy essence or pounded anchovies to colour the sauce a pale pink. Season with pepper and only very little salt.

Egg Sauce—1 small hard-boiled egg, chopped finely.

Parsley Sauce—1 tablespoonful finely chopped parsley. The parsley must be washed and dried thoroughly before chopping.

Onion Sauce—3–4 boiled onions, finely chopped. To remove some of their strong flavour, blanch the onions, *i.e.* put them into cold water and bring to the boil. Drain, put into fresh boiling water and boil gently till tender, about 1 hour. Drain off water, chop the onions very finely and add to the sauce.

Other variations in sauces may be made by the addition of such condiments as vinegar and mustard. The following sauce usually served with grilled fresh herrings or with mackerel will serve as an example:

Mustard Sauce.

Ingredients

½ pint foundation sauce, *i.e.* 1 oz. margarine, 1 oz. flour, ½ pint stock, plus 1 bay leaf. 1 teaspoonful mixed mustard. 2 teaspoonfuls vinegar. Salt, cayenne, pepper.

Method. Cook the flour in the margarine, add bay leaf, mustard and vinegar. Next add stock gradually, bring to the boil and cook gently for 5 minutes. Season and strain.

Brown Sauce.

The making of a brown sauce is distinguished from the making of a white sauce by the fact that (1) the margarine and flour are cooked, either alone or with the vegetables, until they brown, that is, until the flour is dextrinised; (2) brown stock provides the liquid.

Brown Sauce.

Ingredients

1 oz. margarine.
1 oz. flour.
¾ pint brown stock.
1 tablespoonful tomato pulp.
Salt, pepper and cayenne.

1 slice onion or 1 shallot. ½ carrot. 3–4 mushrooms. } optional.

Method. If vegetables are used, chop them finely and cook

them in the margarine until they are a golden brown colour; add flour and brown that also. When the flour is a bright coffee colour, add the stock gradually and finish as for white sauce. Add the tomato pulp and seasonings and strain.

CHAPTER XIV

THE COOKING OF CARBOHYDRATE FOODS: VEGETABLES

Classification of Vegetables.[1]

(1) **Green Vegetables,** *i.e.* the stems, leaves and flowers of plants. *Examples*—Asparagus, spinach, Brussels sprouts, cauliflowers.

(2) **Roots, Tubers and Bulbs,** *i.e.* storage organs of plants.

Roots. Examples—Carrots, parsnips, beetroots.

Tubers, or thickened underground stems. *Examples*—Potatoes, Jerusalem artichokes.

Bulbs, or underground stems bearing leaf-bases storing food materials. *Examples*—Onions, leeks.

(3) **Legumes or Pulse,** *i.e.* pods which enclose seeds. *Examples*—Peas and beans (green and dried); lentils.

Character and Constituents of Vegetables.

From the cook's point of view the important feature of vegetables is the large quantity of cellulose or 'roughage' which forms the cell-walls of the plants. In most vegetables this cellulose is too tough to be eaten raw in any considerable quantity and cooking is necessary to soften it and set free such nutritive material as the cells contain.[2] The other feature is the presence of vitamins and the effects of cooking on them.

Besides providing roughage and vitamins, vegetables contain water and mineral salts, all of which serve to keep the body healthy. Some vegetables have in addition carbohydrates, and some not only carbohydrates but proteins also, though the proteins have not as high a 'biological value' as animal proteins. As a class, however, vegetables lack both proteins and fats.

[1] Cucumbers, marrows and tomatoes, though fruits, are used as vegetables.

[2] For the use of *uncooked* vegetables in salads, see pp. 169 et seq.

Green vegetables, to go into details, provide very little else than roughage, water, mineral salts (particularly iron) and vitamins C with, in certain vegetables, A and B, and it is chiefly for these they are eaten.

Root vegetables, speaking generally, contain a slightly smaller proportion of salts than green vegetables, but provide sugar or starch and very small quantities of protein. In beetroots, carrots, and parsnips sugar is stored; parsnips contain also a good deal of starch. Starch is, of course, abundant in potatoes. As sources of vitamins A and C, root vegetables are not as useful as green vegetables, though carrots are a cheap source of A.

Legumes are by far the most nutritious vegetables. They contain proteins in great abundance; the proportion of starch is larger and that of water smaller than in either green or root vegetables, while they have a good amount of mineral salts. Moreover, they are an important source of vitamin B which, as we know, easily withstands drying.

But in considering the food-value of legumes, it must be borne in mind that vegetable proteins are not as digestible as those obtained from animal substances, probably owing to the large quantity of cellulose with which they are intimately bound up. The indigestibility is greater in dried than in green seeds, and of the three beans and lentils are the least digestible, though they are also the most nutritious. For people who have good digestions, or who lead an active outdoor life, legumes are an inexpensive and nutritious food, particularly when eaten with fats, in which they are deficient. They are most digestible when the cooked seeds are finely divided by being passed through a sieve, as is done in making purée soups or when they are cooked in the form of meal or flour.

COOKING OF VEGETABLES

The problem in cooking vegetables is to soften the cellulose and burst the starch grains, where these are present, and at the same time to lose as little as possible of the cell contents—especially the mineral salts and vitamins A, B, C, the last of which presents the greatest difficulty. Further, it is obviously desirable that the vegetables should be made palatable, and that both their colour and shape should be good.

The presence of tough cellulose limits the choice of cooking processes for most vegetables to those which involve the use of water or steam; hence, boiling or cooking in a small quantity of fat, with or without a small amount of water—a process described as cooking the vegetable conservatively—are mostly employed. Only a few vegetables can be baked or fried.

Steaming vegetables results in the loss of vitamin C and is therefore inadvisable, though sprinkling the vegetable with fresh parsley, coarsely chopped, will compensate for this.

COOKING OF GREEN VEGETABLES

Preparation. (1) Use vegetables as fresh as possible, preferably freshly gathered from the garden.

(2) Remove any discoloured or coarse leaves and tough stalks.

(3) Wash very well in cold water. Soak cabbages, sprouts and all vegetables liable to contain slugs for ½ hour in cold salted water, then rinse.

(4) Burn all vegetable refuse which cannot be used for poultry or pigs or on the garden compost heap.

Boiling Green Vegetables. To soften the cellulose and at the same time lose as little as possible of the salts and vitamins, proceed as follows:

Cabbage. (1) Shred into small strips, using a large and sharp knife.

(2) Pack into a saucepan, adding about ⅜ pt. (one breakfast-cupful) of boiling water and 1 teaspoonful salt. Cover the pan closely to prevent loss of steam which would cause the pan to boil dry.

(3) Cook till tender, about 10–15 minutes. Shake the pan occasionally.

(4) Turn into a colander, drain well, arrange neatly in a hot dish, add a small piece of margarine, sprinkle with pepper, if liked, and serve at once.

(5) Use any water left in the pan for stock.

Brussels Sprouts. Cook and serve as for cabbage, piling high in a hot dish.

Cauliflower. (1) Remove green leaves. Cut flower across into four sections or divide into sprigs. Soak for ¼ hour in cold salted water.

(2) Cook as for cabbage, boiling gently for 10–15 minutes. The leaves, which take longer to cook than the flower, should be put in the pan for about 5 minutes beforehand. Or they may be discarded entirely.

(3) After draining and dishing, $\frac{1}{2}$ pint of white sauce (see pp. 151–152) may be poured over the cauliflower.

Spinach. (1) Double each leaf and tear off the stalk and mid-rib.

(2) Wash very well in several waters, lifting the spinach from one bowl of water to another. Great care is needed to remove all grit and dirt.

(3) If young and tender, lift the spinach from the final rinsing water and pack closely in a saucepan with just the water that clings to it. Add salt.

If spinach is old, put it into the saucepan, adding $\frac{3}{8}$ pint (one breakfastcupful) boiling water and one teaspoonful salt, as in cooking cabbage.

(4) Cook 10–15 minutes, keeping the pan covered.

(5) Drain in a colander, press very dry, add a small piece of margarine, a little pepper, grated nutmeg, if liked, and serve in a hot dish.

It is found in practice that cooking vegetables in a *covered* pan gives the best results. There is very little loss of vitamin C by oxidation as the saucepan is packed with the vegetable and the steam is retained, thus excluding air.

It should be noted that the use of soda, whether washing soda (carbonate) or baking soda (bicarbonate) is to be avoided, since these alkalis tend to destroy vitamin C, especially after cooking is completed. Again, it is important to serve vegetables as quickly as possible after cooking. Keeping vegetables hot, and re-heating them both destroy vitamin C.

BOILING OF FRESH LEGUMES[1]

These are treated in the same way as green vegetables, as is shown by the two examples given below.

Beans (*French and Kidney*). (1) Wash and remove strings. Cut into thin diagonal slices. Very young beans may be cooked whole or snapped in half.

(2) Cook in a small amount of boiling salted water for 10–15 minutes, covering the pan. Shake occasionally.

(3) Drain well and add $\frac{1}{2}$ oz. margarine or 'dress' with parsley and margarine. For this, mix together 1–2 teaspoonfuls chopped parsley and $\frac{1}{2}$–1 oz. margarine for each pound of beans. Put into the pan, add the cooked beans and toss till coated with the margarine. Serve at once in a hot dish.

[1] For cooking dried legumes and pulse see pp. 163–165.

Green Peas. (1) Shell the peas and if not to be cooked at once, cover with a damp cloth.

(2) Cook gently in a small amount of boiling salted water, adding a pinch of sugar and a sprig of mint. Cover the pan and cook for 10–20 minutes.

(3) Drain and remove mint. Serve in a hot dish, adding a small piece of margarine.

COOKING OF ROOTS, TUBERS AND BULBS

In cooking these, as in cooking green vegetables, it is necessary to keep the colour and shape good, and to retain not only the mineral salts and the vitamins, but the carbohydrates (starch or sugar or both) and such small quantities of protein as the vegetables possess. As in cooking green vegetables, boiling and conservative cooking are the most usual methods, but some vegetables may also be baked and fried.[1]

Preparation.

(1) Choose vegetables as far as possible of equal size so that they cook in the same length of time.

(2) If the skin is at all dirty, wash, scrub and rinse the vegetables.

Exceptions. (*a*) *Beetroots* must be washed very carefully to avoid breaking the skin and rootlets; (*b*) *Onions* do not require washing.

(3) Prepare according to the vegetable, peeling it thinly or thickly as the case requires, and removing with the point of a knife all decayed and discoloured parts. Put potatoes and Jerusalem artichokes into cold water as they are peeled, adding vinegar or lemon juice for the latter to keep the colour good. Wash all vegetables after peeling.

I. Boiling Roots, Tubers and Bulbs.[2]

(1) Put the vegetables into a pan and just cover with boiling water. Add one teaspoonful salt to each 2 lbs. vegetables.

The boiling water destroys the active enzymes which cause deterioration of vitamin C.

(2) Cover the pan and let the water boil gently; skim well.

[1] Directions for frying potatoes are given on p. 201.
[2] For detailed directions see pp. 159–161.

(3) Test vegetables with a skewer; when tender, but still unbroken, drain and serve in a hot dish.

The *colour of roots, tubers and bulbs* is maintained:

(*a*) By careful preparation and cleansing.

(*b*) In the case of potatoes and artichokes, by putting them as soon as they are peeled into cold water to avoid exposure to the oxygen in the air which causes a dark-coloured substance to form on the surface of the vegetable. (Cf. the discoloration of peeled apples.)

(*c*) By covering the vegetables with boiling water and cooking them in a covered pan.

The *substance* of roots, tubers and bulbs is maintained by:

(*a*) Cooking the vegetables in their skins when this is possible. If the vegetables are uneven in size, boil the larger ones for a short time before putting the smaller ones into the pan.

(*b*) Cooking peeled vegetables as soon as possible after peeling; if vegetables are left long in cold water some of the substance is dissolved out and lost. (Cf. the clouded appearance of the water in which peeled potatoes have been for some time.)

(*c*) Cooking in a small amount of boiling water to soften the cellulose and cook the starch grains, if these are present, as speedily as possible.

The *shape* as well as the substance of roots, tubers and bulbs is retained by boiling them gently until they are tender without being at all broken.

RECTIONS FOR BOILING ROOTS, TUBERS AND BULBS

egetable	*Preparation*	*Cooking*	*Time*	*Serving*
TI-OKES RU-EM).	Peel thinly. (For a very neat dish the artichokes may be pared to the same shape and size, but this makes them an expensive vegetable.) Put at once into cold water with a little vinegar or lemon juice to keep the colour.	Put into boiling salted water, adding a little vinegar or lemon juice and boil gently till tender.	20–45 minutes.	Drain well and coat at once with white sauce flavoured with lemon juice. If the artichokes are not covered quickly with the sauce they become discoloured.

Vegetable	*Preparation*	*Cooking*	*Time*	*Serving*
BEET-ROOTS.[1]	Wash carefully so as not to break the skin or rootlets.	Put into boiling salted water and boil gently until the beetroot feels soft and like india-rubber. Beetroots must *not* be tested with a skewer.	$1\frac{1}{2}$–$2\frac{1}{2}$ hours.	Put into c water. When q cold, trim a remove the sk Use for a salad for a vegeta entrée (see p. 1
CARROTS (OLD).	Wash, scrape or peel according to the toughness of the skin; wash a second time. If very large, cut lengthwise into quarters, or slice the carrots.	Put into boiling salted water and boil gently until quite tender. Add a little sugar to emphasise the sweetness of the carrots.	1 hour.	Drain and ch finely, re-h with a little m garine. Press i hot moulds or cups and turn into a hot ve table dish.
ONIONS.	Remove outer skin.	Put into boiling salted water and boil gently till tender.	Spanish onions, 2–3 hours. Small onions, $\frac{3}{4}$–1 hour.	Drain and c with white sau Use $\frac{1}{4}$ pint n and $\frac{1}{4}$ pint wa in which onions w cooked for liquid for sauce.
POTATOES (OLD) IN SKINS.[2]	Choose potatoes free from black spots and decay. Scrub well. Prick with a fork, or pare off a narrow strip of peel round the centre to allow of the escape of steam and so keep the potato from bursting.	Put into pan, cover with boiling water, add salt and boil very slowly until the potatoes are tender but still quite whole. Test with a fork or skewer.	20–30 minutes.	Drain and le in the uncove pan by the s of the fire to d Serve in a dish. The sk may be remo first, if desired.

[1] Beetroots may also be scrubbed, peeled thinly and cut into slices before p ting into boiling salted water. The time for cooking by this method is about minutes. Cool in the water.

[2] See note 1 on page 161.

Vegetable	*Preparation*	*Cooking*	*Time*	*Serving*
OTATOES)LD) EELED.[1]	Wash, scrub and pare very thinly so as not to waste the mineral salts and proteins, the greater portion of which lie just under the skin. Remove 'eyes', the buds of the potato stem, and any decayed or discoloured parts. Put into cold water as they are peeled to keep the colour.	Put at once into boiling salted water; boil very slowly in covered pan until quite tender but unbroken.	20–30 minutes.	Drain, return to the pan and put near the fire to dry. Shake the pan occasionally to prevent the potatoes from burning. Serve in a hot dish.
OTATOES)LD) ASHED.	Boil potatoes in usual way, preferably in their skins. Drain, remove skins, and mash with a fork or put through a potato masher.	Add to 1 lb. potatoes $\frac{1}{8}$ pint boiling milk, $\frac{1}{2}$ oz. margarine and a little pepper. Beat with a wooden spoon until the potatoes are light and creamy.	20–30 minutes for boiling.	Pile in a hot vegetable dish.
OTATOES IEW).	Scrape or rub with a rough cloth to remove skins. Put into cold water.	Put into boiling salted water with a sprig of mint and boil very gently till tender.	15–20 minutes.	Drain and remove mint. Return to pan, adding $\frac{1}{2}$–1 oz. margarine to 2 lbs. potatoes. Serve in a hot dish.

[1] Where poverty restricts a diet severely it is important that potatoes, which are largely eaten, should be cooked in the best possible way. In such a diet potatoes may be almost the sole source of vitamin C; hence, cooking should be short, as in boiling, rather than long and slow, as when they are cooked in stews, *e.g.* Irish stew. Re-cooking potatoes (*e.g.* frying cold potatoes) is, in such circumstances, to be deprecated. Cooking potatoes in their skins prevents loss of soluble substance, and the skins, if eaten, provide some vitamin B and also roughage.

II. Conservative Cooking of Roots, Tubers and Bulbs, etc.

This process, which answers well for these vegetables and also for green peas and beans, consists in cooking the vegetables very gently in margarine or other fat with a small quantity of liquid: the constituents of the vegetables are conserved more completely than is the case with other processes. (See p. 163.)

DIRECTIONS FOR BAKING ROOTS, TUBERS AND BULBS

Vegetable	*Preparation*	*Baking*	*Time*	*Serving*
BAKED ONIONS.	Skin and cook in boiling salted water till tender, 1–3 hours, according to size.	For 3 large onions heat about 1½ oz. margarine or dripping in a baking tin. Put in the onions and bake until brown, basting them from time to time.	1–3 hours boiling. 15–20 minutes baking.	Serve in a ho dish. Pour margarine or drippin over the onions.
BAKED POTATOES (IN SKINS).	Take potatoes of medium and equal sizes, scrub well, remove 'eyes' and prick them or pare off a narrow strip of peel round the centre to allow the steam to escape.	Bake in a *hot* oven till quite soft. Turn the potatoes occasionally so that they cook evenly. If the potatoes are baked too slowly they become dry and hard.	45–60 minutes.	Serve in a h dish.
BAKED POTATOES (PEELED).	Scrub and wash well, put into boiling salted water and boil gently for 5–10 minutes. Cool for a few minutes then peel and dredge with flour.	Put in a baking tin sufficient dripping to cover the bottom of the tin and allow for basting the potatoes, and heat till a blue vapour comes off. Put in the potatoes and bake in a hot oven, basting and turning the potatoes from time to time, till they are tender, crisp and browned.	20–30 minutes.	Serve in a h dish or put roun baked meat. I the latter cas the potatoes ca be baked wi the meat.

Examples of stuffed baked vegetables will be found on pp. 167–168.

[1] See also p. 163.

Carrots Cooked Conservatively.

Ingredients

1 bunch new carrots *or* 4 large carrots (old).	$\frac{3}{4}$ oz. margarine or dripping.
	3 tablespoonfuls water.
Salt and pepper.	1 tablespoonful chopped parsley.

Method. Wash the carrots and scrape or peel. Cut new carrots into two lengthwise, old carrots into thin slices. Put into a pan with fat, water and seasoning, cover closely with a lid, and cook gently for from 30–40 minutes, shaking frequently so that the carrots do not stick to the pan. When the carrots are tender, uncover the pan and cook for a few minutes longer to allow the liquid to evaporate. Add the chopped parsley and serve very hot.

Onions Cooked Conservatively.

Ingredients

4 large onions.	$\frac{3}{4}$–1 oz. margarine or dripping.
Salt and pepper.	3 tablespoonfuls water.
1 tablespoonful chopped parsley.	

Method. Peel onions and cut into rings. Put into a pan with salt and pepper, fat, water, and cook slowly for approximately 30 minutes. Toss the pan frequently so that the onions do not stick. When the onion is tender, remove the pan lid and cook for a few minutes till the liquid has evaporated. Add the parsley and serve hot.

III. Baking Roots, Tubers and Bulbs.

Certain vegetables which contain a good proportion of water can be baked successfully and with very little loss of substance. But since steam or water is necessary to soften cellulose, baking is perhaps most used to *complete* the cooking of vegetables which have undergone a preliminary boiling. The high temperature of the oven gives the vegetables a crispness which they lack when cooked wholly by water. Baking is the only process which allows of stuffing the vegetables, treatment which makes them more savoury. Vegetable marrows, tomatoes and onions all lend themselves well to this method of cooking and recipes for preparing them thus will be found on pp. 167,168.

COOKING OF DRIED LEGUMES AND PULSE

Peas, Beans and Lentils.

These are usually boiled or stewed. The general directions are as follows:

Preparation. Wash thoroughly in several waters. Steep for at least 12 hours in a plentiful supply of cold water to replace the water lost in the drying. Split or red Egyptian lentils absorb water and soften so readily in cooking that steeping is not necessary.

Cooking. Put the pulse into cold salted water and boil gently till tender. Skim well, strain, season and serve.

Example 1. **Boiled Haricot Beans.**

Wash the beans well and soak overnight in a good supply of cold water. Boil in the water in which they were soaked, adding more if it is necessary to cover the beans well. Add salt, an onion cut in half, a bunch of herbs and either a few bacon rinds or a bacon bone or a little margarine or dripping (1 oz. to 1 lb. of beans). These latter provide the fat which the beans lack.

Boil the beans gently until tender but unbroken, from 2½–4 hours according to the size of the beans and to their dryness and hardness. Drain, keeping the water for stock, and serve the beans in one of the following ways, first removing skins, if desired:

Method 1. Heat a small piece of margarine in a saucepan and add a little finely chopped parsley. Toss the beans in it, season with pepper and serve in a hot dish.

Method 2. Prepare for each pound of beans cooked from ½–¾ pint of tomato, parsley, brown or curry sauce. Reheat the beans in the sauce, stirring them carefully so as not to break them.

Example 2. **American Baked Beans.**

Ingredients

½ pint haricot beans.
1 tablespoonful golden syrup.
Few bacon rinds *or* bacon *or* ham bone.
Pepper and salt.

Method. Wash the beans and steep overnight, then put them in a stew jar with 1 pint of the water in which they were steeped and the syrup, bacon rinds or bone and seasonings. Cover the stew jar with a lid, put it in a cool oven and cook the beans *very* slowly for 9 or 10 hours.

Beans prepared thus the day before and served with bacon or sausages, cooked separately, make an excellent winter breakfast dish. Or a piece of salt pork may be cooked with the beans and served with it.

Example 3. **Boiled Egyptian Lentils.**

Cover the washed lentils with cold water, add salt, bring to the boil and boil very gently for 10–15 minutes until the lentils are tender. Strain off the water, add a small piece of margarine, a little chopped parsley and salt and pepper.

Cooked lentils may also be mixed with curry sauce (see p. 104) allowing ¼ lb. lentils to rather less than ½ pint of sauce.

VEGETABLE ENTRÉES AND SAVOURY DISHES

Many vegetables are capable of rather more elaborate preparation than that already detailed—preparation which makes them suitable for serving as a course in themselves and not as mere adjuncts to meat. See pp. 165–168.

ROUP 1. VEGETABLE ENTRÉES AND SAVOURY DISHES

getables	Ingredients	Preliminary Preparation	Completion
TI- OKES D ROUTS.	2 lbs. Jerusalem artichokes. 1 lb. Brussels sprouts. *Sauce*: 1 oz. margarine. 1 oz. flour. ½ pint milk. Yolk of 1 egg. 1 teaspoonful lemon juice, salt and pepper.	Boil vegetables (see pp. 159 and 156). Prepare white sauce in the usual way (see pp. 151, 152) adding lemon juice, salt and pepper after the final boiling. Cool slightly, add beaten yolk of egg, stir and cook carefully so that the egg thickens without curdling.	Pile the sprouts high in the centre of the dish and arrange the artichokes round. Coat the artichokes with sauce. Serve very hot.
T- TS) TATOES.	2 beetroots. 1 small tablespoonful vinegar. 1 lb. potatoes. *Sauce*: 1 oz. margarine. 2 small onions (chopped). 2 teaspoonfuls flour. ¼ pint white stock or water. Salt, pepper and sugar.	Boil the beetroots (see p. 160), and when cold, peel them and cut them into slices ¼ inch thick. Sprinkle the vinegar over to set the colour. Boil the potatoes, preferably in their skins, and mash them (see p. 161.)	*Sauce*. Heat margarine, fry chopped onions lightly, remove onions, add flour and cook 3 or 4 minutes without browning. Add liquid gradually and complete the making of the sauce in the usual way. Add the sliced beetroot and simmer 20 minutes. Arrange the mashed potatoes in a border on a hot dish. Put the beetroot and sauce in the middle and serve very hot.

Vegetables	*Ingredients*	*Preliminary Preparation*	*Completion*
CHEESE CAULI-FLOWER (Cauli-flower au Gratin).	1 cauliflower. 3 teaspoonfuls fine browned bread-crumbs. *Sauce*: 1 oz. margarine. 1 oz. flour. ¼ pint milk. ¼ pint water used to cook cauliflower. Salt, pepper and cayenne. 2 tablespoonfuls grated cheese.	Boil cauliflower (p. 156) and drain. Make white sauce in the usual way (see pp. 151, 152), adding the cheese at the last and seasoning the sauce well.	Put the cauliflo into a hot firepr dish, pour sauce o and sprinkle bre crumbs on top. Ba in a hot oven for 10– minutes, or bro under a gas-griller.
SPINACH AND EGGS.	2 lbs. spinach. ½ oz. margarine. ⅛ pint milk. Pepper and salt. 1 round of toast. 1 or 3 hard-boiled *or* 3 poached eggs.	Boil spinach (p. 157), drain, rub through a sieve and re-heat with the mar-garine, milk, etc. Prepare toast, cut it into pieces and 'but-ter' it. Put the eggs into boiling water and boil for 10 minutes or poach them (see p. 72).	*Method* 1. Arra the spinach in pyram shape on the toa Garnish with the wh of 1 egg, chopped fin and with the yolk r bed through a siev *Method* 2. Arra spinach in a flat c on the toast and on top the 3 poac or the 3 hard-boi eggs, quartering latter lengthwise.
NOR-MANDY EGGS.	6 hard-boiled eggs. ½ lb. haricot beans. 3 oz. fat bacon *or* few bacon rinds, *or* 1 oz. beef dripping. Salt and pepper. 1 oz. margarine. *Sauce*: 2 oz. margarine. 2 oz. flour. ½ pint water in which beans were cooked. ½ pint milk. Salt, pepper and lemon juice.	Wash beans and soak overnight in a good supply of water. Cook in the same water, adding more if necessary. Put with them the bacon (cut in small pieces), or bacon rinds, or 1 oz. dripping and boil gently for 2½–4 hours, till tender. Put eggs in boiling water and boil gently 10 minutes.	1. Remove skins a shells from the eggs a cut in half lengthwa 2. Drain bea keeping ½ pint liq for the sauce. Seas with salt and pepp add 1 oz. margari and toss over the for a few minutes. 3. Prepare sauce. in the pieces of egg a let them heat throu Pile up the be on a hot dish, lift pieces of egg out the sauce, lay them top of beans and p the sauce over.

GROUP 2. STUFFED AND BAKED VEGETABLES

Dish	*Ingredients*	*Preliminary Preparation*	*Stuffing and Baking of Vegetables*
TUFFED EGE-ABLE ARROW.	1 medium-sized vegetable marrow. *Stuffing*: 2 small onions. 1 oz. margarine. ½ tablespoonful sage. ¼ lb. bread-crumbs. Salt, pepper, cayenne. Yolk of 1 egg *or* ½ whole egg. ——— ½ pint thickened brown gravy or sauce. (See pp. 97 and 153 respectively.)	Cook the marrow in boiling salted water for 15–20 minutes. Drain, peel thinly, cut into half lengthwise and remove the seeds. *Stuffing*. Peel the onions and cook in boiling water for ¾–1 hour, drain and chop finely. Mix with the remaining ingredients of the stuffing and moisten with beaten egg.	Fill each half of the marrow with stuffing and put them together in their original position. Lay the marrow carefully in a greased baking tin and brush with margarine. Bake in a hot oven ¾–1½ hours according to the age and size of the marrow. Lift carefully on to a hot dish and serve with gravy or sauce.
UFFED OMA-ES.[1]	6 medium-sized tomatoes. 6 mushrooms (optional). 6 pieces of toast. 1 tablespoonful browned crumbs. *Stuffing*. ½ shallot. 1½ oz. cooked ham *or* tongue *or* veal. 1 sprig parsley. 3 tablespoonfuls bread-crumbs. Nutmeg, pepper, salt. 1 oz. margarine.	Cut a small slice from the top of each tomato, scoop out contents with a teaspoon, being careful not to break the case. Put pinch of salt in each and turn upside down on a plate to drain. Put insides of tomatoes through a sieve. Cut up shallot, meat and parsley finely. Heat margarine and fry these in it for a few minutes then add tomato pulp, bread-crumbs and seasonings.	Fill cases with prepared mixture, and sprinkle the browned crumbs on top. Grease a baking tin and sprinkle it with a little stock or water, put in the tomatoes and cover closely with a greased paper. Bake in a moderate oven 10–15 minutes until the tomatoes are tender. If the skins are wrinkled, either the oven has been too hot or the tomatoes have not been covered closely enough. Serve each tomato on a piece of 'buttered' toast, putting under each a fried mushroom, if used.

[1] These are fruits but are usually served as vegetables, hence their inclusion here.

Dish	*Ingredients*	*Preliminary Preparation*	*Stuffing and Baking of Vegetables*
Stuffed Onions.	3 Spanish onions. *Stuffing*: 3 tablespoonfuls bread-crumbs. 3 tablespoonfuls cold minced pork. Pepper and salt. ½ teaspoonful lemon juice. 1 oz. dripping.	Peel the onions, put them into boiling salted water and boil gently from 1–1½ hours till barely tender, then drain. Take out the centres of the onions, removing them with a fork from the top, and mince them finely. Mix with the bread-crumbs, meat and seasonings.	Fill the spaces i the onions with tl stuffing. Heat drippir in a baking tin, put the onions and bake a hot oven for abo 20 minutes, bastir them with the drippi from time to time.

VEGETABLE SAUCES

Horse-radish Sauce. (For serving with Roast Beef.)

Ingredients

2 oz. grated horse-radish.
1 teaspoonful sugar.
½ teaspoonful mixed mustard.
¼ pint milk.
1 teaspoonful white wine vinegar.
Salt and pepper.

Method. Mix horse-radish and seasonings together, add milk and vinegar. If it is to be served with hot meat, the sauce may be warmed.

Mint Sauce. (For serving with Roast Lamb or Mutton.)

Ingredients

2 tablespoonfuls chopped mint.
1 tablespoonful brown sugar.
¼ pint vinegar.
Pinch of salt.
1 tablespoonful boiling water.

Method. Wash the leaves of the mint and chop very finely. Add salt, sugar and boiling water. When the sugar has dissolved, add the vinegar. The sauce should stand for an hour before serving.

Tomato Sauce.

Ingredients

1 pint tinned tomatoes, *or*
1 pint pieces of fresh tomatoes.

1 bay leaf.
1 sprig of thyme.
1 clove of garlic.
1 slice of onion.
Bacon or ham bone.

1 teaspoonful margarine
1 teaspoonful potato flour *or* cornflour.

Salt, pepper, cayenne.
Sugar.
1 teaspoonful vinegar.

Method. If fresh tomatoes are used, cut them up and cook them gently without water till they form a pulp.

Put the tinned tomatoes or the tomato pulp into a pan with bay leaf, thyme, etc., and heat gently for $\frac{1}{4}$ hour to extract flavours. Then take out the flavouring materials, rub the tomatoes through a sieve and reheat the purée till it is almost boiling.

Mix the margarine and potato flour or cornflour together with a knife and add it, a small piece at a time, to the sauce, mixing in each portion thoroughly before adding the next. Cook gently for 10 minutes without allowing the sauce to boil. If it boils, the margarine may form as oil on the top. Add seasonings and vinegar, mix well and serve.

SALADS

It will be convenient to discuss here the making of salads, since vegetables are largely used.

I. Foundation Materials.

1. *Uncooked.*

Vegetables. (*a*) Lettuce, watercress, mustard and cress, endive, chicory, nasturtium leaves, dandelion leaves (young), cabbage (young), etc. (*b*) Carrots and turnips (young), radishes celery. (*c*) Cucumber, tomatoes. (*d*) Apples, oranges, lemons grape fruit. (*e*) Walnuts or other nuts (shelled).

2. *Cooked.*

(1) *Vegetables.* (*a*) Potatoes, carrots, turnips (preferably young), beetroot. (*b*) Green peas, French and kidney beans, haricot beans (fresh), cauliflower (flower only). (*c*) Haricot beans (dried).

(2) *Meat, Fish and Eggs.* (*a*) Chicken, game, rabbit, tongue, ham, sausage. (*b*) Salmon, halibut, turbot or other white fish; sardines; lobster, crab, shrimps, prawns. (*c*) Eggs (hard-boiled), yolks or whites or both.

II. Additions.

1. *Flavouring Materials.* (*a*) Onions, spring onions, shallots. (*b*) Chives, chervil, parsley, tarragon, fennel, mint.

2. *Garnishing Materials.* The best parts of any of the foundation materials named above.

Selection of Materials. Dietetically the most valuable salads are those made entirely or mainly from raw vegetables and fruits whose value as sources of mineral salts and vitamins has not been lessened by cooking. The choice is regulated to some extent by the time of year, but whatever the season it is wise to avoid monotony both in selecting and combining the materials available. Colour, as well as food value and flavour, needs consideration; for example, beetroot does not look attractive with tomatoes, nor yet with carrots.

Salads to be served with hot or cold joints or poultry or game are usually simpler than salads which form a course by themselves.

Preparation of Salad Materials.

Vegetables.

1. *Uncooked Vegetables. Lettuce, watercress and all green salad material* should be young and crisp. (If leaves are at all stale soak in cold salted water for a short time.) Remove stalks and any coarse or discoloured leaves. Wash in very cold water, thoroughly but lightly; avoid breaking or bruising the leaves. Shake lightly in a salad basket or colander, toss gently in a clean soft cloth, and put on a cake tray or sieve till required. *Lettuce*: tear into small pieces with the fingers; for garnishing, a few of the inner leaves can be shredded finely with a knife. *Cabbage*: use only crisp inner leaves and shred finely. *Radishes*: wash, brush if necessary, and cut off the tops. *Young carrots and turnips*: wash, grate finely or cut into shreds. *Celery*: use white crisp part, wash, cut into fine strips or dice. *Cucumber*: peel, cut into wafer-like slices or into dice. *Tomatoes*: cover with boiling water for a few minutes, place in cold water and skin; cut into slices or sections. *Apples*: peel, core, cut into dice or small sections. Prepare immediately before use or else put into cold water after peeling. *Oranges, lemons, grape fruit*: peel, remove pips and every trace of bitter white skin, cut into thin slices. *Walnuts*: cut each half into three or four pieces.

2. *Cooked Vegetables*. Cooked vegetables should be tender but firm, free from discoloured parts and quite cold when used. Cut them into dice or slice thinly.

Meat, Fish, Eggs.

Meat. Remove gristle, skin and tissue, cut into small neat pieces or into dice. *Fish*: remove skin and bones, divide into flakes, using two forks, or in case of salmon, halibut, etc., into neat portions, suitable for serving. *Sardines*: remove tails, skin and backbone. *Eggs*: remove shell and skin, cut into rings or into sections lengthwise; or separate yolk and white, rubbing the yolk through a sieve and chopping the white very finely.

Flavouring Materials.

Onions (*spring*), *onions and shallots.* Prepare in the usual way, then chop finely. An alternative plan is to omit the onion or shallot, and, instead, rub the inside of the salad bowl with a cut piece of onion; or about 1 teaspoonful of very finely chopped shallot may be incorporated with the salad dressing. *Chives, chervil, parsley, fennel, mint*: wash, dry, chop very finely. Again, finely chopped chives with $\frac{1}{4}$ teaspoonful of Paprika pepper may be incorporated with the dressing.

Dressing Salads. Salads are usually 'dressed' with dressing or cream, of which there are three types:

(1) French dressing (uncooked), made of oil, vinegar and seasonings.

(2) Mayonnaise and salad creams, uncooked or cooked, made of the same ingredients as the French dressing, with the addition of yolks of eggs and also of cream or milk (fresh or condensed).

(3) Salad creams made of the same materials as (2) above, with the exception of oil, which is omitted.

The oil and vinegar used should be of good quality. 'Huile de Provence' is less oily in taste than that sold as 'Lucca' or 'Finest Salad' oil. French vinegar and white wine vinegar are best; lemon juice may be used instead and gives a more delicate flavour. Tarragon vinegar may be used, but very sparingly, for flavouring.

French dressing is used with 'green' salads such as are served with hot roast meat, poultry and game, and for salads made mainly of uncooked materials. There are various ways of preparing this dressing, but whichever is chosen the salad must not actually be 'dressed', *i.e.* mixed with the dressing, until it is about to be served, though the salad materials may be prepared beforehand.

Mayonnaise and Salad Creams are used for the more elaborate salads to be served as a course in themselves and made for the most part of cooked vegetables with or without cooked meat or fish. Here the salad materials are best mixed with the dressing an hour or so before serving.

Whatever the salad, and whatever the dressing, salads must be as cold and as fresh as possible when served.

French Salad Dressing.

Ingredients

2 tablespoonfuls Huile de Provence.
1 tablespoonful French *or* white wine vinegar *or* lemon juice.
1 saltspoonful salt.
1 saltspoonful pepper.
1 saltspoonful sugar (optional).
Variations: 1 teaspoonful finely chopped tarragon, parsley or chervil.

Method 1. Put the pepper and sugar (if used) into a salad or silver spoon, fill it twice with oil and sprinkle it over the salad, turning the salad gently over two or three times with a spoon and fork, so as to coat all the leaves, etc., with the oil. Then put the salt in the spoon, add the vinegar and sprinkle it drop by drop over the salad, and turn it a second time.

The dressing must be done very lightly and carefully, so as to moisten every part of the salad without in any way bruising or pressing down the leaves.

Method 2. Put the oil and vinegar in a bowl, and rub them together with a spoon until they thicken and become opaque; add pepper and salt and sugar (if used). Mix the dressing lightly with the prepared salad materials, using just sufficient to moisten them thoroughly.

Method 3. Mix salt, pepper, sugar (if used) with vinegar or lemon juice, pour very gradually on to the oil and mix very thoroughly. Mix the dressing lightly but thoroughly with the prepared salad materials.

Mayonnaise.

Ingredients

1 yolk of egg (in winter) or 2 yolks of egg (in summer).[1]
Pinch of salt and of mustard.
⅜ pint Huile de Provence.
¼ teaspoonful lemon juice.
1 teaspoonful French *or* tarragon vinegar *or* mixture of the two.

Method. Work in a cool place. Wrap a wet cloth round a basin, and fix firmly in place on a table by means of two heavy weights. Or pack the basin in a mixture of broken ice and rough salt.

Beat the egg in the basin till it froths, add salt and mustard. Dip a teaspoon into the oil, and let the oil which clings to it fall

[1] The eggs should be neither absolutely fresh nor yet decidedly stale, so that the albumen has the right degree of tenaciousness.

drop by drop into the egg, and as it falls stir or rub it with a small wooden spoon, so that the oil is divided into fine globules, each coated with egg. When about a teaspoonful of oil has been added thus, add the remainder, still very gradually, from a small jug, stirring and rubbing thoroughly between each addition. The sauce should be firm, smooth and thick; if the oil makes the sauce thin it has been added too quickly, and the sauce must be stirred and rubbed until it thickens again before more oil is added. At the last add the lemon juice and vinegar, also drop by drop, and mix thoroughly.

The sauce when finished should be of such consistency that it will keep its shape when heaped in a spoon. For dressing salads it may be thinned if desired, by means of a little cream and an additional supply of vinegar, both being added very gradually.

Salad Cream No. 1.

Ingredients

1 teaspoonful mixed mustard.
1 teaspoonful castor sugar.
2 tablespoonfuls Huile de Provence.
4 tablespoonfuls cream or milk.
2 tablespoonfuls French *or* white wine vinegar.
Cayenne, salt.

Method 1. Mix mustard and sugar in a basin and add the oil, drop by drop, from a cream jug. Rub in each few drops thoroughly before adding more. (2) Next add very gradually first the cream or milk, then the vinegar, and mix thoroughly. (3) Add seasonings. The dressing should have a smooth creamy appearance. If it curdles the vinegar has been added too quickly.

Salad Cream No. 2. (Cooked salad cream without oil.)

Ingredients

1 egg.
¼ teacupful new milk.
½ oz. margarine.
1 teaspoonful mixed mustard.
¼ teacupful vinegar.
Salt, pepper, sugar.

Method. Beat the egg and mix with the other ingredients. Put into a pan (preferably a double saucepan) and heat, stirring carefully until the mixture thickens. It must not boil lest the egg curdle.

Vegetable Salad.

Foundation. Two or more of the following: Celery (raw). Carrot and turnip (raw or cooked; if raw, use in relatively small amounts). Beetroot, potatoes (cooked). Green peas, kidney beans, haricot beans (cooked). Cauliflower (cooked, flower part only).

Garnish. Mustard and cress, *or* watercress, *or* lettuce, *or* parsley, *or* other green salad material.

Dressing. Mayonnaise or salad cream (see pp. 172–173).

Method. (1) Cut the selected vegetables (other than beans, peas or cauliflower) into dice or slices. Grate or shred finely raw carrot and turnip; divide the flower of the cauliflower into small sections. (2) Season and mix lightly with the salad dressing. (3) Prepare the garnish according to its kind (see p. 170), chopping parsley (if used) very finely. Decorate the salad with it. Raw carrot and turnip may form part of the garnish if desired. (4) Put into a cold place for an hour before serving.

Green Pea Salad.

Foundation. 1 pint green peas (cooked), 2 small round lettuces.

Garnish. 3 tomatoes (skinned).

Dressing. Mayonnaise or salad cream (see pp. 172, 173).

Method. (1) Tear up lettuce leaves, keeping smaller innermost leaves for garnish.

(2) Put torn leaves in salad bowl and mix with *part* of the mayonnaise or salad cream.

(3) Pile peas in the centre of the salad bowl and pour the rest of the dressing over.

(4) Put the smaller lettuce leaves in the centre of the mound of peas and garnish the base with quarters of tomato.

Potato Salad.

Foundation. 1½ lbs. new potatoes.

Garnish. 2 tablespoonfuls parsley, finely chopped.

Dressing. Mayonnaise or salad cream (see pp. 172, 173).

Method. Cut the potatoes into dice or into slices. Mix with finely chopped parsley and mayonnaise or salad cream and arrange in pyramid shape in a salad bowl.

Green Salad.

Foundation. Lettuce, watercress, mustard and cress; chicory; dandelion leaves (very young).

Flavouring. Slice of onion or shallot (optional).

Garnish. 1 teaspoonful each of finely-chopped parsley, chives, fennel.

Dressing. French dressing (see p. 172.)

Method. (1) Prepare foundation materials in the usual way (see p. 170). (2) Rub the inside of the salad bowl with onion or shallot (if used). (3) Put the salad in the bowl and 'dress' it, using silver or salad spoon and fork, and mixing it lightly but thoroughly with the dressing. (4) Scatter the garnish on top of the salad.

Marguerite Salad.

Ingredients

2 small French lettuces.	3–4 tomatoes.
¼ lb. watercress.	1 egg (hard-boiled).

Dressing. French dressing or salad cream or mayonnaise (see pp. 172–173).

Method. (1) Prepare lettuce, watercress and tomatoes as directed on p. 170. (2) Tear outer lettuce leaves into pieces, put into salad bowl and mix with the dressing, then cut inner lettuce leaves into fine shreds and sprinkle on top. (3) Gather the watercress into small bunches and arrange in a border round the bowl. (4) Cut tomatoes into slices and form into a circle inside the watercress, letting the pieces overlap. (5) Rub the yolk of the egg through a gravy-strainer or sieve and cut the white lengthwise into strips. Arrange these in the middle of the bowl to represent the yellow centre and white petals of a marguerite.

Watercress and Orange Salad. (For pheasant or cold mutton.)

Ingredients

¼ lb. watercress. 1 teaspoonful chopped shallot.
1 large orange.

Dressing. French dressing (see p. 172).

Method. Prepare watercress (see p. 170). Remove peel, pith, skin and pips from the orange and cut into thin slices. Mix watercress, chopped shallot and dressing, put into salad bowl, add orange and mix gently. Serve very cold.

Celery, Apple and Walnut Salad.

Ingredients

1 head of celery. 2 oz. shelled walnuts.
3–4 apples.

Dressing. Mayonnaise or salad cream (see pp. 172, 173).

Method. (1) Clean celery (see p. 170) and cut the inner white sticks into shreds (use the remainder as a vegetable or in soup). (2) Cut each half walnut into two or three pieces. (3) Peel apples, core, and cut into ¼ inch dice. (4) Mix celery, walnuts, apple and mayonnaise or salad cream well together. (5) Cover and put into a cold place for an hour before serving.

Fish Salad.

Ingredients

1 lb. cooked fish (*e.g.* salmon, halibut, hake).	½ cucumber.
1 lettuce *or* ¼ lb. watercress.	2 tomatoes (peeled).
	1 hard-boiled egg.

Dressing. Mayonnaise or salad cream (see pp. 172, 173).

Method. (1) Prepare lettuce (or watercress), cucumber and tomatoes, as directed on p. 170. (2) Tear up outer lettuce leaves and put in salad bowl or on a dish. (3) Remove skin and bones from fish, divide into pieces suitable for serving, and arrange on top of the lettuce. (4) Coat each piece of fish with dressing. (5) Cut tomato and cucumber into slices, the latter very thinly, and put alternately round the edge of the bowl or dish, letting them overlap. (6) Put the hearts of the lettuce in the centre of the dish. (7) Chop white of egg finely and put yolk through a sieve or gravy-strainer. Arrange in little heaps, alternately, just inside the circle of tomatoes and cucumber. (8) Put into a cold place for an hour before serving.

Chicken or Veal Salad.

Ingredients

Cold cooked chicken or veal.	Finely chopped chives.
1–2 lettuces.	2 eggs, hard-boiled.
¼ cucumber.	Pepper, salt.

Dressing. Mayonnaise or salad cream (see pp. 172, 173).

Method. (1) Cut chicken or veal into neat pieces, removing skin and gristle. (2) Peel cucumber, cut in half lengthwise and after removing seeds, cut into dice. (3) Wash and dry lettuces, shred inner leaves finely, tear outer leaves into small pieces. (4) Mix chicken (or veal) and cucumber together, season and mix with part of the mayonnaise sauce or salad cream. (5) Put some of this mixture into the salad bowl, then a layer of torn lettuce leaves, then the remainder of the mixture. (5) Arrange shredded leaves on top. (7) Pour over any mayonnaise or cream remaining, and garnish with hard-boiled eggs cut into sections lengthwise. (8) Sprinkle chopped chives over all.

Russian Salad.

Foundation. ½–¾ lb. cold veal, ½ lb. French beans (cooked).

Flavouring. 1 small Spanish onion, rind and juice of 1 lemon, 1 tablespoonful capers, 2 tablespoonfuls parsley (finely chopped), salt and pepper.

Garnish. 2 hard-boiled eggs, 1 beetroot *or* 4 tomatoes (skinned).

Dressing. Mayonnaise or salad cream (see pp. 172, 173.)

Method. (1) Cut veal into slices $\frac{1}{4}$ in. thick and devide into pieces about 1 in. long.

(2) Chop onion, parsley and lemon rind finely.

(3) Mix well together the veal, beans, onion, parsley, lemon rind and juice, capers, salt and pepper, and put in a salad bowl.

(4) Pour mayonnaise or salad cream over.

(5) Garnish with slices of beetroot *or* tomato and hard-boiled egg, cut into sections lengthwise.

Suggestions for Salads.

(1) Tomatoes and chopped parsley; French dressing.

(2) Tomatoes, lettuce, shrimps or prawns; mayonnaise or salad cream.

(3) Beetroot, potatoes, sardines; mayonnaise or salad cream.

(4) Potatoes (new), chopped chives, salad cream.

(5) Potatoes, tomatoes, chopped parsley, chopped onion or shallot, nasturtium leaves and garnish of nasturtium flowers; French dressing.

(6) Beetroot, endive, and small sections of cream cheese; French dressing.

CHAPTER XV

THE COOKING OF CARBOHYDRATE FOODS: FRUITS

Character and Constituents of Fruits.

For the present purposes, the large variety of fruits may be classified as follows:

Group 1. **Sugary Fruits.**

(1) Fruits with pips, *e.g.* apples, pears, lemons, oranges.
(2) Fruits with stones, *e.g.* damsons, plums, cherries, apricots.
(3) Fruits with seeds, *e.g.* gooseberries, raspberries, strawberries.

Group 2. **Nuts,** *e.g.* walnuts, chestnuts, Brazil nuts.

Sugary Fruits. In general character the fruits in this group are alike. Cellulose forms the framework, the watery contents of the cells have a fair proportion of sugar, very small quantities of mineral salts, while in certain fruits vitamins are also found. Fats and proteins are noticeably absent.

The amount of sugar in most fruits is quite small, and only a few fruits, for example, prunes, figs and dates, contain sufficient sugar to make them really nutritious.

In addition to sugar, fruits contain a second carbohydrate substance, or, more probably, a group of substances, known as *pectin*. Pectin resembles gelatin, the protein substance obtained by boiling in water the bones and connective tissues of animals, in that it is soluble in hot water and gelatinises on cooling. For this reason it is often spoken of as 'fruit gelatine'. It is the quantity of pectin present which makes it possible to prepare jelly from such fruits as apples, currants, and damsons.

The juice of fresh citrous fruits, oranges, lemons and grape fruit contains some sugar and is a valuable source of the anti-scorbutic vitamin C which is also present, though in much smaller quantities in fresh raspberries, apples and bananas. In grapes the amount of vitamin C is extremely small, while in dried fruits with the exception of peaches, there is little, if any vitamin C.

Fruits owe their flavour and fragrance to their volatile essences or oils. It is the volatile essence of the rinds of lemons and oranges which makes them useful for flavouring.

Though sugary fruits contain very little actual nourishment they are valuable for the sugar, water, vitamins and roughage they supply, as well as for their pleasant refreshing taste.

Nuts, as a class, are a good source of vitamin B. They contain much less water than do the sugary fruits, and with the exception of chestnuts, are rich in proteins, fats and mineral salts. Chestnuts contain large quantities of starch and sugar. Nuts thus contain a good proportion of nourishment in a concentrated form, but are not, as a rule, digested easily. The difficulty of digestion is overcome to some extent by their preparation as 'nut-foods' or 'nut-flour', both much used in vegetarian cookery. 'Vegetarian butter' is prepared from the fat of nuts.

COOKING OF SUGARY FRUITS

The anti-scorbutic value of fresh fruits, as we have seen, is lessened by cooking and by drying. Hence, as sources of vitamin

C, raw fruits are more valuable than cooked and fresh than dried. For example, fresh oranges contain more vitamin C than oranges eaten as marmalade, raw apples and raspberries more than the same fruits stewed. It is worth noting that when lemon juice is used for purposes of flavouring, its vitamins are better preserved if the juice is added to the mixture *after* instead of *during* the cooking. Similarly, in making lemonade it is well to use cold water to avoid impairing the vitamin value of the lemons.

While uncooked fruits are valuable, many fruits are readily perishable, and moreover are only obtainable at certain periods of the year. Hence cooking is often necessary to preserve them either for short or for long periods or for other reasons. Fruits which are to be preserved temporarily are, in general, cooked at a low temperature in a syrup of sugar and water which is served with them. Apples, pears and bananas can also be baked. When fruits are cooked the cellulose is softened, the contents of the cells set free and the pectin dissolved.

Earthenware, enamel-lined and aluminium pans are best for cooking fruit since they are not liable to the formation of rust, tarnish or verdigris. Both tarnish and verdigris are liable to be acted upon by fruit acids, and if copper and brass pans are used they must be scrupulously clean.

Stewing Fruits.

Preparation. Pick the fruit, rejecting any decayed specimens. Put firm fruits, *e.g.* cherries, gooseberries, which are not to be peeled or skinned, in a colander and rinse quickly in cold water. Wash dried fruits very thoroughly. Remove the peel and tough white skin from oranges. Peel and core apples and pears and leave whole, or cut into halves or quarters, as desired; these fruits should be peeled immediately before cooking. If this is not possible, put them into cold water as soon as they are peeled to prevent discoloration.

Cooking.[1]

A. *Thin-skinned, juicy fruits, e.g.* strawberries, raspberries, currants.

(1) For each pound of fruit, take ¼ lb. sugar and ¼ pint of water. Dissolve the sugar in the water, boil 3–4 minutes, skim and cool.

[1] When it is desired to use less sugar than is prescribed here, the alternative method of stewing fruit, given on p. 181, should be used.

(2) Put the fruit into the cold syrup and, if time allows and the weather is not very hot, let it remain in the syrup for a short time. This absorption of sugar makes the fruit much sweeter, and prevents it from shrinking and losing its shape when it is cooked.

(3) Strain the syrup into a pan and bring it to the boil; reduce the heat slightly and put in the fruit. Simmer very gently until the fruit is tender but unbroken.

(4) Put the fruit in a dish. Before adding the syrup it may be necessary to 'reduce' or thicken it by boiling it for a few minutes.

Note. If strawberries and raspberries are to be used within a few hours, the syrup may be boiled in the first instance rather longer than 3–4 minutes to thicken it sufficiently, and after cooking be poured over the fruit, and the fruit be served without cooking. This method preserves the fragrance and flavour of the fruit, as well as its vitamin content. Oranges and grapefruits can also be prepared in this manner.

B. *Firm, hard fruits, e.g.* apples, pears, rhubarb, plums, gooseberries.

(1) For each pound of fruit (except pears) prepare a syrup with ¼ lb. sugar and ½ pint of water. Bring the syrup to the boil, boil 3 or 4 minutes, and cool slightly.

(2) Put in the fruit and flavouring (lemon peel or cinnamon stick, etc.) and simmer carefully until the fruit is quite tender but unbroken. Serve in a glass dish and reduce the syrup before pouring it over the fruit.

These fruits are improved by being steeped in cold syrup before cooking, but the steeping is not so necessary as for the less firm fruits whose shape is more readily lost.

Apples. Cook with these thin strips of lemon peel. The syrup may be coloured with a little carmine or cochineal colouring before putting the fruit in it.

Rhubarb. Cut into inch lengths and flavour with lemon peel.

Stewing Pears. Cut in halves or, if they are very large, in quarters, and pack closely in a pan. Make syrup, allowing ¼ lb. sugar to each ¾ pint water required, and let it go cold. Cover the pears with syrup and simmer very slowly for 4–5 hours or longer if necessary. Flavour with lemon peel and a small piece of cinnamon stick. The syrup may be coloured with cochineal or carmine, if desired, before putting the pears in it.

C. *Dried Fruits, e.g.* prunes, figs, apricots, apple rings.

Wash the fruit well and soak it overnight in water to replace that lost in the drying. Drain and make syrup with the steeping water, using 4–8 oz. sugar to each pint of water. Allow ½ pint of syrup for each pound of fruit. If the fruit has no skin on it, *e.g.* apple rings, boil the syrup before putting it in. Put fruits with skins on, *e.g.* prunes, apricots, into cold syrup. In both cases let the syrup simmer gently till the fruit is tender. Flavour figs, prunes, and apple rings with lemon peel; prunes may also be flavoured with cinnamon stick (about 1 inch cinnamon stick to 1 lb. of prunes). When the fruit is tender, take it out of the syrup, then reduce the latter before pouring it over the fruit.

Alternative Method of Stewing Fruits.

Fruit may be stewed in water instead of syrup. In this case it is more economical to add the sugar at the end instead of at the beginning of the cooking. Cane sugar added in the initial stages of the cooking is changed by the heat and by the fruit acids into grape sugar which is less sweet.

This method, though simpler, is not generally considered to be as successful as that first described. The shape and colour of the fruit are usually less well retained and the fruit is not sweetened throughout in the same way.[1]

Baking Fruits.

Baked Apples. No. 1. Take good, sound apples of equal size, wipe, remove cores, make an incision round the skin and put sugar in cavities. Put in an earthenware or enamel dish and bake in a moderate oven till they are tender but unbroken. Sift castor sugar over and serve hot or cold.

Baked Apples. No. 2. ('Buttered' Apples.)

Ingredients

4 large apples.	4 tablespoonfuls sugar.
1–2 oz. margarine.	2 tablespoonfuls jam.
4 squares stale bread.	3–4 tablespoonfuls boiling water.

Method. Peel and core the apples and place each on bread in an earthenware or enamel dish. Fill the cavities with sugar and

[1] Bicarbonate of soda added to sour fruits, *e.g.* damsons or rhubarb, neutralises the acid and so diminishes the amount of sugar required. For each pound of fruit stir in slowly ½ level teaspoonful bicarbonate of soda towards the end of the cooking and before adding the sugar.

margarine, and bake in a moderately hot oven till soft but unbroken. When the apples are nearly tender, put the jam in the cavities. Arrange the apples on a hot dish; put the boiling water into the baking dish, mix well and pour the syrup obtained thus over the fruit.

Baked Apples. No. 3. ('Crusted' Apples.)

Ingredients

4 apples.
2 tablespoonfuls jam.
White of 1 egg.

½ tablespoonful ground almonds.
½ tablespoonful castor sugar.
½ tablespoonful sponge-cake crumbs.

Method. Peel and core the apples; beat the white of egg slightly, brush the apples with it and roll them gently in the almond mixture. Fill the cavities with jam. Put the apples in a dish greased with margarine and bake them in a moderate oven till tender. Serve hot or cold.

FRUIT SALADS

Discretion must be exercised in the choice of fruits to form a salad so that their colours and flavours blend well and no one flavour overpowers the others.

The salads should be made some time before they are required so that the flavours of the different fruits may become thoroughly mixed. Salads should be served as cold as possible.

Fruit Salad No. 1.

Ingredients

2–3 oranges.
2–3 bananas.
½ lb strawberries or raspberries.

½ lb. cherries.
½ lb. grapes.

Syrup.
½–¾ pint water.
6–8 oz. sugar.
Strip of lemon peel.

Method. Peel oranges, remove pith, cut into rings, taking out pips. Peel bananas, cut into rings. Remove stalks from cherries and wash. Skin grapes, cut into halves and remove stones. Pick strawberries and raspberries carefully, handling as little as possible.

Put water and sugar into pan with any juice which has come from the fruits, add lemon peel; bring to boil, and boil 5 minutes to thicken syrup. Remove scum and lemon peel, then cool.

Arrange the fruits attractively in a dish, pour over the cooled syrup; put in a cold place for at least an hour before serving.

Fruit Salad No. 2.

Ingredients

½ lb. prunes.	1½ lb. apples.	4–5 Tangerine oranges.
½ pint water.	¾ pint water.	1 oz. almonds.
2 oz. sugar.	6 oz. sugar.	Juice of 1 lemon.
Strip of lemon rind.	Strip of lemon rind.	

Method. Wash prunes and steep overnight in ½ pint water. Peel and core apples. Cook the prunes and apples in their respective syrups (see directions on pp. 181 and 180), keeping the apples as whole as possible. Remove stones from the prunes.

Peel oranges, remove pith, cut across into rings and take out pips. Blanch almonds by covering with boiling water for a few minutes, skin and cut into strips.

Put prunes in the bottom of a dish, and the apples, decorated with strips of almond, in a circle resting on them; then fill the centre with orange. Put prune and apple syrups into a pan, boil gently for 5 minutes, to blend the flavours and thicken the syrup. Cool and remove lemon rind. Add strained lemon juice and pour over the fruit.

MISCELLANEOUS FRUIT DISHES

Apple Charlotte.

Ingredients

1 lb. apples	Margarine.
1 tablespoonful water.	Slices of bread ⅜ inch thick.
2–4 oz. sugar.	½ pint cream *or* custard (pp. 76 *or* 146).
Grated lemon rind.	

Method. (1) Peel, core and slice the apples, stew them with the water till soft then add the sugar and grated lemon rind.

(2) Clarify the margarine, melting it slowly and removing the salt which rises as a scum to the surface.

(3) Cut a piece of bread to fit the bottom of the mould or dish to be used, and cut strips 1 inch wide to line the sides. Dip the pieces of bread in the clarified margarine and place them in position, the 'buttered' sides next to the mould. Fill the mould with stewed apple and cover with a piece of bread dipped in margarine, placing the 'buttered' side outermost.

(4) Bake the mould in a moderately hot oven for about ½ hour, until the bread is a bright golden brown colour.

(5) Turn out on to a hot dish and sift sugar over. Serve with cream or custard.

Fruit Pudding.

Ingredients

Slices of stale bread, ⅜ inch thick.
Or slices of stale sponge-cake, ⅜ inch thick.
Or Sponge Fingers.
1 lb. fruit, *e.g.* (*a*) Raspberries, *or* red currants, *or* both.
(*b*) Plums, damsons, etc.
Water and sugar.
½ pint cream or custard (pp. 76 or 146).

Method. Grease a pint basin and line the bottom and sides with bread or sponge-cake or sponge fingers, splitting the last in halves lengthwise. Pick the fruit, stew it with 1–2 tablespoonfuls water, sweeten it and put it at once, while still hot, into the basin. Cover the top with bread or sponge cake, filling up any spaces. Place a plate or saucer over the pudding and put a weight on top. Put the bowl on a dish which will catch any juice which may overflow. When the fruit is set and the mould quite cold, turn out the pudding. Pour the juice round and serve with custard or cream.

Fruit Whip.

Ingredients

1 pint fruit purée made from raspberries, red currants, plums, damsons, etc.
2 oz. semolina.
Pinch of salt.
Sugar to taste.

Method. (1) Prepare fruit purée in one of the following ways:

(*a*) Stew in the usual way enough raspberries, red currants, plums or damsons, etc., to make 1 pint of purée when passed through a fine strainer or sieve. A small amount of water may be added, if necessary, to make up the pint.[1]

Or (*b*) Heat contents of a 2 lb. jar of bottled raspberries, etc., until the fruit is soft, then treat as (*a*) above.

Or (*c*) Use liquid from bottled or tinned fruit, etc., adding fruit essence if desired, to give the liquid a definite taste of the fruit.

Or (*d*) Put ¾ pint of water with 2 heaped tablespoonfuls of jam into a saucepan, bring to the boil and strain to remove any pips.

(2) Add pinch of salt to semolina and moisten with ¼ pint cold liquid (if liquid prepared with jam is used), otherwise with ¼ pint prepared fruit purée.

(3) Bring remaining ¾ pint purée or liquid to the boil; add to the semolina paste, stirring smoothly. Return to pan and boil gently for about 10 minutes, stirring frequently.

[1] For directions for stewing fruit, see pp. 179-181.

(4) Sweeten to taste and pour into a large bowl; put to cool for 10 minutes or so.

(5) Whisk the mixture vigorously until it is thick, creamy and spongy in texture, then pour into a glass bowl or fruit dish or into individual dishes. Cool thoroughly before serving.

Chestnut Purée.

Ingredients

1 lb. chestnuts.	½ pint of cream.
2 oz. sugar.	1 oz. sugar.
	Vanilla essence.

Method. Prick the chestnuts, put them into boiling water and boil for ¾–1 hour, until they are quite tender. Peel them and rub through a wire sieve. Arrange the purée in a dish and sift 2 oz. sugar over. Just before serving, whip the cream stiffly, add 1 oz. sugar and a few drops of vanilla essence and place it in spoonfuls over the purée.

FRUIT SAUCES

Group 1. Apples and gooseberries, both strongly acid fruits, are sometimes served as sauces to modify the richness of certain kinds of meat and fish.

Apple Sauce. Served with roast duck and pork.

Ingredients

1 lb. cooking apples.	⅛ pint water.
½ oz. margarine.	Sugar.

Method. Peel and core the apples, cut into quarters and slice very thinly. Put into a saucepan with the margarine and water and cook until the apple is reduced to a pulp. Stir or beat well to make the sauce smooth and sweeten it to taste.

Gooseberry Sauce. (Served with mackerel or hot boiled ham.)

Ingredients

1 lb. gooseberries.	¼ lb. sugar.
⅛ pint of water.	

Method. Pick the gooseberries and wash in a colander. Make a syrup of the sugar and water, add the gooseberries and cook gently till quite tender. If desired, the gooseberries may be rubbed through a hair sieve and reheated before serving.

Group 2. Syrup Sauces.

Lemon Sauce.

Ingredients

½ pint water.
4 oz. sugar.
Rind and juice of 2 lemons.
1 teaspoonful cornflour.

Method. Wipe lemons and peel thinly; boil rinds with sugar and water, keeping back a little water with which to mix the cornflour to a smooth paste. Strain the liquid and add to the cornflour paste, mixing smoothly. Return the pan, bring to the boil, and boil for 2–3 minutes to cook the cornflour, stirring all the time. Cool slightly and add the strained lemon juice.

Orange Sauce.

Ingredients

½ pint of water.
1 tablespoonful marmalade.
Juice of 2 oranges.
Juice of 1 lemon.
2 oz. sugar.

Method. Boil water, marmalade and sugar together for 10–15 minutes, until the syrup is reduced to about half its original quantity. Skim well and cool slightly. Add the juice of the oranges and lemons and strain.

Jam Sauce.

Ingredients

½ pint of water.
1 tablespoonful raspberry jam.
1 oz. sugar.
1 teaspoonful lemon juice.

Method. Make as for Orange Sauce. Strawberry, apricot or other jam can be substituted for raspberry jam.

FRUIT DRINKS

Black Currant Tea.

Ingredients

½ teaspoonful lemon juice.
½ pint boiling water.
1 large tablespoonful black currant jam.

Method. Put jam into a jug, add boiling water, cover and cool slightly. Add lemon juice, strain and serve.

Lemonade.

Ingredients

2–3 lemons.
2–3 oz. sugar.
1 pint boiling water.
1 pint cold water.

Method. Wipe lemons, peel thinly, add sugar and boiling water to rinds, cover and set aside till cold. Add lemon juice, cold water and strain.

CHAPTER XVI

THE COOKING OF FATS: THE PREPARATION OF FATS FOR USE IN FRYING: THE FRYING OF FOODS

Fats used in cooking as a medium for frying, or for other purposes may be classified according as they are:

I. Animal Fats.

A. Fats which have formerly been in a state of emulsion. *E.g.* butter, the fat of milk thrown out of emulsion by churning.

B. Fats still in their natural state, a mass of globules, each enclosed in connective tissue. *E.g.* raw fat and suet of beef, mutton, etc.

C. Fats which have been extracted from their connective tissues. *E.g.* (1) Dripping, the fat extracted in cooking beef, mutton, bacon, etc. (2) Lard, extracted from the fat of pork.

II. Vegetable Fats.

These are fats extracted from plant substances. *E.g.* olive oil, nut butter and other vegetarian butters.

Margarine is prepared from both animal and vegetable fats. When animal fat is used, its more solid constituents are removed, leaving a soft fat resembling butter in consistency. The fats, both animal and vegetable, are churned with milk, coloured with vegetable colouring, and salted to resemble butter. Margarine is considerably cheaper than butter, and being prepared under strict supervision, is pure and wholesome, though it does not keep as well as butter.[1]

Food Value of Fats. We have already seen that fats in a dietary are the source of the energy required for the doing of work and for the production and maintenance of heat. Further, animal fats (but not vegetable fats) are for the most part valuable sources of vitamins A and D.

Lard is deficient in vitamin A, partly because the food on which pigs are commonly fed lacks vegetable substances, partly because such vitamin as is present in the fat is liable to be lost in the process of manufacture. Lard has, however, a definite antirachitic action. The vitamin value of *margarine* (though not

[1] The product known as 'Cooking Fat' can also be used for frying food, etc. The sources of this fat are various.

its value as a source of energy) depends on the kind of fat or fats used in its manufacture and the proportion in which each is present. Margarine made largely or wholly from vegetable fat is a less good source of vitamins than that made from animal fats. But it should be remembered that though vegetable fats lack vitamins, a percentage of *synthetic* vitamins A and D is now added to margarine during manufacture. (See p. 60.)

In considering the vitamin value of a given fat, the way in which the fat is treated to prepare it for eating must be taken into account. We have seen that vitamins A and D are affected adversely by heat and oxidation combined, A more readily than D. Hence, fats eaten uncooked, *e.g.* butter, are better sources of these vitamins than others, *e.g.* meat fat, which are not palatable unless cooked. Again, the vitamins of fats which during cooking have some protection from oxidation are less harmed than those which are more exposed; it is probable that the butter on the surface layers of puff pastry covering a beefsteak pie loses more in the baking than that in the under layers. Again, assuming the fat of sausages to contain these vitamins, to cook sausages enclosed in pastry as in a sausage roll would be preferable to frying in an open pan, as far as vitamin value is concerned, especially if, as sometimes happens, the skin bursts. Sausage in its turn is less exposed to oxidation than bacon similarly cooked.

PREPARATION OF FATS FOR FRYING

All the fats already named are used for frying; each has its merits or demerits, as the case may be, and each, with two exceptions, requires special treatment or 'clarifying' in addition to heating, to prepare it for use.

Butter gives a delicate flavour to the food, but it is expensive and unless carefully managed does not give good results. It burns easily and the food quickly becomes discoloured.

Raw Fat is excellent and inexpensive for both shallow and deep frying. Beef or mutton fat or equal quantities of both answer well.

The clarifying necessary to prepare raw fat for use involves two processes: (1) purification, (2) extraction, of the fat.

The purification brings about the removal from the fat of substances which would prevent it keeping good. These are (*a*) the connective tissues which, being nitrogenous matter, quickly decay; (*b*) fatty acids, formed when fats split up, which, if present in any but very small quantities, make the fat rancid.

The extraction completes the removal of the fat from its connective tissues and brings it into a form convenient for heating.

Clarifying Raw Fat. The process is as follows:

Purification. Cut the fat into even-sized pieces, *e.g.* quarter to half-inch cubes, removing all the skin and lean pieces of meat. Put the pieces of fat into a shallow stewpan, just cover with cold water, and boil rapidly in the open pan, removing the scum as fast as it forms. Continue until the fat is soft and milk-coloured and all the water has evaporated.

By this process the tissues are softened so that the extraction of the fat can begin and the fatty acids, probably with some other substances, are removed as scum. It will be noticed that at this stage the fat gives off an unpleasant smell.

Extraction. Melt the fat *slowly* over a gentle heat and stir it frequently so that it does not stick to the pan. Continue to heat it gently, stirring occasionally, until all the tissues have parted with their fat and have become small, shrivelled, gold-coloured objects which sink to the bottom of the clear oil extracted from them. Care must be taken not to overheat the fat at this stage.

When the extraction is complete, cool the fat for a short time before pouring it through a fine strainer covered with muslin; press the tissues with a spoon to extract as much fat as possible.

When cold, the fat forms a solid flavourless cake of a delicate cream colour. Properly treated, it can be used for frying again and again and will keep good for several months. The fat will diminish slightly in quantity each time it is used; the loss must be made up by the addition of fat similarly clarified. All small pieces and trimmings of raw fat can be used for this purpose, so also can cooked fat which is clarified in exactly the same manner as raw fat; the two should, however, be treated separately.

When such pieces of fat (raw or cooked) are not needed to replenish the supply of clarified fat to be used, for example, in deep frying (see p. 194) they may be treated more simply, the fat being merely extracted and purifying omitted. The fat then keeps less well.

Dripping. This form of fat has usually acquired some of the flavour and substance of the meat from which it has been extracted and clarifying is necessary to remove these as far as possible.

To Clarify Dripping.

Method 1. Cover the dripping with three or four times its bulk of boiling water, stir frequently and put to cool. Since oil and water do not make a permanent emulsion, the dripping sets in a solid cake on top of the water, leaving some of its impurities behind. Such impurities as are not in the water form a brown sediment on the under side of the cake. Scrape this away and heat the dripping carefully in a frying pan till it ceases to bubble, when it can be assumed that any water it contains has evaporated. Strain the dripping through a piece of muslin placed over a fine strainer. Since dripping keeps good longer if the mass is unbroken, it is best to strain it into a number of small jars or cups.

Method 2. Heat dripping slowly in a pan and remove the scum; when no more scum forms, strain the fat as in Method 1. When it has solidified, scrape the sediment away from the under side of the cake.

The clarified drippings from beef, mutton, lamb and veal are all used for frying, the first two giving the best results. But as clarified dripping is never quite as pure as clarified fat, it is best used for shallow frying only. As will be explained later, fat used for shallow frying cannot in any case be used as often and does not keep good so long as that used for deep frying.

Lard. This answers well for potatoes and all kinds of batter, but for most foods is a somewhat wasteful frying medium. It tends to cling to the food, making it soft and greasy.

Lard is already clarified and only requires heating before use.[1]

Margarine is not a very satisfactory medium for frying, burning rapidly.

Oil can be heated to a very high temperature and gives excellent results. But good oil is usually considered to be too expensive to be used much for frying. Like lard, it does not require clarifying.

Heating of Fats for Frying.

Fats for frying must be heated slowly and watched carefully to prevent overheating. Four distinct changes are recognisable:

(1) *Melting Point.* At this stage all the heat is used in converting the solid fat into a liquid.

[1] 'Cooking Fat' also does not need clarifying. It can, if necessary, replace lard and dripping for shallow frying.

(2) *Ebullition Point.* When the fat bubbles it is a sign that water, usually still present in it is being expelled. (When the fat contains little or no water, bubbling is not apparent.) As the water evaporates the movement of the fat lessens, and when it becomes almost still, the third stage, a stage at which the temperature of the fat ranges from 171° C. (340° F.) to 204° C. (400° F.), is at hand.

(3) *Frying Point.* When the fat is ready for use, a faint blue vapour rises from its surface. The vapour can be seen most easily by looking at the fat with the eyes on a level with it. This blue vapour must not be confused with the darker vapour which sometimes arises from the heating of fat which has spread to the outside of the pan. As soon as the blue vapour is clearly seen, the food to be fried must be put in the fat. If this is not done, the fourth stage will quickly be reached and the fat spoiled. If the food is not ready, the pan must be drawn back from the heat. Similarly, when the frying of the food is completed the pan must be taken off the heat at once.

(4) *Decomposition Point.* The signs of this are the appearance of a thick brown vapour which is very inflammable, a deepening of the colour of the fat, and the forming of volatile substances which give the characteristic smell of burning fat. Fat which has been overheated thus naturally does not keep good as long as it should.

Importance of Using the Fat at the Right Heat. This is illustrated by the following experiment:

Heat a small quantity of fat, and as it reaches each of the last three stages described above, put into it small dice of white bread; fry each two minutes and notice the results:

(1) *At Ebullition Point.* When the bread is first put in, the fat bubbles round it only slightly. The bread is pale-coloured, sodden and greasy inside.

(2) *At Frying Point.* The fat bubbles vigorously round the bread, which quickly becomes crisp and golden-brown in colour, a change due to the conversion of some of its starch into dextrin. Inside, the bread shows no trace of grease; this is because the heat of the fat was sufficiently great to form a crust, so that no fat could be absorbed.

(3) *At Decomposition Point.* The bread is dark-brown in colour and extremely hard.

If, owing to insufficient light or other causes, there is any difficulty in detecting the appearance of the blue vapour, the heat of the fat should be tested with a small piece of bread as in this experiment.

Straining of Fat after Use. Cool the fat slightly and pour it through a fine strainer covered with muslin to remove from it particles of food which would sooner or later go bad and make the fat unfit for use. Food particles which are too fine to be removed thus sink as the fat cools, and the brown layer which they form on the bottom of the cake must be removed before the fat is next heated.

If, during use, the fat becomes rather dark so that food fried in it is not a good colour, it should be clarified with boiling water according to the method already described for dripping (No. 1, p. 190).

After being in use some time, the texture of the fat changes; it becomes coarse and granulated and resembles dark and oily Demerara sugar. The change is hastened by continuous overheating or by the omission of straining. Fat in this condition is quite useless for frying, making the food greasy and dark-coloured.

PREPARATION OF FOODS FOR FRYING

Before being fried, most foods are coated with substances which harden when they come into contact with the heated fat and make a protective casing. Such casing serves a threefold purpose, preventing (1) the flavour or substance of the food from mingling with the fat; (2) the fat from being absorbed by the food; (3) the outer layers of the food from being hardened unduly before the inner layers are sufficiently cooked.

Protective Casings: (1) *Flour* seasoned with salt and pepper (1 teaspoonful salt, $\frac{1}{2}$ teaspoonful pepper to 1 tablespoonful flour), and mixed with milk to a smooth paste the thickness of cream. The paste must be just thick enough to cling to the food and to coat it smoothly.

(2) *Egg*: usually the yolk and white are beaten together, but each can be used separately. Yolk of egg and whole egg may be diluted slightly with milk.

(3) *Pastry* to enclose food to be fried is usually mixed with egg to make it more tenacious and when the food is wrapped in it, is coated with egg.

(4) *Frying Batter*. This is a special form of paste made of

flour, egg and butter or oil. It is used to enclose fish and fruit (see p. 257).

It will be noticed that in each case one or more of the substances used contain proteins, which, as we know, harden on the application of heat. Thus, flour contains gluten, milk and egg contain albumen, all of which coagulate when the food is put into the heated fat.

Flour-paste and egg coatings are usually completed by covering the food with breadcrumbs or crushed vermicelli; these do not protect the food to any great extent, but serve to roughen its surface and to give it an agreeable texture.

Breadcrumbs are the more generally used of the two and are prepared by (1) rubbing stale bread through a wire sieve, or (2) drying small pieces of bread and light-coloured crusts in a cool oven until they are a pale yellow colour, then crushing them with a china rolling pin or a jar and sifting them. Both kinds of crumbs should be very fine and small, otherwise they absorb so much fat as to make the food greasy and give it a coarse untidy appearance. The crumbs should be seasoned with salt and pepper, sprinkling these over the bread as it is rubbed through the sieve or passed through the sifter.

Vermicelli is prepared by crushing it into very tiny pieces and seasoning it with salt and pepper.

To apply Casings. Put the flour paste or beaten egg on a plate or in a basin, according to the shape of the food to be coated, and have the seasoned crumbs on a sheet of kitchen paper. Using a pastry brush, cover the food uniformly with the paste or egg and hold it for a moment in such a position that any which does not cling to it drains away. Then roll the food gently in the crumbs, pressing them on with a knife; finally, move the food lightly from one hand to the other to shake away loose crumbs.

Crushed vermicelli is applied in similar fashion.

In order that the egg or paste may cling properly to the food, moist surfaces (*e.g.* fish) must be dried with a towel and rubbed with flour before applying the egg or paste.

The casings should be applied as near the time of frying as possible, otherwise the crumbs soak up the egg or paste and become sodden, making the surface of the food less crisp than it should be.

Though many foods may be encased before frying, there are some for which a *protective casing may be used or omitted* at will. Such foods are:

Meat and fish. These already contain albumen and to a certain extent form their own protection. Meat and fish, though they do not, strictly speaking, require it, may be and often are coated with egg or flour-paste and breadcrumbs. For meat, the egg or paste is sometimes omitted, and fine white breadcrumbs, seasoned with salt and pepper, are beaten or pressed into the flesh. The crumbs give a crisp surface to the meat and absorb juices which might otherwise escape. Yet another plan is to coat the meat with dry seasoned flour, again omitting the egg or paste; the flour enables the meat to be browned readily. This last method is also sometimes employed, though less successfully, for fish.

For the following foods a *casing is unnecessary*:

(1) Eggs, pancakes, fritters and all forms of batter. These already contain albumen.

(2) Sausages, bacon. These are usually fried in their own fat, hence there is no object in providing them with a casing. Sausages have the additional protection of a skin.

(3) Potatoes. These are so watery that they do not readily absorb fat, and consequently do not require a casing.

SHALLOW AND DEEP FRYING

Foods prepared according to the directions just given may be fried in one of two ways, known respectively as shallow frying and deep frying.

Shallow Frying. The food is fried, one side at a time, in a quantity of fat just sufficient to cover the bottom of the frying pan and to keep the food from burning.

This method is advisable only for:

(1) Bacon, sausages, which contain in themselves sufficient fat for frying.

(2) Eggs, pancakes, which are required to set in a thin layer.

(3) Steaks, chops, cutlets, all thin flat pieces of meat of firm texture.

Flat fish are often fried by this method, not because it is the better of the two but because their size makes deep frying impossible, unless a special pan is kept for the purpose.

Deep Frying. Sufficient fat is used to cover entirely the food to be fried.

For deep frying 3–4 lbs. of raw fat should be clarified. An

iron stewpan, *without* a tin lining, 4–5 inches deep and 7–8 inches in diameter, is needed; a frying basket of rather smaller dimensions, though not essential, is a great help in lowering the food into and lifting it out of the fat.[1]

Except for the foods mentioned above, deep frying is decidedly to be preferred to shallow frying and in particular should always be used for such things as rissoles, croquettes, fritters. Its superiority depends mainly on the fact that the entire surface of the food is hardened and the food cooked evenly all over at one and the same time, not, as is the case with shallow frying, in two portions. As a result of this it follows that: (*a*) The casing is complete and leaves no junction through which the flavour or substance of the food can escape into the fat or at which fat can be absorbed by the food. (*b*) It is not necessary to turn the food from one side to the other; the food, therefore, seldom breaks and its surface is evenly browned. (*c*) The frying takes rather less attention, as well as less time, and the food is hotter when served.

It is often said that, as compared to shallow frying, deep frying is an extravagant process, and it is, of course, true that the initial cost of the apparatus is greater and that more fuel is needed to heat the larger quantity of fat. But on the other hand, it must be remembered that the results obtained are much better and that, provided it is not used before the right frying temperature is reached and is not overheated, the fat will last for some time and can be used again and again for all kinds of food, meat, fish, fruit fritters, etc., quite indiscriminately. This is not the case with fat used for shallow frying and moreover, the wastage which occurs each time the fat is used is smaller in deep than in shallow frying. This is not wholly because less fat is absorbed by the food; it is partly due to the fact that when only a small quantity of fat is used, the stages of heating succeed each other rapidly and the chances of accidental overheating are thereby increased.

Directions for Frying.

Both in shallow and in deep frying there are certain points which need careful attention:

(1) The fat must be used at exactly the right temperature.

[1] Failing a stewpan, a frying-pan with sides from 2–2½ inches deep can often be made to answer, provided the food is basted constantly with the fat.

Coolness of the fat when the food is first put in cannot be remedied by excessive heat during the frying.

For frying rissoles, croquettes, etc. made from food which has already been cooked once and which therefore needs rapid heating, the fat should be at a slightly higher temperature than is necessary for most foods. The same applies to such foods as fish, which by their wateriness tend to cool the fat.

(2) Anything which might chill the fat at the time of cooking must be avoided, as tending to make the food greasy. For example, the frying basket, if used, must be heated in the fat for a moment before food to be fried is put in it. Again, the portions of food put into the fat at one time must not be so numerous as to cool it to too great an extent or to prevent its surrounding each of them. Finally, when two or more batches of food are to be fried, the fat must be reheated before each time of using.

(3) After frying, the food must be freed completely from fat. To do this, let it drain for a moment over the pan, shaking the basket gently, then place it on a hot plate on pieces of crumpled paper, into the hollows of which the fat will drain, and cover it with paper. Put the plate for a moment or two in a warm oven or on a plate rack over the fire or gas stove, to complete the drying.

Precautions to be taken in Frying.

(1) Avoid putting into the fat very damp foods, *e.g.* slices of potato which have not been dried, and avoid splashing water into the fat. The sudden heating of the water causes a burst of steam which may scald the hands.

(2) Lower the food carefully into the hot fat, lest the fat splash up and burn the hands or catch fire. If fat, which spreads easily, catches fire on the outside of the pan, take the pan from the heat at once and blow out the flame. If any quantity of fat is spilt on the stove and catches fire, throw ashes or earth over it.

(3) Never leave a pan of fat on an open fire unless the pan rests quite steadily on the bars.

(4) Take the pan off the fire or cooker as soon as frying is finished.

FRYING MEAT

For the principle involved in frying meat, see p. 92.

Beefsteak and Onions.

Ingredients

- 1½ lbs. of rump steak (1–1½ inches thick).
- 1 tablespoonful flour.
- 1 teaspoonful salt.
- ½ teaspoonful pepper.
- ¾ pint stock or water.
- 2–3 oz. dripping.
- 3 Spanish onions.
- Salt and pepper.

Method. (1) Peel the onions and slice thinly in rings. Heat the dripping in a frying pan; when the blue vapour appears, put in the onions, season, cover with a plate and cook gently for 20–30 minutes, till tender. Take off the plate and let the onions brown, stirring them so that they do not burn. Take out the onions, put on a hot plate and keep hot in the oven.

(2) While the onions cook, remove the superfluous fat from the meat, wash it, and beat it with a damp rolling pin to bruise the fibres and make the meat more tender; trim neatly. Mix together the flour and seasonings and coat both sides of the meat with the mixture.

(3) When the cooking of the onions is completed, re-heat the fat, adding more if necessary. When it is at frying point, put in the meat. Cook it quickly for the first 2 minutes, turning the meat at the end of 1 minute. Then decrease the heat slightly and cook the meat rather more slowly for the rest of the time, turning it every 2 minutes. Cook in all from 10 to 12 minutes. The degree of cooking may be estimated by the same tests as those already given for grilled meat. (See p. 99).

(4) Put the meat on a hot dish, garnish it with the onions and keep it hot while the gravy is made.

To do this, pour off the fat leaving only 2–3 tablespoonfuls in the pan; be careful to retain any browned meat juices. Add the remainder of the seasoned flour, mix smoothly and cook until the flour is a rich brown colour. Add the stock by degrees, mix well, bring to the boil and boil 2–3 minutes. Season, add browning if required, and strain round the meat.

Mutton Cutlets and Mashed Potatoes.

Ingredients

7 mutton cutlets (best end of neck).
1 egg (optional).
2–3 tablespoonfuls fine white bread-crumbs.
Salt and pepper.
3 oz. dripping.
1 tomato (sliced), *or*
1 tablespoonful tomato pulp.
¾ tablespoonful flour.
½ pint stock.
1–1½ lbs. mashed potatoes[1] (see p. 161).

Method. (1) Prepare the piece of best end of a neck of mutton thus: (*a*) Saw across the long bones to make the cutlets of even length (3½–4 inches); (*b*) cut down between the cutlets with a sharp knife, then, using a chopper, chop through the chine bone; (*c*) remove piece of chine bone left on each cutlet; (*d*) trim off most of the fat, and bare about ½ inch of bone at end of each cutlet; (*e*) scrape inside curve of bone clean, first removing skin.

(2) Wash the cutlets, dry and coat with beaten egg and seasoned breadcrumbs, or omit the egg and press the bread-crumbs into the meat.

(3) Heat the dripping and fry the cutlets in it for from 7–10 minutes, following exactly the method described on p. 197 for beefsteak.

(4) Pile the mashed potatoes in pyramid shape on a hot dish, arrange the cutlets round them and keep hot.

(5) Pour off some of the fat, cook the tomato in the remainder for a few minutes, add the flour and cook until it browns. Add the stock gradually, bring the gravy to the boil, season it and add browning, if required. Strain a little of the gravy round the dish and serve the rest in a tureen.

Fillets of Veal and Tomato Sauce.

Ingredients

¾ lb. fillet of veal.
Bacon dripping.
1 egg.
Salt, pepper and lemon juice.
{ 6 tablespoonfuls breadcrumbs.
2 oz. lean cooked ham, finely chopped.
2 teaspoonfuls parsley, finely chopped. }
8 small slices of fat bacon.
8 lemon 'butterflies'
3 tablespoonfuls small cooked sprouts *or*
3 tablespoonfuls cooked green peas (see pp. 156 and 158).
½ pint tomato sauce (see p. 168).

Method. (1) Wash the veal and cut it into 8 oblong pieces of even thickness and size, flatten them with a damp rolling pin

[1] Green peas, kidney beans, boiled haricot beans and other vegetables may be substituted for potatoes.

and trim into shape. Season these fillets with salt, pepper and lemon juice, coat with beaten egg and roll in the breadcrumb, ham and parsley mixture.

(2) Remove rinds from bacon, roll into small rolls and put on a skewer. Bake or grill.

(3) Heat bacon dripping and fry the fillets briskly for 4–5 minutes, turning them once or twice, then cook slowly for a further 5 minutes.

(4) Arrange the fillets down the centre of a hot dish, garnish each with a lemon 'butterfly' and a bacon roll.

(5) Arrange the sprouts or green peas (previously cooked) round the dish in a decorative manner and pour tomato sauce round.

Fried Liver and Bacon.

Ingredients

1 lb. calf's or lamb's liver.
Lemon juice.
6 oz. bacon.
1 tablespoonful flour *or* fine oatmeal.
1 teaspoonful salt.
½ teaspoonful pepper.

Method. (1) Remove outer skin, gristle and blood vessels, and cut the liver in slices ¾ inch thick. Wash the pieces well in a colander, drain and dry them on a cloth. Sprinkle a little lemon juice on them and coat with flour or oatmeal, salt and pepper.

(2) Cut the bacon into thin slices, trim, fry, and put on a hot dish.

(3) Add a little lard, if required, to the bacon fat and heat it until it smokes quite strongly. Dip the pieces of liver into the flour or oatmeal, seasoned with salt and pepper, and fry them for 3 minutes, turning the pieces at the end of 1½ minutes. If the fat has been at the right temperature and the liver cut to the right thickness, it will be crisp and tender. Put it on the dish with the bacon and serve at once. If gravy is required, prepare it beforehand. If the liver is kept hot while gravy is being made it will be tough.

Sausages and Bread Sauce.

Ingredients

½ oz. bacon dripping.
1 lb. sausages.
2–3 slices of bread.
¾ pint bread sauce, *i.e.* ¾ pint milk.
3 cloves.
1 small onion.
4 peppercorns.
1 blade of mace.
3 oz. fine white crumbs.
½ teaspoonful salt.
Cayenne pepper.
Lemon juice (optional).
¾ oz. butter or margarine.

Method. (1) **Bread Sauce.** Put the cloves into the peeled onion and put it with milk and peppercorns and mace in a pan. Place the pan near the fire for 15–20 minutes. Strain this flavoured milk and, if necessary, add a little more to make up $\frac{3}{4}$ pint. Put the crumbs into the milk and let the sauce simmer slowly for $\frac{1}{4}$ hour, stirring it frequently. Then bring it to the boil, season with salt, cayenne pepper and a very little lemon juice, add the butter or margarine a little at a time, and let it melt.

(2) **Sausages.** Prick the sausages so that their skins do not burst and put them into boiling water for two or three minutes. Heat dripping in a frying pan, put in the sausages and fry them rather slowly for about 15 minutes till they are a rich brown colour; move them about so that they cook evenly. Put on a hot plate and keep them hot.

(3) **Bread.** Cut the bread into finger-shaped pieces, rather wider and longer than the sausages. Heat the fat from the sausages and fry the pieces of bread in it until they are crisp and brown. Arrange the pieces of bread on a hot dish, put a sausage on each, and serve very hot, with the bread sauce in a tureen.

FRYING FISH

1. **Whole Fish:** *Plaice, Soles, Whiting.*

Remove the dark skin of soles; that of plaice may be left on, if desired. Wash fish well, dry with a cloth and rub with flour. Sprinkle lemon juice over the fish, coat it with beaten egg or flour-paste and seasoned breadcrumbs. Fry in shallow fat, having the fat slightly hotter than usual at the beginning of the cooking. Decrease the heat a little after the first few minutes. Fry the fish 7–10 minutes, according to the thickness, turning it when the first side is browned. Drain the fish well, put on a hot dish and garnish with sprigs of parsley and very thin slices of lemon.

2. **Fillets of Fish,** *e.g. Plaice, Soles, Fresh Haddock.*

Remove the skin from fillets of haddock, and the dark skin from fillets of sole and plaice. Wash and dry the fillets, rub with flour and season with a little lemon juice.

Method. (*a*) Cook the fillets as they are, cutting long fillets across into pieces of a suitable size. Or, (*b*) roll up the fillets round the left thumb beginning at the head and putting the skin side inwards; tie loosely with cotton. Or (*c*) cut the fillets in half lengthways and tie each piece in a knot.

In all three cases, coat the fish with flour-paste or egg and seasoned breadcrumbs, or dip it into frying batter. (See p. 257.)

Fry the fillets in deep fat, having the fat rather hotter than usual to begin with and reducing the heat slightly after the first few minutes. Flat fillets as in (*a*) may also be cooked in shallow fat. Drain the fish well, put on a hot dish, garnish with parsley and slices of lemon; serve very hot.

3. **Steaks or Cutlets of Fish,** *e.g. Cod, Halibut.*

Cut the fish into steaks about 1½ inches thick; wash and dry them, rub with flour, season with lemon juice and coat with beaten egg or flour-paste and seasoned breadcrumbs. Fry in deep or shallow fat. Have the fat thoroughly hot when the fish is put in and reduce the heat slightly towards the end of the time. Fry for 7–10 minutes according to the thickness of the pieces. Drain, put on a hot dish, garnish, and serve very hot.

4. **Frying Fish in Batter.** See p. 258.

5. **Oven-Fried Fish.**[1]

This process is useful when there is a shortage of fat for frying; the finished appearance resembles that of fried fish.

Ingredients

1 lb. fillets plaice, sole, etc. *or* 1 lb. cutlets of cod, hake, etc.
Flour paste (1 tablespoonful flour, etc., see p. 192) *or* 1 beaten egg.
Browned crumbs (see p. 46).
1 oz. dripping, lard or cooking fat.
½ pint sauce (parsley, anchovy, etc.—see pp. 151–153).

Method. Wash and dry the fish and coat either with flour-paste or with beaten egg, then toss in browned breadcrumbs. If the fillets are long they should be cut into two or more pieces before coating. Heat the fat in a shallow fireproof dish or in a baking tin; when hot, put in the fish and bake in a hot oven for 20–30 minutes, according to the thickness of the pieces. Serve with sauce.

FRYING VEGETABLES

Raw Potatoes. (Chip Potatoes.)

Scrub the potatoes, peel them thinly, wash, cut them either into thin oblique slices ⅛ inch thick, or into match-like pieces ¼ inch thick and 1½–2 inches long. As the potatoes are cut, put the pieces into cold water. Just before cooking, drain well and dry thoroughly on a clean soft cloth. The frying is best done in

[1] It will be noted that these directions somewhat resemble those for baking fish by Method 2 on p. 118 but the greater quantity of fat used in the preparation of Oven-fried Fish and the fact that the fish is not covered during cooking increase the resemblance to the results obtained by frying.

deep fat and a double frying is required, the first to make the pieces of potato tender, the second to make them crisp and brown.

1*st Frying*. Heat the fat, put in the frying basket and when the blue smoke *just* begins to appear, drop in the pieces of potato, taking care not to put in so many as to chill the fat unduly. Reduce the heat slightly and cook the potatoes till they are quite tender but still white. Take out and drain.

2*nd Frying*. Reheat the fat till it smokes rather strongly, put in the potatoes and fry for a moment or two till they are a golden brown colour; they should be crisp but not at all hard. Drain well, sprinkle a little salt over and serve on a hot uncovered dish. If the potatoes are covered they quickly become sodden.

Cooked Potatoes. (See p. 276.)

Frying Pancakes, Fritters, etc. Directions for these will be found on pp. 257–258.

CHAPTER XVII

THE COOKING OF FATS: THE USE OF FATS AS SHORTENING

In addition to being used for frying, fats are used in the making of pastries, suet puddings and cakes. Fats 'shorten' these flour mixtures, making them crisp and tender. The action of fats used as 'shortening' is most conspicuously demonstrated in the making of shortbread, where the proportion of butter used is large and the shortbread extremely crisp.

PASTRY MAKING

Kinds of Pastry. *Short Pastries.* (*a*) Short Crust.
(*b*) Suet Crust.
Flaky Pastries. (*a*) Flaky Crust.
(*b*) Puff Paste.

In *short pastries* the shortening is divided into very small pieces which are distributed evenly throughout the flour. These pastries are rolled once only. In *flaky pastries*, the flour and fat are arranged in alternate layers and several rollings are required to do this.

All four kinds of pastry are baked; short crust can also be

fried, while suet crust can be boiled and steamed as well as baked.

Pastry Materials.

(1) *Flour.* Household or 'seconds' flour should be used except for puff pastry, for which 'pastry' or Austrian flour, with its larger proportion of starch, answers better.

(2) *Salt.* Use 1 teaspoonful salt to each pound of flour, sifting the two together.

(3) *Shortening.* The nature of the fat used and the proportion it bears to the flour depend on the kind and richness of the pastry. The proportion of shortening to flour is noted below. As to the kind of fat used, butter (usually for puff pastry only), margarine, lard, clarified beef dripping and clarified bacon dripping are all used: the last three, however, though they 'shorten' mixtures well, are liable to have too pronounced a flavour to be altogether agreeable to the taste and some margarine is usually used with them.

(*a*) Puff paste. Butter or butter with a small quantity of lard. *Proportion*: 1 lb. butter to 1 lb. flour.

(*b*) Flaky Crust. Margarine with lard. *Proportion*: 8 to 12 oz. shortening to 1 lb. flour. 8 oz. is a very usual amount.

(*c*) Short Crust. Margarine with either lard or clarified beef or clarified bacon dripping. *Proportion*: 6 to 8 oz. to 1 lb. flour, though as much as 12 oz. is sometimes used.

If, as is sometimes done in making a very plain short crust, the shortening takes the form of dripping, unmixed with margarine, it is not desirable to use more than 6 oz. to the pound of flour because of its taste.

All the fats are difficult to manipulate in hot weather, lard particularly so.[1]

(*d*) Suet Crust. 6–8 oz. beef suet to 1 lb. flour.

(4) *Sugar.* ½–2 oz. sugar is added to each pound of flour for short pastry for sweet dishes.

(5) *Baking Powder.*[2] 1 teaspoonful of baking powder to 1 lb. flour is used for short and suet crusts when the weight of the shortening is half the weight of the flour. When it is less than half, *e.g.* 6–7 oz. shortening to 1 lb. flour, 1½ teaspoonfuls baking powder is the proportion.

[1] *Cooking Fat.* Most samples of the product known as 'Cooking Fat' shorten pastry well and it can, in general, be used in place of lard and dripping.

[2] *Self-Raising Flour.* This has baking-powder already incorporated with it.

Flaky and puff pastries do not require baking powder, air being introduced in the folding and rolling of the paste.

(6) *Liquid.* Water is most commonly used. Egg, either the yolk only or the whole egg, is sometimes substituted for part of the water in mixing puff pastry, or in making a good short crust for sweet dishes, or for enclosing food to be fried. The egg enriches the pastry and causes the particles to stick firmly together. The *proportion* of liquid used averages ½ pint to 1 lb. flour, but varies somewhat with the quality of the flour.

The Making of Pastry.

All pastry must be made in a cool place; the materials used must be cool and must be handled as little as possible. If the fat becomes in any degree soft and oily it is difficult to manipulate and does not 'shorten' the paste well, with the result that it is tough and heavy instead of crisp and light.

Short Pastries. The shortening for these pastries is either rubbed into the flour so that it is divided into fine particles or is chopped finely before being mixed with it. The latter plan is adopted in making suet crust, suet being too hard to be divided by rubbing.

Short Crust. *Method.* (1) Sift the flour and salt into a bowl and add the shortening. Cut it into small pieces with a knife, then rub it between the tips of the fingers (*not* with the palms of the hands) making first a backward and forward movement to work the fat into flakes, then a circular movement to crumble it. Lift the flour some distance out of the bowl each time and handle it lightly, yet with sufficient pressure to make the shortening mix with the flour. Continue until the two can no longer be distinguished from each other, and the mixture looks like fine breadcrumbs.

(2) Sift sugar and baking powder, if used, and mix well with the flour.

(3) Pour three-quarters of the water or beaten egg and water into the flour and mix with a knife, handling the paste as little as possible. Add the remainder of the liquid gradually, using just enough to make the dough firm, without being in any degree dry and crumb-like on the one hand, or sticky and clinging on the other. If the pastry is the right consistency it forms a dough with which the bowl can be wiped out cleanly.

(4) Sift a little flour on to the pastry board and rolling pin, make the paste into a compact oblong cake and first press, then

roll it out. One rolling should suffice. Roll with quick, short strokes, rolling always straight backwards and forwards and stopping short at the ends of the paste. If the extreme ends are rolled all the time, or if the rolling pin is moved in a slanting direction, the thickness of the paste will be uneven.

For pies and tarts, the pastry should be rather less than $\frac{1}{4}$ inch thick; for lining patty tins, or for tartlets, $\frac{1}{8}$ inch thick.

(5) Make up the pastry and bake in a moderate oven till it is firm, crisp and a delicate brown colour.

(6) Examine the pastry as seldom as possible during the baking. When examination *is* necessary, open the oven door only a little way and shut it quietly. When the pastry is baked, put it where it will cool gradually. All these precautions are necessary to prevent pastry from being made heavy and sodden by the collapse of air bubbles formed in it.

Suet Crust.

In essentials, the making of suet crust is precisely similar to that of short crust. The two differ only in that (1) the suet is chopped finely before being added to the flour; (2) 4 tablespoonfuls breadcrumbs are added to each pound of flour to make the crust lighter than it would otherwise be.

Method. (1) Sift the flour well, add breadcrumbs and baking powder. (2) Chop the suet finely. To do this, remove the skin and tissues and cut the suet into fine flakes. Sprinkle over it some of the flour to be used for the crust, roll it with a rolling pin, then chop it with a sharp knife. When it resembles very fine breadcrumbs, put it in the bowl with the flour. (3) Mix the chopped suet with the flour, breadcrumbs, etc., and make into a firm paste with the water. Put the paste on a floured board and roll it out to the required shape.

Directions for making up and using suet crust are given on pp. 218, 219.

Flaky Pastries.

These require careful manipulation to arrange the flour-paste and shortening in regular layers, so that the pastry rises evenly. In puff pastry *all* the shortening is rolled into the flour; in flaky crust a small portion is first rubbed into it, as in making short crust.

Flaky Crust. There are various ways of arranging the flour and shortening in alternate layers; the method given is one of the simplest and most successful.

Method. (1) Sift the flour and salt.

(2) Divide the shortening into four parts, first mixing the margarine and lard together on a plate. Rub one part into the flour, mix with the liquid as in making short crust and roll the paste into an oblong shape, about three times as long as it is broad. The edges must be straight and the corners square; stretch the parts slightly if necessary.

(3) Take a second portion of shortening, cut it into small pieces and distribute them evenly over the paste. Sift a little flour over and fold the paste in three from end to end, so that it is one-third of its original length. Place on the board with the folded edges at the side. With the rolling pin, press the open edges together to enclose air, press the paste across two or three times, then roll it out, stopping short at the open edges. When the paste is an oblong, three times as long as it is broad, roll the ends to the same thickness as the rest of the paste.

(4) Repeat (3) until the two remaining portions of shortening are used. Then fold into three again, and roll the paste to the required shape, making it $\frac{1}{8}$–$\frac{3}{8}$ inch thick, according to the use to which it is to be put.

In rolling both flaky and puff pastes, it is important:

(1) To roll with even pressure, so that the paste is a uniform thickness and the edges straight.

(2) To roll with short, quick strokes, using sufficient pressure to increase the size of the paste, yet not so much as to cause the shortening to break through. If this occurs, sprinkle the place with flour.

(3) To fold the paste accurately, making the corners square and the edges even.

In hot weather, put the paste in a cold place for a short time between the rollings. If the paste becomes at all warm, the shortening will be rolled into it instead of the two forming separate layers, and the pastry will be tough and heavy.

Baking Flaky Crust. The oven should be slightly hotter than for short crust; the amount of heat necessary for baking increases with the richness of the pastry.

Puff Paste. *Method.* (1) Sift the pastry flour, add salt and mix with water or egg and water to a paste about the same consistency as that of the butter to be used. Knead the paste lightly until it forms a smooth elastic piece of dough, then roll it out into an even oblong $\frac{3}{8}$–$\frac{1}{2}$ inch thick, making the corners quite square.

(2) Sift a little flour on one corner of a clean cloth, lay the butter on it and knead it into a flat cake, the size of half the pastry. This removes water from the butter and makes it easier to manipulate. If the butter is very hard the pressure of the rolling pin makes it come through the paste; if, on the other hand, it is too soft, it is difficult to avoid rolling it into the paste.

(3) Lay the cake of butter on one half of the paste, fold the other half over and press the edges together. Place the folded edges of the paste to one side, press it with the pin two or three times, then roll it into a long, even, oblong strip.

(4) Fold the paste into three, as for flaky pastry, keeping the edges straight and the corners square, and press the edges together as in making flaky pastry. Press and roll out the pastry as before, continuing until it has been folded and rolled five or six times in all, when the flour-paste and shortening should no longer be distinguishable as separate layers. Then fold the paste into three again for the last time and roll it to the required shape, making it about $\frac{3}{8}$ inch thick for pies and tarts, and $\frac{1}{8}$ inch thick for lining patty tins.

Puff pastry, even more than flaky crust, needs to be kept cool and should be put in a cold place for 15 minutes or so between each rolling. It is advisable to let a still longer interval elapse between the last rolling and the making up and baking. When it is convenient, the pastry may with advantage be made the day before it is to be baked.

Baking Puff Pastry. Puff pastry requires a very hot oven. The door should not be opened for the first 7 or 8 minutes, and then only very slightly and must be shut quietly. When the pastry is baked, it must be put in a warm place to cool gradually.

Making up of Short, Flaky and Puff Pastry.

For the making up of short, flaky and puff pastries into pies, tarts, etc., certain general instructions may be given:

(1) Grease plates, patty tins and the edges of pie-dishes to keep the paste from sticking. This is not necessary when puff pastry, with its large proportion of shortening, is used.

(2) To prevent burning at the edges, line the edges of pie-dishes, plates, etc., with strips of pastry $\frac{1}{2}$–1 inch wide, unless both a lining and a cover of pastry are to be used, as in making mince pies, when the strips are not required. Place the cut edges of the strips outwards. To join two strips, moisten the ends with a pastry brush damped slightly with water, and make

them overlap for about ½ inch. Damp the lining strip slightly in the same way before putting on the sheet of pastry.

(3) To cover a pie-dish or line a plate, roll the paste to the required size and fold it in half. Lay the doubled paste on one half of the dish, open it out and press gently on to the strips. The pastry shrinks slightly in baking and must not be stretched in any way. Hold the dish or plate on the palm of the left hand and cut away the superfluous pastry, slanting the knife outwards, so as to make the cover amply large. Decorate the edges.

(4) To give a good finish, glaze the pastry before baking it. For savoury dishes, *e.g.* pastry enclosing meat, etc., brush the paste with beaten egg, using the whole egg or the yolk of an egg diluted with a little milk or water; milk alone may also be used. For sweet pastries, *e.g.* fruit tarts, etc., brush the pastry with the white of an egg, beaten slightly and diluted with 2 teaspoonfuls water; sift castor sugar over. An alternative plan is to brush she paste lightly with cold water to remove any dry flour and to scatter over it a liberal supply of granulated sugar.

Instead of being glazed before cooking, sweet pastries may be covered after baking with a meringue mixture. (See p. 80.)

RECIPES FOR PIES, TARTS, ETC.

For convenience for reference we may first summarise the ingredients required for the different kinds of pastry.

Table of Ingredients for Pastries

Ingredient	*Short Crust*	*Flaky Crust*	*Puff Pastry*
Flour.	½ lb. household flour.	½ lb. household or 'pastry' flour.	½ lb. 'pastry' flour
Salt.	½ teaspoonful salt.	½ teaspoonful salt.	Pinch of salt.
Shortening.	3–4 oz. margarine with lard *or* clarified beef *or* bacon dripping.	4–6 oz. margarine with lard.	½ lb. fresh butter *or* 6 oz. butter with 2 oz. lard
Baking powder.	½ teaspoonful (4 oz. shortening).	—	—
	⅔ teaspoonful (3 oz. shortening).	—	—
Additions.	¼–1 oz. castor sugar for sweet pastry only.	—	—
Liquid.	¼ pint of water *or* yolk of egg and water to make up ¼ pint.	¼ pint of water.	¼ pint of water *or* yolk of 1 egg and water to make up ¼ pint

SWEET PASTRY DISHES

Fruit Tarts.

Ingredients

Fruit or mixtures of fruit to fill 1 pint pie-dish.
2–4 tablespoonfuls sugar to 1 lb. of fruit.
1–2 tablespoonfuls water to 1 lb. of such hard dry fruits as gooseberries, plums.

Short crust *or* puff pastry (5–6 oz. flour).
White of 1 egg, 2 teaspoonfuls water and castor sugar, } For glaze.
Or, Cold water and granulated sugar, }

Method. Prepare the fruit. Put half of it in the pie-dish, add sugar and water, if required, and cover with the remainder of the fruit. Pile up the fruit to support the crust and if necessary, put a pie-crust holder or an inverted egg-cup in the middle. If there is nothing for the paste to rest on, it will sink before it has had time to set and will be sodden and heavy.

Line the edges of the dish with pastry, put on the cover and ornament the edges. Make one or two slits in the cover to let out steam which would otherwise make the pastry sodden. Glaze the pastry and bake the tart in a moderate oven for about ¾ hour, until the pastry is crisp, firm and lightly browned. If the oven is too cool, the pastry will be tough and leathery. If, at the end of ¾ hour, there is reason to suspect that the fruit is still not perfectly tender, put the tart in a cooler part of the oven to complete the cooking. Cover with greased paper to prevent undue browning.

Alternative Methods.

(1) *Fruit tarts* may also be made by lining a deep plate with pastry, putting in the sweetened fruit (*e.g.* raspberries, black currants, red currants, cherries) in the usual way and covering it with pastry.

(2) *Fruit Sandwiches.* For 1 lb. fruit (*e.g.* apples, sliced thinly, or stoned Valencia raisins with a layer of sliced apple on top), make short crust with 6 oz. flour, etc. Roll the pastry into a square or oblong and divide it in two. Put one piece on a greased baking sheet and cover with a layer of prepared and sweetened fruit. Damp the edges and cover the fruit with the second piece of pastry, pressing it down lightly. Glaze the pastry, cut slits here and there, and bake in a moderate oven for 20–25 minutes. When cool, cut the sandwich into square or oblong pieces.

Eccles cake mixture (see p. 211) can be used in the same way.

Apple Dumplings.

Ingredients

6 large apples.
2–3 tablespoonfuls Demerara sugar.
6 cloves *or* lemon juice and grated lemon rind.

Short crust (8 oz. flour, etc.).
White of 1 egg, 2 teaspoonfuls water and castor sugar, } For glaze.
Or, Cold water and granulated sugar,

Method. Roll out the pastry thinly and cut into 12 rounds, each large enough to cover half an apple. Damp the edges. Peel and core the apples; place each on a round of pastry and put sugar with a clove or a little lemon juice and rind into each cavity. Bring the paste up the sides of the apple and cover it with the *second* round of pastry, pressing the edges together at the join. Glaze the pastry and bake the dumplings on a greased tin in a moderate oven for 30–40 minutes according to size. Test the tenderness of the apples with a skewer.

Note. (1) These dumplings should be made only with apples which are known to bake quickly. (2) Very tender pears may be prepared in the same way.

Apple Meringue Tart.

Ingredients

2 lbs. apples.
2 oz. margarine.
3 oz. sugar.
Grated rind of 1 lemon (optional).

Short crust, *or* flaky, *or* puff paste (6 oz. flour).
Whites of 2 eggs } Meringue.
4 oz. castor sugar

Method. (1) Line a deep plate with the pastry, first putting strips round the edges; prick the pastry on the bottom of the plate and bake for 15–20 minutes in a moderate, hot or very hot oven, according as it is short crust, flaky or puff paste.

(2) Peel the apples, cut into quarters and slice thinly. Put them in a pan with the margarine, sugar and grated lemon rind and cook slowly, tossing occasionally, until they are quite tender.

(3) Put the apple in pyramid shape on the cooked pastry case and sift a little sugar over. Prepare the meringue according to the directions given on p. 80 and pile it on top of the apple. Sift icing or castor sugar over and bake in a very cool oven for $\frac{3}{4}$ hour or longer, till the meringue is faintly browned and crisp on the outside.

The tart may be served either hot or cold.

:ccles Cakes.

Ingredients

$\frac{1}{4}$ lb. currants.	1 oz. margarine.
$1\frac{1}{2}$ oz. candied peel.	$\frac{1}{4}$ teaspoonful allspice.
2 oz. castor sugar.	Pinch of grated nutmeg.

Short *or* flaky crust *or* puff pastry (6 oz. flour, etc.).
White of egg, 2 teaspoonfuls water and castor sugar, } For glaze.
Or, Cold water and granulated sugar, }

Method. Clean and pick the currants, chop the candied peel very nely and mix both with sugar, margarine, allspice and nutmeg.
The mixture is improved by being put in a jar and heated in pan of boiling water for $\frac{1}{4}$ hour. It must be cool before being ut in the pastry.

Roll out the pastry thinly; cut into rounds $3\frac{1}{2}$–$4\frac{1}{2}$ inches cross, place the rounds on sugared paper and damp the edges. ay a spoonful of the mixture on each round and gather the dges together. Make two slits on the top of each cake, glaze, ut on a greased tin and bake 10–15 minutes in a fairly hot oven.

Iince Pies.

Make good short crust *or* flaky *or* puff pastry and roll it out ıinly. Cut the rounds for the covers first, and line patty tins ith the rounds cut from the pieces of pastry left over and re-olled. Put in the mincemeat, piling it up; damp the edges of e paste and put on the covers. Glaze and bake for 15–20 ıinutes in a moderate, quick or very quick oven according to ıe kind of pastry used.

pen Jam Tarts or Tartlets.

Line a plate or patty tins with short crust *or* flaky *or* puff astry, first putting strips of pastry round the edges. Decorate e edges, then put in the jam. Place twisted strips of pastry, oout $\frac{1}{4}$ inch wide, across the tart from edge to edge, giving an fect of lattice work. Bake 10–20 minutes in a moderate, quick r very quick oven, according to the kind of pastry used.

yrup Tart.

Ingredients

$\frac{1}{4}$ lb. syrup. 1 teacupful breadcrumbs. Grated rind $\frac{1}{2}$ lemon *or* $\frac{1}{2}$ teaspoonful ground ginger.	Short crust (6 oz. flour), etc.

Method. Make as for Jam Tart, substituting the syrup and readcrumb mixture for jam.

Lemon or Orange Cheese Tarts.

Line patty tins with good short crust *or* with flaky *or* puff pastry, first putting strips of pastry round the edge. Prick the pastry to prevent it blistering and leaving the plate. Bake in a quick oven for 8–10 minutes. When baked, fill the shells with the cheese mixture (see p. 74). If the shells are filled immediately after baking, the cheese should be warmed slightly.

SAVOURY PASTRY DISHES

Beefsteak, Veal and Ham, or Rabbit Pie.

Beefsteak Pie	*Veal and Ham Pie*	*Rabbit Pie*
1½ lbs. beefsteak.	1½ lbs. fillet of veal.	1 young rabbit.
¼ lb. beef kidney,	¼ lb. ham *or* bacon.	¼ lb. ham *or* bacon.
Or 2 hard-boiled eggs,	2 hard-boiled eggs.	2 hard-boiled eggs.
Or 5 or 6 mushrooms.		
¾ tablespoonful flour.	¾ tablespoonful flour.	¾ tablespoonful flour.
1½ teaspoonfuls salt.	1½ teaspoonfuls salt.	1½ teaspoonfuls salt.
¾ teaspoonful pepper.	¾ teaspoonful pepper.	¾ teaspoonful pepper.
	Cayenne, pinch nutmeg, grated lemon rind.	Grated lemon rind.
Stock *or* water.	Stock *or* water.	Stock *or* water

Puff *or* flaky *or* short pastry (6–8 oz. flour).
Beaten egg (whole egg, *or* yolk of egg with 1 tablespoonful milk).

Method. (1) *Beef or Veal.* Wash the meat and cut it across th grain into rather thin pieces about 2 inches long and 1½ inche wide. (If the beef is at all likely to be tough it should be cut int ½ inch dice.) Dip each piece in seasoned flour and roll up putting a morsel of fat in each.

Rabbit. Cut into pieces, wash and dry well. Dip each piec into seasoned flour.

(2) Cut the kidney or ham into pieces. Shell and skin the egg and cut into slices or quarters. Peel the mushrooms and tri the stalks.

(3) Arrange the contents of the pie in layers in a dish (abou 1 pint capacity for the quantities given); heap them up and pu a pie-crust holder or an inverted egg-cup in the middle, necessary. Pour in stock or water to come rather more tha half-way up the sides of the dish.

(4) Roll out the prepared pastry. Grease the edges of the dish, line them with strips of pastry, damp the strips and put on the cover. Chip the edges of the paste with the blade of a sharp knife to separate the flakes a little. Decorate the pie with leaves, roses, or other ornaments cut out of the pastry. Cut one or two slits in the paste to let out the steam which would make it sodden. Glaze with beaten egg.

(5) Bake from 1½–2 hours, putting the pie at first in a fairly hot oven. When the crust has risen well and is set and lightly browned, cook at a rather lower temperature so that the meat may cook slowly for the remainder of the time. When the crust has nearly acquired the desirable rich brown colour, cover it with a greased paper sufficiently large to protect both the top and sides of the pie.

(6) Just before serving add a little hot well-seasoned stock or gravy; put it in by means of a funnel or small jug, through a hole made in an inconspicuous position in the pastry.

Sausage Rolls.

Ingredients

½ lb. sausages.
Flaky *or* short pastry (7 oz. flour).
Beaten egg *or* milk.

Method. Slit the sausage skins from end to end, remove the contents and shape them into 8 small rolls of even length.

Roll out the pastry, cut it into 8 squares and damp the edges. Wrap a portion of sausage in each piece, making the edges overlap on top and closing up the ends. Brush with egg or milk, cut slits in the paste, put on a greased baking tin and bake in a fairly hot oven for 20–25 minutes.

Cornish Pasties.

Ingredients

8 oz. steak.
1 teaspoonful chopped onion.
½ teaspoonful salt.
¼ teaspoonful pepper.
1 potato.
2 teaspoonfuls stock *or* water.
Short crust (8 oz. flour).
Beaten egg *or* milk.

Method. (1) Wash the meat, cut into small pieces and mix with chopped onion and seasonings. Peel the potato, keep in water till required, cut into dice and mix it with the meat, etc. and stock.

(2) Roll out the pastry thinly and cut into 7 or 8 rounds or squares. Damp the edges and put a spoonful of the meat and

potato mixture on each; gather the edges together on the top, forming them into a frill. Cut slits in the paste.

(3) Brush the pasties with egg or milk, put on a greased baking tin and bake 35 minutes. Have the oven fairly hot for the first 15 minutes, then moderate the heat slightly.

Egg Patties.

Ingredients

4–5 hard-boiled eggs. (See p. 70.).
Salt, pepper, powdered mace.
1 tablespoonful finely chopped parsley.
½ pint white sauce (1 oz. margarine, 1 oz. flour, ½ pint milk, etc. pp. 151, 152).

Short *or* flaky crust (6 oz. flour).
Beaten egg *or* milk.

Method. Shell and skin the eggs and chop finely. Mix egg, parsley, seasonings and sauce together. Roll out pastry thinly, cut 12 rounds and line patty tins with 6 of them. Fill with the egg mixture, piling it up high. Damp the edges and press the covers into place. Brush the pastry with beaten egg or milk and bake in a fairly quick oven 15–20 minutes.

Note. These patties may be eaten hot or cold. Remains of cold sauce (*e.g.* savoury white, parsley, anchovy sauce) can be substituted for the freshly made sauce.

SUET PUDDINGS

There are two distinct types of these:

(1) Puddings in which the suet forms part of a crust or case in which the remaining ingredients *e.g.* meat, fruit, syrup are enclosed. *Example*: Beef-steak Pudding, Roly-poly Pudding.

(2) Puddings in which the suet is distributed evenly throughout the mixture. *Example*: Plum Pudding.

Type 1. In puddings of this type the suet crust is used:

(1) To line a basin into which the meat or fruit is put and to form a lid or covering for these so that they are enclosed completely.

Or (2) to form a roll consisting of alternate layers of crust and jam or syrup, etc.

Directions for the making of suet crust have already been given on p. 205 and methods of using it are illustrated by recipes on pp. 218, 219.

Type 2. There is an infinite variety of puddings of this type, but all have certain features in common. Their basis consists of the same ingredients as those of a suet crust, but other substances are added to enrich and vary the mixture, which is moistened with eggs and milk instead of with water.

The ingredients for puddings of this type may be classified as follows:

Basis.	1 lb. flour *or* flour and breadcrumbs[1] *or* flour and steeped breadcrusts or pieces of bread. 1 teaspoonful salt.
Shortening.	6–16 oz. of suet.[2]
Baking powder.	2 teaspoonfuls when the weight of the shortening is half the weight of the flour, etc., forming the basis; $2\frac{3}{4}$ teaspoonfuls when the proportion of shortening to flour is less than half.
Additions.	(*a*) $\frac{1}{4}$–$1\frac{1}{2}$ lbs. currants, sultanas, Valencia raisins, candied peel, figs, dates *or* mixtures of these. $\frac{1}{4}$–$\frac{3}{4}$ lb. sugar. *Or*, (*b*) 1 lb. marmalade, jam, treacle or syrup. 2–4 oz. sugar (if required).
Flavourings.	Ginger, nutmeg, allspice, etc.
Liquids.	For plain puddings: milk / For richer puddings: 2–8 eggs with milk } to give the required consistency.

To prepare the pudding:

(1) Make all the preparations for cooking the pudding (see pp. 216, 217).

(2) Sift flour, add salt and breadcrumbs or steeped crusts or pieces of bread. If crusts or pieces of bread are used, cut them into small pieces, put them into a basin and cover with cold water; put a plate over the basin and let the crusts soak $\frac{1}{2}$ hour or longer until they are perfectly soft. Then press them in a strainer to remove as much water as possible and beat them up lightly with a fork.

If time is short, or the bread very stale, use boiling water.

(3) Chop the suet very finely and add it to the flour, etc.

(4) Pick currants and sultanas, stone and chop Valencia raisins, cut figs or dates into small pieces, candied peel into dice, and add to the flour and suet.

(5) Add baking powder and remaining dry ingredients to flour and suet; mix all together thoroughly.

[1] The use of breadcrumbs makes the pudding lighter.

[2] A smaller proportion of suet suffices when steeped breadcrusts or pieces of bread form the basis.

(6) Beat up the eggs, add milk if required, and mix the pudding to a batter just sufficiently stiff to remain heaped up in a spoon, yet so soft that it cannot be handled.

(7) Pour the mixture into a greased mould or dish and cook at once. Illustrative recipes are given on pp. 220–223.

Cooking of Suet Puddings.

Suet puddings of both types can be steamed, boiled or baked

(1) Steaming Suet Puddings.[1]

Puddings in Moulds or Basins. Put the pudding mixture into the greased mould or basin, allowing room for it to swell and expand.[2] Cover with a greased paper to keep out condensed steam which would otherwise collect on the top of the pudding and soak into it.

Roll Puddings. Cover the pudding first with a greased paper then with a thin cloth so that it can be lifted out of the steamer

Roll puddings cannot be steamed except in the regulation steamer or in a large potato steamer.

To Steam Puddings. The water in the boiler must be boiling when the pudding is put in the steamer. Watch carefully that the water does not stop boiling and add more boiling water as often as is necessary. Cover the pan closely to retain the steam.

(2) Boiling Suet Puddings.

Since the pudding will be covered with water, measures must be taken to prevent as far as possible (1) the water from soaking into the pudding, (2) the substance of the pudding from being extracted by the water.

Puddings in Moulds or Basins.

Fill the mould or basin quite full, so that the water cannot get in. Cover it first with a greased paper, then tie over it a pudding cloth of strong unbleached calico. Wring the cloth out of boiling water and dredge with flour whose starch grains will swell and burst, filling up the crevices of the cloth.

Roll Puddings. Wrap the roly-poly loosely in a scalded and floured pudding cloth. Tie it close up to the ends of the roll so that the pudding can expand widthways but not lengthways. Fasten the open edge of the cloth along the roll with two or three stitches.

[1] For preparations for steaming see pp. 51, 52.

[2] This does not apply to puddings of Type 1 (*e.g.* Beefsteak Puddings) which do not rise to any appreciable extent.

To Boil Puddings. Have sufficient boiling water to cover the pudding completely and watch that it boils continuously the whole time. Add more boiling water when necessary.

Both in boiling and steaming puddings a steady heat must be maintained. Variations in the temperature must inevitably interfere with the proper cooking of the puddings and make them less light than they should be.

(3) Baking Suet Puddings.

Puddings of Type 1, made of suet crust with a filling of fresh fruit, etc., are usually baked in basins, but those of Type 2 are best baked in a shallower vessel, such as a pie-dish. The oven must be moderately hot.

Time required for the Cooking of Suet Puddings.

Two factors determine this: (1) the size of the pudding, (2) the proportion of suet in the mixture. The richer the pudding, that is, the greater the proportion of suet it contains, the longer cooking will it require.

Suet, as compared to other shortening, needs long cooking, because however finely it is chopped, the connective tissues with which the fat is bound up have to be softened before the fat can 'shorten' the mixture.[1]

Time for Boiling.

(1) Plain suet mixture, sufficient to fill a ½ pint basin, 1¼–1½ hours.

(2) Moderately rich mixture, sufficient to fill 1–1½ pint basin, 1½–2½ hours.

(3) Rich suet mixture (*e.g.* Plum Pudding), 8 hours.

Time for Steaming. One-third to one-half as long again as the time allowed for boiling.

Time for Baking. One-half the time allowed for boiling.

Relative Merits of Methods of Cooking Suet Puddings.

Steaming and Boiling.

When a pudding is boiled, the water tends to soak into it, extracting its substance and making it sodden, while its pressure keeps the pudding from expanding to its full extent. Further, the movements of the water shake the pudding and may make it close and heavy. Cooking by steam is thus, as a general rule,

[1] If margarine or other soft fat is used to make a so-called 'suet' pudding, it is rubbed into the flour, as in making pastry and the time for cooking is reduced, *e.g.* 1½–2 hours for steaming instead of 2–2½ hours. See p. 222.

much to be preferred to boiling and is especially suitable for very light mixtures, those with a basis consisting largely of breadcrumbs and with a good proportion of egg.

The difficulty of time often makes it necessary to boil puddings which have a large quantity of suet. Cf. Plum Pudding No. 1, p. 220.

Baking. A baked suet pudding has a crispness of texture which is lacking in boiled and steamed puddings. No loss of suet or other substance of the pudding occurs, and the process takes less time than boiling or steaming.

ILLUSTRATIVE RECIPES. SUET PUDDINGS. (TYPE I.)

A. Suet Crust for 1 pint Basin.

¼ lb. flour.
Pinch of salt.
1 tablespoonful breadcrumbs.
2 oz. suet (finely chopped).
¼ teaspoonful baking powder.
⅛ pint of water.[1]

For Fruit Pudding.

1 lb. apples, plums, or gooseberries, etc.
2–4 tablespoonfuls sugar.
1–2 tablespoonfuls water.

For Beefsteak Pudding.

6 oz. steak.
2 oz. kidney *or* 6 mushrooms.
1 teaspoonful flour.
½ teaspoonful salt.
¼ teaspoonful pepper.
Stock *or* water.

Method. (1) Prepare fruit in the usual way, beef as for beefsteak pie (see p. 212).

(2) Mix flour, salt, breadcrumbs, suet and baking powder together, add cold water and mix to a stiff paste.

(3) Turn on to a floured board, cut off about ⅓ of the paste to make the cover of the pudding. Roll both pieces into rounds about ¼ inch thick, making the larger one about 1½ times the diameter of the basin. Line a greased basin with this, pressing it evenly up the sides and leaving only a small piece projecting above the rim. Put in the contents of the pudding. If these are fruit, put in half of it, add sugar and water, omitting the latter for juicy fruits, then add the remainder of the fruit, heaping it up in the centre. Arrange meat in similar fashion, pouring in stock to come about half-way up the basin. Wet the edges of

[1] It will be noticed that the ingredients are precisely the same as those used to make suet dumplings to serve with boiled meat. See p. 95. Compare also Savoury Dumplings (p. 105).

the paste and put on the cover; press the two edges of paste together and turn them inwards so that they do not stick to the basin and make it difficult to turn out the pudding.

(4) Steam or boil the pudding as directed on pp. 216 and 217.

Times	*Boiling*	*Steaming*
Beefsteak Pudding - - -	2–2½ hours.	2¾–3¼ hours.
Fruit Pudding - - - -	1½–2 hours.	2–2¾ hours.

B. Roll Puddings.

To ½ lb. suet crust (½ lb. flour, 2 tablespoonfuls breadcrumbs, 4 oz. suet, ½ teaspoonful of baking powder, ¼ pint of water) use for:

(*a*) *Jam Roly-poly* - - ½ lb. jam.
(*b*) *Treacle Roly-poly* - - ½ lb. treacle, 3 tablespoonfuls fine white breadcrumbs, grated rind of 1 lemon.
(*c*) *Orange Roly-poly* - - ½ lb. orange marmalade, 1–2 oranges, sliced thinly, 2–3 tablespoonfuls fine white breadcrumbs, 1 oz. sugar.
(*d*) *Lancashire Roly-poly* - ½ lb. mincemeat.

Method. (1) Prepare the suet crust as already directed, and roll it into a paste ¼ inch thick, making it oblong in shape.

(2) Leaving a clear space of about 1¼ inch all the way round, spread the jam or treacle mixture or mincemeat on the paste; for Orange Roly-poly, arrange the ingredients in layers on the paste in the order given.

(3) Moisten the edges with a pastry brush, roll up the paste rather loosely, press down the outer edges and tuck in the ends securely.

(4) Steam or boil as directed on pp. 216 and 217, allowing 1½–2 hours for boiling, 2–2¾ hours for steaming.

(5) A boiled roll-pudding is sufficiently cooked when the cloth begins to show small wrinkles. A much wrinkled cloth is a sign that the pudding has begun to boil away; if the cooking is continued beyond this point more and more water will get in and soak into the pudding.

'Suet' Puddings Made with Soft Fat (*e.g.* margarine, lard or dripping).

The following recipes serve as examples of the use of soft fats to make so-called 'suet' puddings. They show also how a very small proportion of fat can, if necessary, be used, with additional baking powder as compensation for the lack of shortening. [Continued on pp. 222-223.

Kind of Pudding	*Basis*	*Shortening*	*Additions*	*Liquid*
PLAIN SUET PUDDING.	4 oz. flour. 4 oz. bread-crumbs. Salt.	3–4 oz. suet. 1⅓–1 tea-spoonful baking-powder.[2]		1 egg. ⅛–¼ pint milk.
TREACLE PUDDING.	4 oz. flour. 4 oz. bread-crumbs. Salt.	3–4 oz. suet. 1⅓–1 tea-spoonful baking-powder.	2 oz. sugar. 2 oz. currants. 2 large tablespoonfuls treacle. Juice and rind of 1 lemon. ⅛ teaspoonful nutmeg.	2 eggs. ⅛–¼ pint milk.
MARMALADE OR GOLDEN PUDDING.	2 oz. flour. 6 oz. bread-crumbs. Salt.	3–4 oz. suet. 1⅓–1 tea-spoonful baking-powder.	2 oz. sugar. 3 large tablespoonfuls marmalade.	2 eggs *or* 1 and ⅛–¼ pint milk.
LEMON PUDDING.	4 oz. flour. 4 oz. bread-crumbs. Salt.	5–6 oz. suet *or* 4 oz. suet and 1 teaspoonful baking-powder.	4–6 oz. sugar. Rind of 1½ small or 1 large lemon. Juice of 3 small or 2 large lemons.	2 eggs. Milk if quired.
PLUM PUDDING, No. 1 (Rich).	1 oz. flour. 1 lb. bread-crumbs. Salt.	1 lb. suet.	¾ lb. sugar. 1 oz. sweet almonds. 2 bitter almonds. ½ teaspoonful nutmeg. 1 lb. currants. 1 lb. Valencia raisins. ¼ lb. candied citron. ¼ lb. candied lemon.	6 eggs. 1 wineglas ful bran
PLUM PUDDING, No. 2.	¼ lb. flour. ¾ lb. bread-crumbs. Salt.	¾ lb. suet.	½ lb. sugar. 1 teaspoonful allspice. ¼ lb. candied peel. ½ lb. currants. ½ lb. Valencia raisins. Juice of 1 lemon.	4–5 eggs. Milk, if quired. ½–¾ wine-glassful brandy.
TREACLE SPONGE PUDDING.	¼ lb. flour (plain). Salt.	1½–2 oz. suet. ¼ teaspoonful bicarbonate of soda.	1 oz. brown sugar. ½ teaspoonful ground ginger. ½ teacupful treacle.	½ teacup milk.

[1] For *general* directions see p. 215. [2] If baking pow

litional Directions for Mixing[1]	Cooking	Sauce, etc., for Serving
Mix the dry ingredients to-her thoroughly, add beaten egg l sufficient milk to make a stiff ter.	Steam 2–2½ hours. Boil 1½–2 hours.	Pour over or serve with the pudding warmed jam or syrup. Dilute jam with water if necessary.
Varm treacle if it is stiff, and l with the grated lemon rind, ained lemon juice, beaten eggs l milk to the remaining in-dients. Put into a quart mould.	Steam 2–2½ hours. Boil 1½–2 hours.	Serve with ½ pint of sweet white *or* melted butter sauce (pp. 151, 152) *or* with ½ pint custard (pp. 76 or 146).
Mix the dry ingredients to-her, add marmalade, beaten and milk, if required. Mix to stiff batter and put into a ased mould.	Steam 2–2½ hours.	Warm 2 or 3 table-spoonfuls of marmalade with an equal quantity of water and pour over the pudding.
Mix together sugar, grated on rind, strained lemon juice, l add to the flour, suet, etc. isten with beaten eggs; add k if necessary to make a stiff ter.	Steam 2–2½ hours. Boil 1½–2 hours.	Serve with ½ pint lemon sauce (p. 186) *or* with ½ pint sweet white or melted butter sauce (pp. 151, 152).
Blanch the almonds and chop ly, stone the raisins. Put all the ingredients together and let m stand for 24 hours. Then isten them with the beaten eggs l brandy. Put into basin, cover h (1) greased paper, (2) flour l water paste, (3) pudding cotlh.	Boil 8 hours.	Serve with ½ pint melted butter sauce (pp. 151, 152), *or* beat to a cream 2 oz. butter and 2 oz. castor sugar and put in a cold place to stiffen. Serve with the pudding.
Make and cook as for Plum ding No. 1.	Boil 6–8 hours.	As for Plum Pudding No. 1.
ift the bicarbonate of soda h the flour and warm the cle. Mix together the dry in-dients, add treacle and milk l mix thoroughly. Put into a t mould.	Steam 1½–2 hours.	Serve with brown sugar and ½ pint sweet white *or* melted butter sauce (pp. 151, 152), *or* with ½ pint custard (pp. 76 or 146).

. 2 (see pp. 227, 228) is used, double the quantity.

Kind of Pudding	*Basis*	*Shortening*	*Additions*	*Liquic*
BREAD PUDDING.	2 oz. flour. 6 oz. pieces of bread *or* bread-crusts. Salt.	2 oz. suet. ½ teaspoonful bicarbonate of soda.	2–4 oz. currants *or* raisins. ½ oz. candied peel. ½ teaspoonful ground ginger. 2 oz. treacle.	Milk, if quired if wate mainin breadi sufficie make a batter.
FIG, DATE OR RAISIN PUDDING.	2 oz. flour. 8 oz. pieces of bread or breadcrusts. Salt.	3–4 oz. suet. 1⅓–1 tea-spoonful baking-powder. [1]	½ lb. figs, dates or stoned Valencia raisins. 3 oz. sugar. Grated rind of 1 lemon.	1 egg. ⅛ pint mi
BAKED PLUM PUDDING.	8 oz. pieces of bread. Salt.	2–4 oz. suet. 1⅓–1 tea-spoonful baking-powder. [1]	2 oz. currants. 2 oz. raisins. 2–4 oz. sugar. Grated rind of ½ lemon.	2 eggs *or* 1 and ⅛–¼ pint milk.

Ginger, Chocolate or Jam Pudding.

Foundation Ingredients for All

½ lb. flour.
Pinch salt.
{3 oz. margarine, lard or dripping.
{2⅔ teaspoonfuls baking powder.[1]
Or
{2 oz. margarine, lard or dripping.
{4 level teaspoonfuls baking powder.[1]
1 oz. sugar.
1 egg.
¼ pint milk *or* milk and water (bare measure).

Additional Ingredients

Ginger Pudding
1 dessertspoonful syrup.
4 teaspoonfuls ground ginger.

Chocolate Pudding
1½–2 oz. sugar.
3 level tablespoonfuls cocoa.
or powdered chocolate.

Jam Pudding
1 oz. sugar.
2 tablespoonfuls jam.

Method. (1) Sift flour and salt and rub in the shortening as in making pastry. Add sugar and baking powder.

(2) Beat egg and mix with milk or milk and water.

[1] If baking powder No. 2 (see pp. 227, 228) is used, double the quantity.

...litional Directions for Mixing	Cooking	Sauce, etc., for Serving
...ft the bicarbonate of soda ... the flour and warm the ...cle. Steep the bread ½ hour or ...ger; squeeze dry and beat with ...rk. Mix with remaining in-...lients, adding treacle at the ... Put into 1½ pint mould.	Steam 2–2½ hours. Boil 1½–2 hours.	Serve with ½ pint jam sauce (p. 186), *or* with ½ pint custard (pp. 76 *or* 146).
...eep the bread or crusts ½ hour ...onger, squeeze dry and break ...vith a fork. Mix all ingredients ...ther and moisten with egg and ... Put into 1½ pint mould.	Steam 2½–3 hours.	Serve with ½ pint custard (pp. 76 *or* 146).
...ut into (*a*) greased shallow dish, *or* into (*b*) 5 small ...sed cups or dariole moulds.	Bake in a moderate oven (*a*) 1–1¼ hours; (*b*) ½ hour.	Turn out and sift sugar over.

(3) *Ginger Pudding*. Add sifted ginger and syrup (slightly warmed) to dry ingredients.

Chocolate Pudding. Add additional sugar and sifted chocolate powder or cocoa to dry ingredients.

Jam Pudding. Add additional sugar to dry ingredients and put jam at the bottom of a greased pudding basin.

(4) Mix all ingredients well together and add egg and sufficient milk or milk and water to make the mixture a stiff consistency.

(5) Put into a greased basin and steam for 1½ hours.

(6) (*a*) Serve with *Ginger Pudding* some warmed syrup diluted with a little boiling water and flavoured with lemon juice.

(*b*) Serve with *Chocolate Pudding* ½ pint custard (see p. 146).

(*c*) Serve with *Jam Pudding* ½ pint Jam Sauce (see p. 186).

CHAPTER XVIII

THE AERATION OF DOUGHS: (1) BAKING POWDER AND ITS CONSTITUENTS

The aeration of doughs depends on the introduction of a gas or gases, which when heated expand and force a way out, making the dough porous. Any gas, provided it had no harmful effect on the dough, would answer the purpose, but carbon-dioxide and the mixture of gases known as air are most generally used.

Air is already to hand and only requires to be enclosed in the dough by some such mechanical means as beating or whisking.

Carbon-dioxide can be produced by means of:

(*a*) Bicarbonate of soda (baking soda).

(*b*) Baking powder or its constituents.

(*c*) Yeast.

Combinations of these methods are often employed; cakes, for example, are frequently lightened partly by beating in air and partly by baking powder.

Production of Carbon-dioxide by the use of (1) Bicarbonate of Soda.

Experiment 1. (*a*) Put a little bicarbonate of soda in a test tube and add cold water.

(*b*) Heat the test tube.

In (*a*) bicarbonate of soda dissolves with difficulty.

In (*b*) effervescence takes place, denoting the formation of a gas. When this gas is led into lime water it causes the latter to become milky and is thus proved to be carbon-dioxide.

Conclusion. Carbon-dioxide is set free from bicarbonate of soda by the action of heat.

(2) Baking Powder and its Constituents.

Experiment 1. Take 2 test tubes A and B. In A put ¼ teaspoonful cream of tartar; in B put ¼ teaspoonful tartaric acid.

Moisten each with a little cold water and test the solution with litmus paper.

Experiment 2. Take 2 test tubes A and B. In A put ¼ teaspoonful cream of tartar, in B put ¼ teaspoonful tartaric acid.

Moisten each with a little hot water, noticing in each case whether the substitution of hot for cold water affects the solubility of the powder.

Experiment 3. Take three perfectly dry test tubes A, B and C. In A put $\frac{1}{2}$ teaspoonful bicarbonate of soda and a small $\frac{1}{2}$ teaspoonful tartaric acid. In B put $\frac{1}{4}$ teaspoonful bicarbonate of soda and $\frac{1}{2}$ teaspoonful cream of tartar. Shake the test tubes to mix the contents thoroughly and examine.

In C put $\frac{1}{4}$ teaspoonful prepared baking powder, *e.g.* Borwick's, Miller's or any other make.

Put in each test tube a little cold water, shake well and notice the result.

Experiment 4. Take three test tubes A, B and C, and put $\frac{1}{4}$ teaspoonful bicarbonate of soda in each. Add to A a little lemon juice. Add to B a little vinegar. Add to C a little sour milk or buttermilk.

Experiment 5. Take two test tubes A and B. Put in A 1 teaspoonful raspberry jam mixed with 1 teaspoonful water. Put in B 1 teaspoonful treacle mixed with 1 teaspoonful water. Test both with litmus paper and add to each $\frac{1}{4}$ teaspoonful bicarbonate of soda.

Experiment 6. Repeat Experiments 3, 4 and 5, in each case heating the mixtures gently.

These experiments demonstrate that:

(1) Dry mixtures of bicarbonate of soda and acids have no effect on each other.

(2) (*a*) Mixtures of bicarbonate of soda and acid cream of tartar or tartaric acid with liquids (*b*) Mixtures of bicarbonate of soda with acid liquids (*e.g.* lemon juice, vinegar, sour milk) or acid semi-liquids, (*e.g.* black treacle or jam)	effervesce, showing the formation of a gas which by use of lime water can be proved to be carbon-dioxide.

Moisture is necessary to bring the acids into close contact with the bicarbonate of soda. Without this close contact they are unable to act on each other. Effervescence is aided by the application of heat. The increased formation of gas is especially noticeable when cream of tartar is the acid used, for the reason that this substance, as we saw, is only slightly soluble in cold water.

Carbon-dioxide, therefore, for the purpose of aeration may be produced by the action of (1) heat, (2) acids on bicarbonate of soda. The second method is the more common of the two. Bicarbonate of soda used alone produces the necessary gas, but the carbonate of soda which remains when carbon-dioxide has been driven off gives the dough a somewhat unpleasant taste and a yellowish colour. A further objection to this means of producing carbon-dioxide is that the carbonate left in the dough, being an alkaline substance, interferes with the work of the acid digestive fluids of the body. Bread and cakes aerated by this means are thus unwholesome if eaten in any quantity.

Action of Carbon-dioxide in Aerating Doughs.

When heat is applied to a dough into which carbon-dioxide has been introduced, the bubbles of the gas expand and try to force a way out. Carbon-dioxide is thus instrumental in starting the process of aeration, even if, as is possible, it does not complete it. It may be that the bubbles formed in the dough by the gas become filled with water vapour, and that the expansion of this water vapour continues and completes the aeration begun by carbon-dioxide.

Experiment. The changes in a dough as the result of aeration are illustrated by the following experiment:

Mix 2 tablespoonfuls flour (A) to a dough with a little cold water. To a second 2 tablespoonfuls flour (B), add a pinch of baking powder and mix with the same quantity of water as was used for (A). Cook the two pieces simultaneously in a greased frying pan over a fairly good heat.

Notice the changes in A and B. A remains practically unaltered. B swells and puffs out and the formation of bubbles can be seen to be taking place below the surface. If a small portion of the dough is opened to show the interior, the bubbles can be seen to be burrowing passages and forcing themselves upwards. At the end of the cooking A is close and sodden, with its particles clinging heavily together; B is light and porous, with its particles separated by numerous holes.

The *successful aeration of doughs* depends very largely on the application of the right degree of heat at the right moment. The capacity of a dough to expand as the bubbles formed in it grow larger is due to the elasticity of gluten, the protein constituent of flour. Gluten, like other proteins, is hardened by heat. It is important that the heat used should be just sufficient to set the gluten when the bubbles, whose walls become thinner as they expand, reach the point at which they burst. If the heat is insufficient, the bubbles break before the gluten has set sufficiently to hold them. If, on the other hand, the heat is too great, the gluten sets and a crust forms before the bubbles have expanded as much as they should. The result in either case is a close, heavy, and therefore indigestible mass, instead of a porous, light and digestible one.

The Preparation and Use of Baking Powder.

As we have already seen, to produce carbon-dioxide for the purpose of aeration, bicarbonate of soda and acids are frequently employed. The salt they leave behind in the dough must, of course, be harmless, at least in small quantities. The two acids most frequently used are cream of tartar and tartaric acid, which, with bicarbonate of soda, form respectively sodium potassium tartrate (Rochelle Salts) and tartrate of soda. Both these salts are practically harmless, though not entirely tasteless. The slight bitterness they give to the dough is more noticeable in the case of tartrate of soda than of sodium potassium tartrate. In cakes containing spices or other substances with a decided flavour, the bitter taste is not noticeable and in plain cakes and scones it is often concealed by means of lemon juice, sour milk or buttermilk.

Bicarbonate of soda and acids may be made up in the correct proportions as baking powder and used as required, or they may be added separately to the flour at the time of making the scones, or whatever mixture is to be aerated.

Recipes for Baking Powder.

Ingredients

No. 1.	No. 2.
4 oz. bicarbonate of soda.	2 oz. bicarbonate of soda.
3 oz. tartaric acid.	4 oz. cream of tartar.
4 oz. rice flour.	6 oz. rice flour.

Method for Both. Sift each of the ingredients in turn. Mix the bicarbonate of soda and the acid thoroughly, then add rice flour to keep the powder from becoming lumpy and from absorbing moisture which would cause slight effervescence and so lessen the strength of the baking powder. Put the baking powder through a sifter two or three times to ensure thorough mixing. Store in airtight tins in a dry place.

Proportions for Use.[1]

For scones and plain cakes, use to each pound of flour 2 teaspoonfuls baking powder No. 1, and 4 teaspoonfuls baking powder No. 2.

For rich cakes, use to each pound of flour 1 teaspoonful baking powder No. 1, and 2 teaspoonfuls baking powder No. 2.

The cost of the two kinds is about the same, but No. 2 will, of course, go only half as far as No. 1. On the other hand, No. 2 does not give up its carbon-dioxide to any extent until the dough containing it is heated, while No. 1, made with tartaric acid, effervesces as soon as it is moistened.

When bicarbonate of soda and an acid are added separately to the flour in making scones, etc., cream of tartar is the acid usually chosen. The proportions are 2 teaspoonfuls cream of tartar and 1 teaspoonful bicarbonate of soda to each pound of flour. Both are sifted with the flour used in making the scones, etc.

'*Self-raising' flour* is simply flour containing baking powder or its constituents in the correct proportions.

MAKING SCONES, BUNS AND PLAIN CAKES

The mixtures used for all these are the same in essentials. The table opposite gives an analysis of the ingredients and of the proportions they usually bear to one another. Slight variations will, of course, be found in many recipes.

Method. The putting together of the ingredients is the same for both these mixtures; the variations occur in the making up and cooking of the dough. In both cases this should be done as rapidly as possible. All preparations should be made beforehand in order not to delay the work at the critical stage.

Preparations.

Oven: Prepare a hot oven.

Baking Trays. Grease with dripping, lard, etc., or dredge lightly with flour.

Cake Tins. Line the tins with greased paper; if the mixture contains only a small amount of fruit, greasing the tins will suffice.

Girdle for Scones. Put the girdle on the stove some time before it is required and let it heat gradually. Grease it slightly

[1] Recipes in cookery books usually require baking powder No. 1. If No. 2 baking powder is used, the quantity given in the recipe should be doubled.

Manufactured baking powder should, as a rule, be added in the same proportion as baking powder No. 1.

Ingredients	*Scones*	*Buns and Plain Cakes*
Flour.	½ lb. flour.	½ lb. flour.
Salt.	Pinch of salt.	Pinch of salt.
Shortening.[1]	1–2 oz. margarine *or* clarified beef *or* bacon dripping, *or* lard.	2–4 oz. margarine, *or* clarified beef *or* bacon dripping, *or* lard.
Sugar.	½–1 oz. sugar (optional).	2–4 oz. sugar.
Fruit.	½–1 oz. sultanas *or* currants (optional).	4–6 oz. currants *or* sultanas *or* candied peel *or* any mixture of these.
Flavourings.	—	Small quantities of grated lemon rind, ginger, nutmeg, allspice, or caraway seeds.
Raising Agent.[2]	1 teaspoonful baking powder No. 1. *Or* 2 teaspoonfuls baking powder No. 2. *Or* 1 teaspoonful cream of tartar and ½ teaspoonful bicarbonate of soda.	As for Scones.
Liquid.	¼ pint milk (approximate).	1–2 eggs, with milk to make up rather more than ¼ pint liquid (approximate).

with a piece of suet. If the girdle is sufficiently hot, the fat will at once give off a faint blue vapour.

Making of Scone, Bun or Cake Mixtures.

For all: (1) Sift flour, add salt and rub in shortening as in making short crust (p. 204).

(2) Add sugar (if any) and sift in bicarbonate of soda and cream of tartar *or* baking powder, whichever form of raising agent is used.

(3) Add to the flour the cleaned fruit and the peel, if any, cutting the latter into dice or chopping it finely.

(4) Mix all the dry ingredients together thoroughly and beat up the eggs (if any).

(5) Moisten the dough, adding first egg then milk.

A. Scones. Make the dough just stiff enough to handle. Turn it on to a floured board and make it up by one of the following methods: [Continued on p. 232

[1] See p. 203 as to choice of shortening. Here, also, 'cooking fat' can, if necessary, replace lard or dripping.

[2] Self-raising flour has the raising agent already added to it.

Kind	*Flour, etc.*	*Shortening*	*Sugar*	*Fruit and Flavour*
CURRANT OR SULTANA SCONES.	½ lb. flour. Pinch of salt.	1½ oz. margarine, *or* lard, *or* clarified bacon dripping.	1 oz. sugar.	1 oz. currants or tanas.
FINGER SCONES.	½ lb. flour. Pinch of salt.	2 oz. margarine *or* lard.	1 oz. sugar.	———
BROWN SCONES.	6 oz. wholemeal flour. 2 oz. white flour. Pinch of salt.	1–2 oz. margarine, *or* lard, *or* clarified bacon dripping.	———	———
GIRDLE SCONES.	½ lb. flour. Pinch of salt.	1 oz. margarine.	1 oz. sugar.	———
RASPBERRY BUNS.	½ lb. flour. Pinch of salt.	2 oz. margarine *or* lard.	2 oz. sugar.	1 tablespoonful ra berry jam.
LEMON BUNS.	½ lb. flour. Pinch of salt.	2 oz. margarine *or* lard.	2 oz. sugar.	1–2 oz. candied lem peel. Grated rind of lemon.
BATH BUNS.	½ lb. flour. Pinch of salt.	2 oz. margarine *or* lard.	2 oz. sugar.	2 oz. candied peel. 2 oz. sultanas.

[1] When manufactured baking powder is used, the amo

[2] For *general* directic

Raising Agent[1]	Liquid	Additional Directions[2]
teaspoonful bicarbonate of soda. teaspoonful cream of tartar.	¼ pint of milk.	Divide dough into two portions, knead each into a round cake and mark into quarters. Brush with milk and bake in a quick oven 15–20 minutes. *Or* roll out the dough till it is ½ inch thick, and cut into rounds with a cutter; glaze and bake about 10 minutes. *Or* omit glaze and cook on girdle for 10 minutes.
teaspoonful baking powder No. 1, *or* teaspoonfuls baking powder No. 2.	1 egg. Milk to make up with egg ¼ pint.	Turn the dough on to a floured board, roll lightly to a paste about ½ inch thick and cut into finger-shaped pieces, about 2 inches by ¾ inch. Brush with egg or egg and milk and bake in a quick oven 10–15 minutes.
½ teaspoonful bicarbonate of soda. 1 teaspoonful cream of tartar. - 1 teaspoonful baking powder No. 1.	¼ pint of milk (good measure).	Roll the dough lightly to a paste about ½ inch thick, and cut into rounds with a cutter. Brush with milk and bake in a quick oven for 10–15 minutes.
) ½ teaspoonful bicarbonate of soda. { ½ teaspoonful bicarbonate of soda. 1 teaspoonful cream of tartar.	(*a*) ¼ pint buttermilk or sour milk. (*b*) ¼ pint sweet, new milk.	Roll the dough lightly on a floured board and cut into three-cornered pieces. Bake on a hot greased girdle for 10–15 minutes, turning the scones over with a knife at the end of 6–7 minutes, when the under sides should be a pale brown colour.
teaspoonful bicarbonate of soda. easpoonful cream of tartar.	1 egg. 3–4 tablespoonfuls milk.	Divide the dough into 8 pieces and mould them into buns. With the floured handle of a wooden spoon make a hole in the centre of each, put in a little jam and draw the dough together to cover it. Brush with milk, sift sugar over and bake in a quick oven 15–20 minutes.
teaspoonful baking powder No. 1, *or* easpoonfuls baking powder No. 2.	1 egg. About ¼ pint milk.	Make into a fairly stiff dough and divide into 10 buns. Brush with milk, sprinkle coarse sugar over and bake in a quick oven 15–20 minutes.
teaspoonful bicarbonate of soda. easpoonful cream of tartar.	1 large egg. ⅛–¼ pint of milk.	Divide into 10 buns, brush with milk, sprinkle coarse sugar over and bake in a quick oven 15–20 minutes.

ould, as a rule, be that given for baking powder No. 1.
pp. 228-229.

Kind	*Flour, etc.*	*Shortening*	*Sugar*	*Fruit and Flowerin*
ROCK BUNS.	½ lb. flour *or* 6 oz. flour and 2 oz. ground rice. Pinch of salt.	2–3 oz. margarine, *or* lard, *or* clarified bacon *or* beef dripping.	3 oz. sugar.	3 oz. currants. 1 oz. candied peel (strips). ½ teaspoonful grou ginger. Nutmeg.
PLAIN FRUIT CAKE, No. 1.	1 lb. flour. ½ teaspoonful salt.	8 oz. margarine, *or* 4 oz. margarine plus 4 oz. lard.	½ lb. Demerara sugar.	½ lb. currants, *or* su tanas, *or* Valenc raisins. ¼ lb. candied peel. 1 tablespoonful treacle (warmed)
PLAIN FRUIT CAKE, No. 2.	1 lb. flour. ½ teaspoonful salt.	8 oz. margarine *or* lard *or* 4 oz. margarine plus 4 oz. lard.	½ lb. Demerara sugar.	¼ lb. currants. ¼ lb. sultanas. 2 oz. candied peel. 2 teaspoonfuls a spice. 1 tablespoonful treacle (warmed)
QUICK JAM SANDWICH.	(*a*) ½ lb. self-raising flour *or* (*b*) ½ lb. plain flour.	3 oz. margarine *or* lard.	3 oz. sugar.	1 tablespoonful jam

(*a*) Divide the dough (½ lb. flour) into two, form each piece into a round, and mark it with a knife into quarters.

Or (*b*) press the dough lightly with a rolling-pin into a flat paste about ½ inch thick and cut into rounds with a cutter about 1¼ inches in diameter.

Or (*c*) roll lightly into a paste about ½ inch thick, cut the edges straight with a sharp knife, then cut into 1¼ inch squares, or into finger shapes about 2 inches by ¾ inch.

The size of the scones should increase considerably in cooking.

Raising Agent	*Liquid*	*Additional Directions*
teaspoonful baking powder No. 1, *or* teaspoonfuls baking powder No. 2.	1 egg. 3–4 table-spoonfuls milk.	Make into an extremely stiff dough and put on to the baking sheet in 10–12 high and rock-like buns, with strips of candied peel on each. Brush with milk and sift sugar over. Bake in a very hot oven for 10–15 minutes. *Note.*—If the dough is too moist or the oven too cool, the cakes do not keep their shape.
teaspoonfuls baking powder No. 1, *or* teaspoonfuls baking powder No. 2.	2 eggs. Milk to make up with the egg rather more than ½ pint.	Mix into a rather stiff dough with warmed treacle, beaten eggs and milk. Bake in a fairly quick oven for 1–1½ hours. Let the heat of the oven decrease gradually so that the cake bakes slowly the latter half of the time.
teaspoonful baking powder No. 1. teaspoonful bicar-bonate of soda. teaspoonfuls vinegar.	1 pint milk (bare mea-sure).	Rub the shortening into the flour, add baking powder, bicarbonate of soda and all the dry ingredients. Stir the vinegar into milk, then add it and the warmed treacle to the flour, etc. Put into a greased cake-tin and bake in a slow oven for about 1 hour.
Nil for self-raising flour. 1 teaspoonful bak-ing powder No. 1, *or* teaspoonfuls baking powder No. 2 for plain flour.	1 egg. ⅛ pt. milk (approx.).	Make into a soft, light dough, turn on to a floured board and cut into two. Mould one half lightly into a round cake about ½ inch thick. Put on a greased baking sheet, cover to within ½ inch of edge with jam and damp edges. Mould the second portion similarly and place on top of the first. Brush top with water, sprinkle little sugar over. Bake in a hot oven 20–30 minutes.

Remove superfluous flour and brush the scones with beaten egg, or egg and milk, or milk only to glaze them. Bake in a quick oven 10–15 minutes.

Alternative Plan. Omit glazing, and cook the scones on a hot greased girdle for about 10 minutes, turning them when the under sides are slightly browned.

Scones are best split open, spread with butter or margarine immediately after baking and served hot. Scones which are not newly baked should be warmed in the oven for a few minutes before being eaten.

B. Buns and Small Cakes.

Mix the flour, etc., to a rather soft dough, just stiff enough to be handled. *Exception*: Rock Buns, the dough for which must be as stiff as it can be made, so that the buns are rock-like in shape when baked.

Using two forks, put the dough in small even-sized portions on the baking tray; ½ lb. flour makes 10 or 12 cakes.

Brush with beaten egg, or egg and milk, or milk only; sift sugar over and bake at once in a quick oven for 10–20 minutes.

C. Large Cakes.

Make the dough fairly stiff, put it into the cake-tin and bake at once in a fairly quick oven. When the cake has risen well and is browned slightly, reduce the heat a little and let it decrease gradually for the rest of the baking. When the cake is sufficiently baked the centre will feel firm and a bright skewer pushed in at the thickest part will come out quite clean, with its brightness undimmed.

As soon as they are taken from the oven, small cakes and scones should be put on a cake tray or on a sieve, so that the steam escapes. Large cakes should not be turned out of their tins for 10 minutes or so, lest they break. All should be left in a warm place till they are set. If they are put in a cold place, they become heavy and close.

Recipes for typical scones, buns and cakes are given on pp. 230–233.

The following recipes are of interest as being rather different from the usual type.

Potato Cakes.

Notice that shortening takes the form of suet; baking powder is omitted and the moisture in the potatoes makes the use of other liquids unnecessary.

Ingredients

1 lb. mashed potatoes (preferably freshly prepared. See p. 161).
4 oz. flour.
2 oz. suet.

Method. Remove the skin from the suet and shred it finely. Put it with the flour on a board and roll the two together, till they can no longer be distinguished from each other. Add the potatoes and press the ingredients together well. Turn the mixture on to a floured board, divide into 6 or 8 equal pieces, and form each into a round. Roll these into thin flat cakes. Cook the cakes on a heated and greased girdle or in a heated and greased frying pan. When the underside is a light brown colour, turn the cakes over and brown the other side. Put on a hot plate, one on top of the other, spreading each with margarine and cutting it into quarters. Serve at once.

The cakes may also be baked.

Ginger Cakes.

In these cakes, the shortening is not rubbed into the flour as in other plain cakes, but is melted with the treacle and sugar, which are then mixed with the dry ingredients.

Ingredients	*Ginger Cake No.* 1	*Ginger Cake No.* 2	*Ginger Cake No.* 3
Flour.	¾ lb. flour. Pinch of salt.	10 oz. flour. Pinch of salt.	10 oz. flour. Pinch of salt.
Shortening	¼ lb. margarine.	3 oz. margarine.	¼ lb. margarine.
Sugar.	¼ lb. Demerara sugar.	1 oz. Demerara sugar.	2 oz. Demerara sugar.
Spice.	¼ oz. ground ginger (about 2 teaspoonfuls).	½ oz. ground ginger.	1 oz. ground ginger. 1 teaspoonful Jamaica ginger. ½ oz. allspice.
Fruit, etc.	1½ oz. candied peel.	2 oz. citron. 2 oz. glacé cherries. 2 oz. almonds.	¼ lb. sultanas. 2 oz. almonds.
	1 teacupful treacle (10 oz.).	¼ pint treacle (½ lb.).	¼ pint treacle (½ lb.).
Raising Agent.	½ teaspoonful bicarbonate of soda.	½ teaspoonful bicarbonate of soda.	½ teaspoonful bicarbonate of soda.
Liquid.	1 large *or* 2 small eggs. ⅛ pint of milk.	1 large *or* 2 small eggs. ⅛ pint of milk.	2 eggs. Rather less than ¼ pint of milk.

Method for All. (1) Cut candied peel into small pieces; halve cherries, clean sultanas, blanch almonds, *i.e.* cover with boiling water and leave for about 5 minutes so that the skins can be slipped off, then split them.

(2) Sift the flour, salt and bicarbonate of soda; add spice and fruit and mix together well.

(3) Put margarine, sugar and treacle in a pan and stir over the fire till hot.

(4) Beat the eggs well and add milk.

(5) Add margarine, sugar and treacle, then eggs and milk to the dry ingredients and mix together well.

(6) Put into greased and papered tins and bake in a moderate oven for 1 to 1¼ hours.

Oatmeal Biscuits.

Ingredients

4 oz. flour.	3 oz. margarine *or* dripping.
6 oz. fine oatmeal.	1 egg.
Pinch of salt.	¼ teaspoonful bicarbonate of soda.

3–4 oz. Demerara sugar.

Method. (1) Sift flour, salt and bicarbonate of soda. Add sugar and oatmeal. Mix well.

(2) Make the margarine or dripping hot and beat up the egg.

(3) Add first the shortening, then the egg to the dry ingredients, adding just sufficient egg to make a rather stiff paste.

(4) Roll the paste till it is about ¼ inch thick, cut it into rounds with a cutter or into squares or oblongs with a knife. Put the biscuits on a greased tin and bake in a moderate oven for 10–15 minutes till they are crisp and a pale brown colour.

Ginger Biscuits.

Ingredients

4 oz. flour.	1½–2 oz. margarine.
Pinch of salt.	1½ oz. sugar.
1 oz. rolled or flaked oats.	1½ tablespoonfuls golden syrup.
1 level teaspoonful bicarbonate soda.	1½–1 teaspoonfuls ground ginger.

Method. (1) Sift flour, salt, bicarbonate of soda and add oats.

(2) Melt margarine, sugar, syrup and ginger in a pan and add to dry ingredients; mix well.

(3) Cool slightly then roll into small balls, flouring hands.

(4) Place the balls some distance apart on a well-greased baking sheet and bake in a moderate oven for about 20 minutes, when the biscuits should be firm, crisp and a golden brown colour.

CHAPTER XIX.

THE AERATION OF DOUGHS: (2) YEAST[1]

Microscopical Examination of Yeast. Dip the tip of the finger in water and touch a piece of yeast cake lightly with it. Draw

[1] In this connection, parts of Chapter I should be re-read.

the finger over a glass slide, place the slide under the microscope and examine the yeast cells. Notice how exceedingly numerous they are; examine their shape and appearance and see if any are 'budding', or forming new plants.

Nature and Growth of Yeast. A yeast plant is a single colourless cell of microscopic dimensions, which, under the right conditions, grows and multiplies, putting out 'buds' which grow larger and larger and eventually detach themselves, becoming separate plants.

Yeast plants, so small and light that they are distributed by the wind, are present in the air in great numbers and are known as 'wild' yeasts. For bread-making it is more convenient to use 'cultivated' or 'commercial' yeast, of which there are three forms: (1) brewer's or liquid yeast, (2) dried yeast, (3) compressed yeast. Of these, the last is most widely used, as it aerates the dough most readily and in other ways gives the best and most uniform results.

A cake of compressed yeast, containing millions upon millions of yeast plants, is a firm, pale, buff-coloured mass, slightly resembling putty. In a fresh yeast cake most of the plants are alive and do their work of raising the dough vigorously and rapidly. If the cake is kept for a day or two the plants die by degrees and the action of the yeast goes on less well. If it is not possible to use yeast at once it should be kept in a cool, dry place.

Conditions of Growth of Yeast.

Experiment	*Observation*
Experiment 1. Take 3 test tubes or tumblers *A*, *B*, *C*. Put in *A* ½ teaspoonful fresh yeast cake, crumbling it with the fingers. Put in *B* ½ teaspoonful yeast cake and ½ tablespoonful lukewarm water (i.e. 2 parts cold and 1 part boiling water). *C*. Prepare yeast 'cream' by mixing together until they liquefy ½ teaspoonful yeast and ¼ teaspoonful sugar; add ¼ teaspoonful flour and ½ tablespoonful lukewarm water. Mix and put into the test tube *C*. Put *A*, *B* and *C* in a warm place or in lukewarm water for 10–15 minutes, then examine and compare.	*A*. No change. *B*. Yeast and water mix, but no other change takes place. *C*. Surface of yeast cream is covered with a froth of tiny bubbles of gas. This is carbon dioxide formed by the growth of the yeast plants.

Experiment	*Observation*
Experiment 2. (1) Prepare a little yeast 'cream' as above, and put equal quantities into three test tubes, *A*, *B*, *C*. To *A* add lukewarm water and keep warm as in the previous experiment. To *B*, add cold water and place in a bowl of cold water to which ice or salt has been added. To *C*, add boiling water. Leave *A*, *B* and *C* for 10–15 minutes, then examine and compare.	*A*. Yeast grows vigorously and bubbles of carbon dioxide form. *B* and *C* show no sign of the formation of gas.
(2) Keep *B* and *C* under the same conditions as *A* for 10–15 minutes. Examine and compare.	Yeast in *C* still shows no change, but that in *B* froths as it becomes warm.

It will be clear from these experiments that in order to grow and form carbon-dioxide, yeast requires (1) food, (2) moisture, (3) moderate warmth.

(1) *Food*. Belonging as it does to the group of colourless plants, yeast requires organic food for its life. Among other substances it requires sugar. The flour of which bread-dough is made already contains a small quantity of sugar; it contains also gluten, starch and a substance known as diastase. In the process of bread-making diastase converts some of the starch of the dough into sugar, so that the yeast has an ample supply.

(2) *Moisture*. Yeast requires a considerable amount of moisture; this is provided by the water or milk with which the flour is mixed into a dough.

(3) *Warmth*. Moderate and uniform warmth is necessary for the growth of yeast. Cold checks its growth, though warmth will revive it even when it has been chilled to freezing-point. Too great heat also checks growth and may kill the plants outright.

Results of Yeast Growth. Two distinct changes take place in the dough during the process of bread-making, the first being a preparatory change without which the second could not take place: (1) Diastase changes a portion of the starch into sugar (2) Yeast plants grow and multiply, feeding on the sugar thus prepared, and ferment it, that is, form from it two other substances, carbon-dioxide and alcohol. The bubbles of carbon dioxide collect in the dough and make it swell. When a sufficient quantity of gas has been formed the dough is baked. It i probable that as the gas-bubbles expand in the baking they become filled with water-vapour, the expansion of which completes the aeration of the bread. The heat of the oven drives off the small amount of alcohol formed in the dough and at the same time kills the yeast plants, so that no further supply of gas is formed.

It is noticeable that in addition to raising the dough and so making it more digestible, yeast gives the bread a pleasant flavour which is lacking in bread lightened by the use of the inorganic substances which constitute baking powder.[1]

BREAD-MAKING

The processes of making the different kinds of fermented bread, white, brown, currant, etc., are the same in essentials, and are arranged to provide for the yeast plants the conditions under which they can best do their work of raising the dough.

WHITE 'HOUSEHOLD' BREAD

Ingredients.

Flour. A good quality of household or 'seconds' flour is best for bread which is to constitute a large part of the daily food.

Shortening. 1 oz. lard or bacon dripping to 3 lbs. of flour is sometimes used to enrich the bread.

Salt. 2 teaspoonfuls salt to 3 lbs. flour.

Yeast. 1 oz. compressed yeast to 3–3½ lbs. flour.

Fresh yeast is an even, buff colour, free from brown spots and when broken is slightly moist, though not sticky, inside. If mixed with a little sugar the two rapidly form a creamy liquid, as in Experiment 1.

Sugar. 1 teaspoonful sugar to each ounce of yeast is used to assist fermentation.

Liquid. Water alone is usually used, though occasionally milk is added; bread mixed with water only keeps moist best.

To bring the dough to the temperature at which yeast grows, the liquid must be lukewarm, about 37° C. (98° F.) *when it is used*—not when it is prepared. If a thermometer is not available, the approximate temperature can be obtained by mixing one part of boiling water with two parts of cold water.

[1] Since yeast is a valuable source of vitamin B, it largely compensates for the loss of the vitamin which occurs in milling the flour. It is probable, moreover, that the vitamin is little harmed by the baking of the bread.

We may summarise the ingredients required thus:

No. 1.	*No.* 2[1].
3 lbs. flour. 2 large teaspoonfuls salt. 1 oz. yeast. 1 teaspoonful sugar.	1 lb. flour. 1 small teaspoonful salt. ½ oz. yeast. ½ teaspoonful sugar.
1½ pints lukewarm water *or* milk *or* equal parts of both (approximate).	½ pint lukewarm water *or* milk *or* equal parts of both (approximate).

Processes of Bread-making.

Throughout the work the yeast must be kept at the right temperature for growth; the 'sponge' and dough must be kept warm and must not be exposed to draughts, while the mixing, kneading and moulding of the dough must be done as speedily as possible.

(1) **Mixing.** In this process fermentation begins.

Sift the flour into a warm bowl and put it to warm either near the fire or in a cool oven. If shortening is used, rub it into a small portion of the flour and add it to the remainder. Add salt, crushing out the lumps and mixing well. Make a cavity in the flour.

Method (*A*). Cream yeast and sugar, add about half the lukewarm liquid; mix and pour into the cavity in the warmed flour. Stir in enough flour from the edges to make a thin batter and sprinkle flour on top. This process is known as 'setting the sponge'.

Cover the bowl with a clean, warm tea towel; if the kitchen is cold or draughty, it may be necessary to cover the bowl with a warm rug, in addition to the tea towel. Put the bowl in a warm place for 15–25 minutes, at the end of which time the yeast, if fresh, will be fermenting vigorously, covering the surface of the batter with frothy gas bubbles. Add by degrees the rest of the liquid, re-warming it first if necessary; mix with a wooden spoon, stirring the pond of batter round and round and gradually taking in flour from the sides. Continue until no more can be mixed with the spoon. The dough should be rather soft at this stage; yeast grows more readily in a soft than in a stiff

[1] No. 2 gives the proportions for a small quantity of bread suitable for making in a cookery lesson when time is limited. This quantity of dough is best mixed by Method (*B*) and will take about 1 hour to rise; it can be made up into 6 small twists or cottage loaves, etc. which will take about 20 minutes to bake.

dough. The next process, kneading, will make the dough firmer.

Method (*B*). Cream yeast and sugar in a small bowl, add 1 teaspoonful flour and 4 or 5 tablespoonfuls of lukewarm liquid, cover and put in a warm place for a few minutes till the yeast froths. Then pour the yeast into the cavity in the bowl of flour, add the rest of the lukewarm liquid and moisten the whole of the flour, as in Method (*A*).

(2) **Kneading.** This is done (1) to distribute the yeast evenly throughout the dough; (2) to moisten the flour completely; (3) to make the dough elastic and capable of expansion; (4) to work in air, which will assist fermentation.

To knead the dough, flour the hands lightly; for a small piece, use the fingers and fold the dough from the edges inwards to the centre, tucking each piece down firmly to enclose air. To knead a large piece of dough, clench the hands and manipulate the dough in the same way, throwing the weight of the body on to each hand in turn. In both cases the kneading must be done quickly and vigorously to avoid chilling the dough.

The dough is sufficiently kneaded when it (1) no longer sticks to the sides of the bowl or to the hands; (2) is firm, smooth and shows no dry flour when cut across; (3) feels spongy and elastic and quickly regains its shape when indented. Dough made with 3 lbs. of flour will require 10–20 minutes vigorous kneading; if, after a reasonable time, the dough still clings to the hands, work in a little more flour.

When the kneading is complete, flour the bottom of the bowl, and put back the dough, smooth side uppermost, dredging the top lightly with flour. If a deep cross is cut on the top of the dough, it will be useful later in determining if the dough has risen sufficiently.

(3) **Rising.**[1] This is to allow time for the formation by the yeast of a quantity of carbon-dioxide sufficient to aerate the dough.

Cover the dough with the warmed towel and rugs and put it to rise as before in a warm place. The temperature should be about 21° C. (70° F.) in summer and about 32° C. (90° F.) in winter. If the dough is put near the fire, turn the bowl round from time to time so that each part is warmed in turn.

[1] The mixing, kneading and rising can also be carried out by means of a bread-making machine, which is easily manipulated and makes it unnecessary to handle the dough until it is ready for moulding.

The dough has risen sufficiently when it is so filled with gas bubbles that it feels tense and is swollen to twice its original size; by this time the cross cut on the top will have almost disappeared. The length of the rising varies with the freshness and quantity of the yeast used and with the temperature of the dough. Dough made with 1 oz. fresh yeast to 3 lbs. flour and kept at the right temperature has usually risen sufficiently in from 1¼ to 2 hours.

The importance of letting the dough rise at the right temperature and for the right length of time can hardly be overestimated, for on these, more than on any other factors, depend not only the lightness but also the texture and colour of the bread. If the right degree of moderate and uniform warmth be maintained, the dough will rise as it should and in the normal length of time. But mistakes in gauging the temperature (when a thermometer is not available) and misjudgment of the signs of sufficient rising have serious results.

Insufficient rising, by curtailing the time for the formation of carbon-dioxide, causes the bread to be heavy. Over-rising spoils the colour and texture of the bread and may make it sour. Chilling the dough and overheating it both check the growth of the yeast; if overheating is carried to a sufficient extreme the yeast will be killed outright and the bread be heavy.

Causes of Sourness in Bread. The main cause of souring in bread is the activity of certain bacteria which are present in the yeast in spite of the careful purifying it receives during cultivation. In the normal course of events the yeast plants are so strong and so numerous that the bacteria are overpowered, and the yeast plants can do their work undisturbed and with good results. But when, for any reason, the yeasts become weakened or inactive the bacteria get the upper hand and form acids which make the dough sour.

Souring, then, may be caused by:[1]

(1) Overheating the dough. This causes carbon-dioxide to form so rapidly that the dough rises in less than the normal time; the very rapidity of its own growth weakens the yeast, for, like other organisms, its growth is first checked, then stopped by the substance which it itself forms.

(2) Keeping the dough at the right temperature but allowing it to rise for too long a time. Again the activity of the

[1] We shall see later that sourness may also result from baking the bread in too cool an oven.

yeast becomes exhausted so that bacteria are able to overpower it.

(3) Rendering the yeast inactive by allowing it to become so chilled either in the mixing, kneading or moulding of the dough that it has to be re-warmed before fermentation can begin.

(4) Using stale yeast. In a stale yeast cake the number of living plants is diminished so considerably that the dough takes unduly long to rise and a chance is thus given for the development of bacteria, whose numbers increase as the yeasts die.

The signs of sourness are the sour smell and taste of the dough, which becomes stringy and collapses in the middle.

(4) **Moulding.** The purpose of this is (1) to break up any too large gas bubbles or colonies of bubbles which would cause large holes in the bread, (2) to divide the dough into pieces of a suitable size and shape for baking.

Before moulding the dough, warm the bread tins or baking-sheets slightly and grease them. Flour the fingers, put a piece of dough the required size on a floured board and fold the edges inwards, moulding the dough into a smooth shape as quickly and as lightly as possible. Turn the dough over and knock it lightly with the hands to distribute the air thus enclosed.

Tin-loaves. Make oval-shaped pieces of dough large enough to fill the tins rather more than half full.

Cottage Loaves. Mould the dough into two rounded pieces, one about half the size of the other and put the smaller one on top. Press the handle of a wooden spoon through the centre of both.

Coburg Loaves. Mould the dough into oval shapes and cut deep gashes across the top to give the required crustiness.

(5) **Proving or Second Rising.** This is to make good any loss of warmth in the dough as a consequence of moulding and to complete the process of rising.

Cover the tins or baking sheets warmly, and put them in a warm place as for the first rising. Let the dough rise for 15 minutes or rather longer if necessary. The dough in the tins should rise till it is almost level with the top.

(6) **Baking.** Put the bread into a hot oven and keep the oven door shut for the first third of the time allowed for baking. At the end of this time, moderate the heat slightly and let it decrease very gradually. If the bread rises or colours unevenly, turn it round.

The hot oven is necessary to cause full expansion of the gas bubbles and to kill the yeast plants which by this time have done all the work required of them. If their growth is allowed to continue the bread will be poor in flavour, if not actually sour.

If, therefore, the bread rises very much after it is put into the oven, the oven is too cool. If, on the other hand, the bread browns before it has been in the oven ¼ hour, the heat is too great. When the bread is fully risen and the crust formed, the heat must be diminished to allow the interior of the loaf to cook without the crust being burnt. If the oven door is opened before the gas bubbles have had time to expand fully and the crust to form, the cold draughts may check the rising.

As the bread bakes, the gluten of the flour is hardened and caused to combine with the contents of the burst starch grains. The browning of the crust is the result of the dextrinisation of some of the starch.

Time for Baking. This naturally depends on the size of the loaf. A loaf made from ¾ lb. flour will take about ¾ hour to bake; 1½ lbs. flour, 1¼–1½ hours, and other quantities in proportion.

Tests for Baking. When sufficiently baked the loaves sound hollow when tapped on the bottom. They have a firm and springy crust and only a very faint smell of yeast. They also shrink away from the sides of the tin in which they have been baked.

When the loaves come out of the oven, turn them upside down and rear them up so that the steam may escape. They should cool gradually; bread which is put in a cold place so that it cools rapidly is often heavy.

BROWN BREAD

Ingredients

¾ lb. white flour.
1½ lbs. brown *or* wholemeal flour.
1 large teaspoonful salt.
1 oz. yeast.
1 teaspoonful castor sugar.
1¼ pints lukewarm water *or* water and milk in equal parts.

The making of brown bread differs from that of white only in the following particulars:

(*a*) In proportion to flour, more yeast and rather more liquid are used.

(*b*) The increased proportion of liquid makes the dough so moist that at first it is often necessary to beat it with a wooden spoon instead of kneading it by hand. Afterwards it is kneaded lightly and rapidly, using only the ends of the fingers, so that the dough does not stick.

(*c*) The dough is moulded into small flat cakes or tin loaves. Dough made with brown flour is not suitable for moulding into fancy shapes and if baked in too large loaves or cakes is apt to become dry on the outside before the middle is cooked.

(*d*) The oven should be slightly cooler than for white bread.

The quantity given in the recipe makes four loaves, which will take about 30 minutes to bake.

MILK OR DINNER ROLLS, TEACAKES, CURRANT OR SULTANA BREAD

Milk or Dinner Rolls	*Teacakes*	*Currant or Sultana Bread*
Flour. 1 lb. Vienna *or* 'Household' flour.	*Flour.* 1 lb. Vienna *or* 'Household' flour.	*Flour.* 1 lb. Vienna *or* 'Household' flour.
Salt. 1 teaspoonful.	*Salt.* 1 small teaspoonful.	*Salt.* ½ teaspoonful.
Yeast. ½ oz.	*Yeast.* ½–¾ oz.	*Yeast.* ¾–1 oz.
Sugar. 1 teaspoonful.	*Sugar.* 1 teaspoonful.	*Sugar.* 2–4 oz.
Liquid. ½ pint milk.	*Liquid.* 1 egg and rather less or rather more than ½ pint milk, according as fruit is omitted or added.	*Liquid.* 1 egg and rather more than ½ pint milk *or* 2 eggs and ½ pint milk.
Additions. 1–2 oz. lard or margarine.	*Additions.* 2 oz. margarine or lard. 2 oz. currants *or* sultanas (optional).	*Additions.* 2 oz. margarine or lard. 3–6 oz. currants *or* sultanas. 1–2 oz. candied peel.

It will be noticed that (1) the richer the dough, the greater is the proportion of yeast and of sugar and the smaller the proportion of salt; (2) the proportion of liquid to flour is greater in rich than in plain doughs, making them softer.

(1) **Milk or Dinner Rolls.** Rub the fat into a small portion of the flour and add it to the remainder, previously put to warm. Cream the yeast with sugar, 1 teaspoonful flour and a little warm milk and put it in a warm place to ferment. Moisten the

flour with the fermenting yeast and the remainder of the lukewarm liquid; knead the dough and put it to rise for 1–1½ hours until it is twice its original size. Then mould the dough into 16 rolls. Put to prove for 10–15 minutes and bake in a quick oven for about ¼ hour. Either immediately before or immediately after baking, brush the rolls with beaten egg or beaten egg and milk to glaze the crust.

(2) **Teacakes.** Rub the fat into a small portion of the flour, add it to the remainder, previously mixed with the salt and put to warm. Cream the yeast with the sugar, add the beaten egg and about half the lukewarm milk. Make a cavity in the flour, pour in the yeast-liquid, and stir in a little flour from the edge; cover warmly and put to rise in a warm place for about ½ hour. Then add the remainder of the milk, re-warming it if necessary and mix with a wooden spoon to a rather soft dough. Instead of kneading the dough by hand, beat it with the spoon until it is perfectly smooth and elastic. Put the dough to rise for 1¼–1¾ hours until it has swollen to twice its original size. If fruit is used, warm it slightly and mix it into the dough before moulding. Mould the dough into 6 round flat cakes, using a knife instead of the fingers if necessary. Put to rise 15 minutes, brush with egg or egg and milk and bake in a quick oven 15–20 minutes.

(3) **Currant or Sultana Bread.** Mix the yeast with 1 teaspoonful sugar, 1 teaspoonful flour and 3–4 tablespoonfuls lukewarm milk and put into a warm place till it froths. Rub fat into a small portion of the flour, add it to the remainder previously warmed. Mix in salt and rest of sugar and make a cavity. Pour in yeast, warm milk, and beaten eggs, mix well and beat as for teacakes till the dough is smooth and even. Work in warmed fruit, mould the dough into two pieces and put into warmed greased tins. Cover and put to rise in a warm place for about 2 or 2¼ hours or until the dough is about twice its original size. Brush with egg or egg and milk and bake in a hot oven for ¾–1 hour.

CHAPTER XX

THE AERATION OF DOUGHS: (3) THE MECHANICAL INCLUSION OF AIR

We have already discussed the aeration of doughs by means of carbon-dioxide produced by the chemical action of such substances as those which constitute baking powder, or by the action on sugar of the organism yeast. We come now to the third and much simpler method, aeration by the inclusion, not of one gas, but of several, by the inclusion of the mixture of gases known as air. When, as in making cakes or batter, a dough is lifted up by a spoon or whisk, air fills the spaces left; the beating or whisking is continued until a quantity of air sufficient to make the mixture light and porous has been enclosed. The air expands in the dough when it is cooked, and aeration takes place exactly as it does when carbon-dioxide is used. Again it is probable that the bubbles formed in the dough by the expansion of the air beaten into it become filled with water vapour whose subsequent expansion completes the aeration.

Doughs aerated thus usually have a large proportion of egg in their composition. Eggs are used, not only on account of their power of frothing, *i.e.* of entangling air in their meshes when beaten, but because by their property of hardening on the application of heat they help to set the bubbles in their expanded state.

The white of an egg, it will be remembered, holds air more readily than does the yolk, and for this reason the two are sometimes beaten and added separately to the mixture to be aerated.

THE MAKING OF POUND AND SPONGE CAKES

In a previous chapter we have discussed the making of plain cakes, mixtures with only a moderate amount of shortening which are aerated almost solely by means of baking powder or its constituents. The richer cake mixtures, usually lightened either by the inclusion of air alone or by air aided by small quantities of baking powder, are of two kinds, pound cakes and sponge cakes.

Pound Cakes. The ingredients for these are of similar nature to those used for plain cakes, but the proportions they bear to one another are different, necessitating different treatment and giving different results. Originally pound cakes were made with equal quantities of butter, sugar, flour and eggs, one pound of each, hence the name, and these proportions are kept to more or less, as is shown in the following table of the ingredients forming the basis of cakes of this class:

Foundation for Pound Cakes.

8 oz. flour.
6–8 oz. butter or margarine.
6–8 oz. castor sugar.
} i.e. roughly the weight of the eggs in butter or margarine, sugar and flour.
3–4 eggs (6–8 oz.).
⅛ pint of milk, if required to make a soft batter.
½ teaspoonful baking powder No. 1 *or* 1 teaspoonful baking powder No. 2.

It will be noticed that (1) the proportion of fat to flour is considerably greater in pound cake mixtures than in plain cakes, so much so that it is not practicable to rub it into the flour, the plan adopted in making the latter type of cake; (2) the proportion of egg is such that very little, if any, milk is required.

The general directions for making pound cakes are as follows:

Mixing of Pound Cakes.

(1) For large cakes line the cake-tin with greased paper. For small cakes (*e.g.* Queen Cakes) grease the tins with melted (not hot) margarine.

(2) Prepare any ingredients to be added in the final stages of the mixing so that the beating of the cake can go on uninterruptedly.

(*a*) Clean and pick sultanas, currants, etc. and cut up candied peel.

(*b*) Cut cherries into half and other crystallised fruits into pieces of similar size.

(*c*) Blanch almonds, *i.e.* cover with boiling water and leave for about 5 minutes; remove skins, dry, and cut into halves or strips or chop them, as required.

(*d*) Beat up the eggs.

(3) Put the margarine and sifted sugar into a bowl and beat them until the mixture is light and creamy and drops easily from the spoon.[1]

(4) Put the flour in a sifter and add it alternately with beaten egg to the creamed margarine and sugar. After each addition, stir the mixture until it is uniform, then beat it for a moment or two.

[1] In very cold weather, heating the bowl by putting it in hot water for two or three minutes, facilitates the 'creaming' of the margarine and sugar.

When all the egg and flour have been added thus, the mixture should be the consistency of thick sauce, too stiff to pour and yet much too soft to handle. If required, a little milk must be added to bring the mixture to this consistency.

(5) Beat the cake mixture vigorously for ten minutes, or if no baking powder is to be used, for 15–20 minutes, when it should be light and creamy.

(6) Add the remaining ingredients, fruit, flavourings, etc. and sift in the baking powder, if it is used. Mix thoroughly, givc a final rapid beating and put the mixture quickly into the tin or tins, as the case may be. The tins should not be more than two-thirds full, so that there is room for the cakes to rise. If almonds are included among the ingredients, scatter them on top of the cake and sift sugar over.

Baking of Pound Cakes.

Rich cakes take a longer, slower and more careful baking then the plainer variety.

For baking *large pound cakes* have the oven moderately hot and keep the heat uniform until the cake has risen to its full extent and is lightly browned; this will take from half to three-quarters of the time allowed. Then cover it with a doubled piece of greased paper to keep it from becoming too brown, and let the heat of the oven decrease gradually. The time required to bake the cake depends on its richness and thickness; the thicker the cake and the richer the mixture, the longer baking it will require.

During the baking, and particularly before it is set, the cake should not be moved; neither should the oven door be opened widely nor shut with a bang. Draughts of cold air and movement both tend to destroy the lightness of the cake.

For baking *small cakes, e.g.* Queen Cakes, have the oven rather hotter than for large cakes, but still only moderately hot and bake them for 15–20 minutes.

The cakes, whether large or small, are cooked sufficiently when they feel firm in the centre and when a bright skewer pushed in the thickest part comes out quite clean and un-dimmed.

After baking, put the cakes on a cake tray or on a sieve to cool. Large cakes should not be taken out of the tins for about ½ hour after they are taken from the oven, lest they break.

Illustrative recipes are given below.

Kind.	*Foundation.*			*Eggs, etc.*
	Shortening.	*Sugar.*	*Flour.*	
SEED OR SULTANA CAKE.	6 oz. butter. or margarine.	6 oz. castor sugar.	½ lb. flour. Pinch of salt.	3 eggs, plus ⅛ pint m ½ teaspoonful bak powder No. 1, *or* 1 teaspoonful bak powder No. 2.[1]
PINE-APPLE, GINGER OR CHERRY CAKE.	As above.	As above.	As above.	As above.
MADEIRA CAKE.	½ lb. butter or margarine.	½ lb. castor sugar.	½ lb. flour. Pinch of salt.	4 eggs.
GENOA CAKE.	½ lb. butter or margarine.	½ lb. castor sugar.	¾ lb. flour. Pinch of salt.	4 eggs, plus ⅛–¼ pin milk. ¾ teaspoonful bak powder No. 1, *or* 1½ teaspoonfuls bak powder No. 2.
HEIDEL-BERG CAKE.	½ lb. butter or margarine.	¾ lb. castor sugar.	1 lb. flour. ¼ teaspoonful salt.	5 eggs. 1 teaspoonful crean tartar. ½ teaspoonful bi bonate of soda.
CHOCO-LATE CAKE.	Butter or margarine equal to the weight of two large eggs.	Castor sugar equal to the weight of two large eggs.	Flour equal to the weight of two large eggs. Pinch of salt.	2 large eggs plus n if required. ¼ teaspoonful bak powder No. 1, *or* ½ teaspoonful bak powder No. 2.

[1] When bought baking powder is used, the amount should, as a rule, be t No. 2 are given on p. 227.

Distinctive Ingredients.	*Additional Directions.*
oz. candied lemon peel in dice). z. caraway seeds, *or* z. sultanas.	Put mixture into greased and papered tin, and bake in a moderately hot oven, decreasing the heat gradually when the cake has risen well and is lightly browned. Time, 1½–2 hours.
z. crystallised pineapple *or* ginger *or* glacé herries.	Cut the pineapple, ginger, or cherries into pieces and add to the mixture before the final beating. Bake in a moderately hot oven for about 1½–2 hours.
ated rind of 1 lemon, *or* aspoonful vanilla ssence. z. citron (in dice). ices of citron for top.	Prepare in the usual way, beating the mixture for 15–20 minutes as no baking powder is used. Put into the prepared tin and lay the slices of citron on top. Bake in a moderately hot oven for 1½–2 hours.
. currants. . sultanas. . mixed peel. ated rind of ½ lemon. oz. almonds, blanched nd split.	Put into a square tin to the depth of 2½–3 inches. Sprinkle the almonds on top and sift sugar over. Bake in a moderately hot oven for 1½–2 hours.
b. preserved pineapple optional). nilla essence. oz. almonds, blanched nd split.	Mix crushed cream of tartar and bicarbonate of soda with 1 tablespoonful flour and add at the last. If pineapple is used, chop it and add it just before the final beating. Put the mixture into the cake-tin to the depth of 2 inches. Sprinkle almonds on top, sift sugar over and bake in a fairly hot oven for 1 hour, decreasing the heat after the first 20 minutes.
oz. grated *or* powdered hocolate *or* cocoa. aspoonful vanilla ssence. *itter' icing.* ½ oz. butter *r* margarine. ½ oz. castor sugar, ½ oz. grated hocolate, vanilla essence. *gar icing.* 1 oz. lump ugar, 1 teaspoonful vater.	Mix chocolate or cocoa with the flour and add it alternately with beaten egg to the creamed fat and sugar. Add the vanilla at the last, put the mixture in a sandwich tin and bake in a moderate oven for ¾–1 hour. When cold, split and spread with the 'butter' icing. 'Butter' icing. Beat the butter or margarine and sugar to a cream, then work in the grated chocolate and vanilla essence. *Sugar icing.* Dissolve sugar in water, draw pan back from the fire, add chocolate or cocoa and beat till smooth. The icing must be warmed without

en for Baking Powder No. 1. The recipes for Baking Powder No. 1 and

Kind.	*Foundation.*			*Eggs, etc.*
	Shortening.	*Sugar.*	*Flour.*	
CHOCOLATE CAKE *continued.*				
QUEEN CAKES.	4 oz. butter or margarine.	4 oz. castor sugar.	6 oz. flour. Pinch of salt.	2 eggs, plus milk if quired. 1 teaspoonful bak powder No. 1, *or* 2 teaspoonfuls bak powder No. 2.
RICE CAKES.	4 oz. butter or margarine.	4 oz. castor sugar.	4 oz. flour. 4 oz. ground rice. Pinch of salt.	2 eggs, plus milk required. ½ teaspoonful bak powder No. 1, *or* 1 teaspoonful bak powder No. 2.
FAIRY CAKES.	4 oz. butter or margarine.	4 oz. castor sugar.	5 oz. flour.	2 eggs. Small ½ teaspoo baking powder N *or* 1 small teaspoo baking powder N

Cake Pudding Mixtures, *e.g.* Bakewell pudding, Madeleine puddings, will be found to bear a close resemblance to pound cakes both in the ingredients used and in the method of putting them together. The mixtures may be baked either alone or in combination with pastry and may also be steamed. Recipes for puddings of this kind will be found in any good cookery book.

Sponge Cakes.

If the recipes for these very light cakes are examined it will be noticed that (1) no butter or other fat is used; (2) the amount of flour is less than in other cake mixtures; (3) in the genuine sponge cakes, eggs alone form the liquid; in the more economical variety, eggs are reinforced with milk and baking powder is used.

The methods of combining the ingredients, as would be expected, differs from that adopted for plain and pound cakes.

Distinctive Ingredients.	*Additional Directions.*
oz. grated chocolate *or* cocoa. w almonds blanched and split.	being made at all hot or it will be dull instead of glossy. Pour it evenly over the cake and decorate it with the almonds.
z. currants. ated rind of ¼ lemon.	Put the mixture into 12–14 Queen-cake tins, filling them about half full. Bake at once in a moderately hot oven for 15–20 minutes.
nilla essence, *or* ated lemon rind.	Mix the flour and ground rice together and add alternately with beaten egg to the creamed fat and sugar. Grease about 18 small tins and dust them with a mixture of flour and castor sugar in equal parts; fill the tins half full and bake in a moderately hot oven 15–20 minutes.
w drops of almond essence. z. glacé cherries } z. angelica } cut into small pieces.	Prepare mixture in the usual way and bake in greased Queen-cake tins, putting 1 large teaspoonful of it in each tin. Sprinkle pieces of cherry and angelica on top and bake in a moderately hot oven for 15–20 minutes.

No. 1. Economical Sponge-Mixture. (for Swiss Rolls, Sandwich Cakes, etc.)

Ingredients

2 eggs.
3 oz. castor sugar.
2 oz. flour.
2 tablespoonfuls milk.
½ teaspoonful baking powder No. 1, *or*
1 teaspoonful baking powder No. 2.

No. 2. Sponge Cakes.

2 eggs.
4 oz. castor sugar.
3 oz. pastry flour (bare measure).
Vanilla essence *or* grated lemon rind.

No. 1. Swiss Roll or Sandwich Cake.

Method. For the quantities given, the Swiss roll tin should measure about 12 inches × 7 inches × 1 inch, and the sandwich tin be 8 inches in diameter.

(1) Brush the tin with warm, not hot, margarine. Prepare a mixture of 1 teaspoonful fine flour and 1 teaspoonful castor sugar. Sift this thickly over the tin, moving it about so that every

part is covered; empty out any which does not stick to the tin. The tin must always be prepared beforehand to give time for the coating to set and to prevent delay in baking the cake.

(2) Break the eggs into a bowl and remove the 'specks'. Add sifted sugar and whisk until the mixture is light and creamy and sufficiently stiff to keep its shape for a moment when it is dropped from the whisk.

(3) Sift the flour into the bowl and fold it in, stirring the mixture as little as possible. Add the sifted baking powder and milk, mix and put at once into the prepared tin.

(4) Bake in a fairly quick oven for about ten minutes. To test the baking, press the centre of the cake lightly with the tip of the finger. If the cake is baked sufficiently, it will at once regain its shape; it will also shrink away slightly from the sides of the tin.

(5) *Swiss Roll.* Loosen the edges of the roll and reverse as quickly as possible on to a sugared paper laid on a cloth previously wrung out of hot water. Trim the sides of the roll, spread with warmed jam or lemon cheese and roll up lightly and speedily. Sift castor sugar over.

The hot cloth helps to keep the cake supple and to prevent its cracking in the rolling. If the cake is over-baked or if there is delay in the rolling, it will probably crack.

Sandwich Cake. Let the cake remain in the tin for a few minutes to allow it to shrink from the sides, then loosen it round the edges if necessary and turn it carefully on to a sieve. When it is cold, split it open and spread on it lemon cheese or jam. Replace the upper part of the cake and sift castor sugar over.

Raspberry or Strawberry Cake. Spread on the cake crushed raspberries or strawberries, sweetened with sugar (½ lb. fruit, 1½–2 oz. sugar). If the cake is not to be eaten while it is quite fresh, the fruit should be stewed slightly.

No. 2. Sponge Cakes. Make in the same way as Swiss Rolls. Put the mixture into a mould prepared in the same way as the tin for Swiss Rolls, with the addition of a piece of greased paper tied round so that it projects a few inches above the top. Bake in a very moderate and steady oven for from ½–¾ hour. When the cake has risen well and is coloured lightly, cover it with greased paper. To prevent undue browning of the bottom of sponge cakes, put in the oven a dripping tin containing a thick layer of salt or fine sand and place the cakes on it.

Sponge cakes should stand for a few minutes before being turned out, so that they may shrink away from the sides of the mould. They must be turned out on to a sieve and kept in a warm place till set.

BATTERS

These are semi-fluid mixtures of eggs and flour to which are added milk or water and melted butter or oil, according as the batter is:

Type 1. Batter to be used for Yorkshire pudding, pancakes, etc. (Recipes 1, 2, 3, below.)

Type 2. 'Frying batter' to be used to coat fish, fruit, etc., to be fried. (Recipe 4 below.)

In both types, aeration is brought about solely or mainly by mechanical means. When the proportion of egg is small, as it is in an economical batter, it is well to use a small quantity of baking powder to assist aeration.

Recipes for Batters.

No. 1 *Batter*	*No.* 2 *Batter*	*No.* 3 *Batter*	*No.* 4 *Batter*
Flour. ½ lb.	*Flour.* ½ lb.	*Flour.* 1½ oz.	*Flour.* 4 oz.
Salt. ¼ teaspoonful.	*Salt.* ¼ teaspoonful.	*Salt.* A pinch.	*Salt.* A pinch.
Eggs. 2.	*Eggs.* 4.	*Eggs.* 1.	*Eggs.* Whites of 2 eggs.
Milk. 1 pint.	*Milk.* ⅞ pint (bare measure).	*Milk.* ¼ pint.	*Water.* ¼ pint.
Baking Powder. 1 teaspoonful.			*Melted Butter* or *Salad Oil,* 1 tablespoonful

Batter No. 1, the least rich, is suitable for Yorkshire pudding, baked batter pudding, or pancakes of the plain and fairly substantial order.

Batter No. 2, as will be seen by comparing the proportions of the different ingredients, is a lighter and richer batter than No. 1 and can be used for the same purposes.

Batter No. 3 (6 oz. flour, 4 eggs, 1 pint milk) is as rich as No. 2, but rather less solid and makes very light pancakes.

Batter No. 4, frying batter, is considerably thicker than any of the others so that it will cling to the food to be fried. Yolks of eggs are omitted and the whites are beaten stiffly to make the batter crisp.

Mixing of Batters. All batters are best mixed some hours before cooking to allow time for the starch grains of the flour to become soaked and swollen. In this condition they burst more readily in the cooking than if the batter were used at once. Beaten white of egg and baking powder cannot, of course, be added until immediately before the batter is cooked.

To mix Batters Nos. 1, 2, 3.

(1) Sift the flour into a bowl, add salt and make a hollow in the centre.

(2) Beat the eggs slightly and add rather less than half the milk to be used; pour these into the hollow in the flour. With a wooden spoon, stir the liquid gently round and round, so that the flour from the sides is worked in gradually, making a *smooth* batter, semi-fluid, but stiff enough to be beaten easily.

(3) Beat or whisk the batter vigorously for about 10 minutes, until it is full of air bubbles, the bigger ones of which burst as fast as they form.

(4) Mix in the remainder of the milk and leave the batter to stand for 1 hour, or longer if possible.

(5) Add sifted baking powder, if used, immediately before cooking the batter and mix it in thoroughly.

Alternative Method. Use only the yolks of eggs in mixing the batter. Just before the batter is cooked, beat the whites stiffly and fold them carefully into the batter, adding the baking powder, if used, at the same time.

To use Batters Nos. 1, 2, 3.

Yorkshire Pudding. For the quantity of batter given put 1 oz. dripping in a baking tin and heat it in the oven till a faint blue smoke comes from it. Pour in batter No. 1 or No. 2 to the depth of about ¾ inch. Bake in a hot oven ½–¾ hour until the pudding has risen well and is lightly browned. Serve at once.

Baked Batter and Fruit Pudding.

Ingredients

Batter No. 1 or No. 2.
1 oz. castor sugar.
1 lb. apples, *or* 1 lb. ripe juicy cherries or other fruit.

Method. Peel and core the apples and cut them into neat even-sized pieces. If cherries are used, take off the stalks and wipe with a damp cloth.

Grease a pie or soufflé dish thickly with margarine, fill it two-thirds full with the sweetened batter and drop in the prepared fruit. Bake in a hot oven for ¾–1 hour.

Pancakes.

Ingredients

Batter No. 2 or No. 3.
1–2 oz. lard.
Lemon and castor sugar.

Method. (1) Melt the lard in a frying pan, pour it into a cup, keep it warm and use as required.

(2) Put into a frying pan just sufficient melted lard to form a thin film over the surface, and heat it till a blue vapour rises from it.

(3) Put some of the batter into a small jug with a lip. Pour into the middle of the pan enough batter to make a thin layer. If the fat is sufficiently hot, the batter will spread all over the pan at once; if it does not do this, tilt the pan from side to side. Cook the pancake fairly quickly.

(4) When the batter has set, loosen it round the edges with a knife, then shake the pan or pass a palette knife under the pancake, so that it does not stick at any point.

(5) When the pancake is lightly browned on the underside, toss it or turn it with a knife and brown the second side.

(6) Turn the pancake on to a sugared paper, putting undermost the side cooked first; sprinkle a little lemon juice and sugar over; roll up and serve as soon as possible on a hot dish.

Note. If the frying pan is new or has not been used for some time, 'season' it before use to keep the pancakes from sticking. To do this, put in it ½ oz. lard or dripping and heat it till it smokes strongly. Pour the fat away and wipe the pan with paper. The pan is then ready for use.

To Mix Batter No. 4 (*Frying Batter*).

Ingredients

4 oz. flour.
Pinch of salt.
Whites of 2 eggs.
¼ pint of water.
1 tablespoonful melted margarine or salad oil.

Method. (1) Sift the flour into a basin, add salt and make a hole in the centre of the flour. Pour in the melted margarine or oil and add gradually the water, tepid or cold, according as margarine or oil is used. If melted margarine is used the tepid water should follow it at once so that the margarine does not harden and make the mixing of the batter difficult.

(2) Mix the batter smoothly, then beat as before till it is full of air bubbles.

(3) Leave uncooked for 1 hour or longer; immediately before use beat the whites of eggs stiffly and fold them uniformly into the batter.

To use Frying Batter.[1]

Fruit Fritters.

(1) *Oranges.* Remove peel and white skin, cut into transverse slices $\frac{1}{4}$ inch thick and take out the pips.

Apples. Peel, core and cut into transverse slices $\frac{1}{4}$ inch thick.

Bananas. Cut into halves lengthways and divide into pieces about 2 inches long.

(2) Heat the fat till the blue vapour appears, then draw it aside for a second or two. Dip the prepared fruit in the batter and put the pieces into the fat, three or four at a time, replacing the pan over the fire or heat. Fry gently till the fritters are crisp and golden.

(3) Lift out on a flat egg-beater or with a skewer and drain carefully, first over the fat, then on crumpled pieces of absorbent paper. Arrange on a hot dish, sprinkle thickly with castor sugar and serve at once.

Fish Fried in Batter.

Ingredients

Fillets or other small sections of fish.
Salt, pepper and lemon juice.
Batter No. 4.
Lemon and parsley for garnish.

Method. Cut the fillets or whatever fish is to be fried into neat pieces, wash, dry, rub with flour, season with salt and pepper and dip into the frying batter to which a little lemon juice has been added. Fry exactly as for fruit fritters. Drain well and serve on a hot dish garnished with parsley and lemon.

[1] Fat used for frying batters must not be dark or discoloured or the colour of the fritters will not be good. It is inadvisable to use a frying basket, as the batter clings to the wires. The fat must always be strained carefully after use to remove all the pieces of batter.

CHAPTER XXI

THE UTILISATION OF COOKED FOODS

It is undeniable that, in most cases, food is in every way at its best when it is freshly cooked, and in arranging meals a housekeeper usually orders food in such quantities as she expects will be required for immediate use. But because, among other reasons, the human appetite is a factor upon which it is difficult to calculate with any degree of certainty, it frequently happens that some portion, large or small, of the food provided remains uneaten; such food has, as a rule, to undergo further treatment to convert it into a presentable dish and to ensure its providing the maximum of nourishment.

Generally speaking, it is advisable to re-heat food for three reasons:

1. *To increase its digestibility.*

Food which has already been cooked has usually suffered some loss of flavour and cold food is not unseldom most unattractive in appearance. Skilful re-heating, by remedying these defects, makes it more digestible, for the reason that ill-flavoured and uninviting food fails to stimulate the glands whose business it is to secrete the substances necessary to bring about digestion. Lack of warmth also makes cold foods indigestible, since digestion cannot begin until the food is at the temperature of the body. When cold food is eaten, heating it to this temperature is bound to use up some of the heat of the body, heat which, in winter particularly, can ill be spared.

2. *To provide variety.*

It is a well-authenticated fact that monotony in a diet makes for indigestibility. The avoidance of monotony is particularly difficult in housekeeping for small families. Good réchauffés provide welcome variety. But the word "hash" has a sinister meaning and it is important to realise that the making of réchauffés requires imagination, care and skill if they are to be successful.

3. *From motives of economy.*

Small portions of meat, fish or vegetables, which are too unsightly or in too small quantities to be served as they are, can often be combined with sauce or gravy, also left over, and can be reinforced with such economical additions as macaroni, rice, haricot beans, potatoes.

We have already indicated in Chapter V the kinds of foods which, in the daily inspection of the larder, should be set aside for further treatment, and it now remains to show how these may best be utilised.

RÉCHAUFFÉS OF MEAT

In making these certain points are of importance:

1. *The condition of the meat must be taken into consideration in deciding the method of re-heating.*

(*a*) If the meat is already well cooked, the re-heating must not be too prolonged. Such meat is best made into croquettes, rissoles or similar dishes, for which a rapid frying provides the necessary heat.

(*b*) For undercooked meat, the slower methods are more suitable, and the meat should be heated in sauce or gravy in the form of curry, hash or mince, etc.

(*c*) If the meat is in small and unsightly scraps, a method of re-heating should be chosen which will involve its division into fine pieces and so disguise its appearance. Such meat can be converted into Shepherd's Pie, Croquettes, Mince, etc.

2. *The loss of flavour must be made up.*

This may be done by the addition of:

(*a*) Good well-flavoured gravy or stock. The jellied meat juices which collect under the cake of dripping obtained from a baked joint should always be used thus.

(*b*) One or more of the following, if they are available:

(1) *Other Meats*	(2) *Vegetables*	(3) *Herbs, Seasonings*	(4) *Flavouring Essences*
Ham. Tongue. Bacon. Sausage meat. Kidney. Liver.	Onion or shallot. Mushrooms. Tomatoes, etc.	Parsley. Thyme. Marjoram, etc. Salt. Pepper. Cayenne.	Anchovy essence. Tomato essence. Worcester sauce, etc.

The proportion of ham, tongue, etc., to the foundation meat should be as 1–3. Onions and shallots should be used only in small quantities and the amount of flavouring sauces and essences should also be small. Their flavour must merely be suggested and must never predominate.

The following list gives successful combinations of meat and flavourings; the list is by no means exhaustive.

By 'meat' in the recipes given, such mixtures of meat as are described in this list are implied.

(*a*) *Beef* (*fresh or salt*) may be re-heated with additions of tongue or ham or bacon or liver or sausages and flavoured with (*a*) tomatoes or tomato sauce, or (*b*) mushrooms or mushroom ketchup, or (*c*) anchovy sauce.

(*b*) *Mutton and lamb* may be re-heated with additions of game, liver, kidney or sausage meat and flavoured with (*a*) tomatoes or tomato sauce, or (*b*) mushrooms or mushroom ketchup, or (*c*) Worcester or similar sauce.

(*c*) *Veal, chicken and game* may be re-heated with additions of ham or bacon or sausage meat or forcemeat and flavoured with button mushrooms or mushroom ketchup, lemon juice and a pinch of nutmeg.

(*d*) *Small portions of meat of several kinds*, *e.g.* beef, mutton, veal, etc., may be re-heated together, preferably with the addition of a little flavouring meat, *e.g.* sausage, tongue, etc.

3. *Steps must be taken to ensure that the réchauffé is made thoroughly hot and its different flavours intimately blended, without at the same time overcooking the meat.*

(*a*) Uncooked materials, *e.g.* onion or other vegetables, starch-thickened sauces must be cooked well before being mixed with the meat.

(*b*) The meat must be protected in some way from receiving too great heat. Such protection is given by (1) gravy or sauce with which the meat is mixed, (2) casings of pastry, batter, or egg and breadcrumbs in which the meat is enclosed, (3) coverings of mashed potatoes, boiled rice, etc.

In this connection it should be remembered that all foods are bad conductors of heat and that it takes a longer time than is generally realised for réchauffés to become thoroughly hot; meat hash or mince and fish kedgeree, in particular, are often served in a tepid state. When the food is made into rissoles, croquettes, etc., which are fried, the heat of the fat is so great that there is not the same difficulty in making it perfectly hot.

Methods of Re-heating Meat.

Almost all the many ways of disguising and re-heating cold meat can be classified as belonging to one or other of the following types or as being variations of them:

Type 1. *A*. Meat sliced or minced and re-heated in a well-flavoured sauce or gravy ($\frac{1}{2}$–$\frac{3}{4}$ pint sauce or gravy to 1 lb. meat).

B. Meat sliced or minced, mixed with a smaller proportion of sauce or gravy or stock than in *A* ($\frac{1}{4}$–$\frac{1}{2}$ pint to 1 lb. meat) and baked in a dish with a covering of mashed potato or pastry.

Type II. A. Slices of meat encased in or covered with batter and fried or baked.

B. Minced meat bound together with sauce or egg or both, moulded into shape, and covered with beaten egg and bread-crumbs or enclosed in pastry. Such mixtures are fried or, if the pastry casing is used, may be fried or baked.

Type III. A. Minced meat with additions of breadcrumbs, etc. moistened with gravy or egg or both, and steamed or baked in moulds. The moulds are turned out and served hot or cold.

B. Minced meat prepared as above, but baked inside hollowed vegetables; *e.g*. vegetable marrows, tomatoes, onions.

C. Minced meat prepared as above, formed into balls, covered with sauce and baked in the oven.

Type IV. Small pieces of meat, preferably chicken or veal, put into a mould previously decorated with ham, etc. and covered with stock in which gelatine has been dissolved. The moulds are turned out when the stock has set to a jelly and are served with or without salad.

Making of Réchauffés of Meat.

Preparation of Meat. The first steps in the preparation of the meat are the same for dishes of all types and consist in the removal of uneatable parts, skin, gristle, bone and superfluous fat. Bones and gristle should be put into the stock-pot; fat should be clarified and melted for use as dripping.

Type I. A. Meat re-heated in Sauce or Gravy, e.g. Hash, Mince.

For dishes of this type, meat which is rather underdone is best. For hash or curry, cut it into small neat slices; for mince cut it up finely, preferably by hand. Mincing machines reduce the meat to an uninviting pulp.

The re-heating is best done in a double pan and for meat in

slices at least 1 hour should be allowed. It will be obvious that the more finely the meat is divided the more readily will it become hot, the more thoroughly will the different flavours blend and the less will be the danger of over-cooking. It is for this reason that minced meat is, as a rule, a greater success than meat in the form of hash. Illustrative recipes are on pp. 264–267.

Type I. B. Meat sliced or minced and baked.

Shepherd's Pie.

Ingredients

1 lb. cooked meat.
1 tablespoonful sauce (Anchovy, Worcester, etc., according to kind of meat).
Salt, pepper, cayenne.
¼ pint gravy prepared as for mince (p. 266).
1–1¼ lbs. mashed potatoes (p. 161).
3–4 slices of bacon, *or*
½ oz. margarine.

Method. Cut up the meat finely as for mince, or into small slices as for hash. Season it well and mix with the sauce and gravy. Grease a pie or other fireproof dish and put a layer of potato on the bottom. Put in the meat and gravy and cover with the remainder of the potato. Smooth the potato with a knife heated in hot water for a moment or roughen it slightly with a fork. Put pieces of bacon or small pieces of margarine on top and bake in a moderate oven for ¾–1 hour, by which time the potatoes should be browned.

Plainly boiled potatoes put through a masher may be substituted for potatoes mashed with margarine and milk, provided an additional ¼ pint of gravy be used.

Squab Pie.

Ingredients

8 oz. cooked meat, freed from skin, gristle and superfluous fat.
½ lb. onions.
1½ lbs. apples.
Salt and pepper.
Stock.
Short pastry (6 oz. flour, etc.—see pp. 208, 204).

Method. Cut meat into thin slices; peel onions, slice thinly or chop; peel and core the apples and cut into slices. Put meat, onions and apple in layers in a pie dish, seasoning each layer of meat and onion with salt and pepper; the top and bottom layers should be apple. When the dish is full, pour in stock to come about half-way up the dish.

Cover the pie with short pastry, make a slit in the top and bake in a fairly hot oven for about 1¼ hours. Reduce the heat slightly towards the end of the time, covering the pie, if necessary, with a greased paper to prevent burning.

Type II. A. Slices of Meat cooked in Batter.

Meat Fritters (Meat fried in Batter).

Ingredients

6 oz. cooked meat.
1 tablespoonful chopped parsley.
Salt, pepper.
Little tomato sauce or mushroom ketchup.

COMPARATIVE RECIPES FOR COLD MEA

Dish.	*Meat.*	*Gravy.*	*Additions.*
CURRY OF COLD MEAT. (BEEF, OR MUTTON, OR VEAL, OR FOWL.)	1 lb. cooked meat (beef, mutton, veal or fowl, plus suitable flavouring meat).	1½ oz. margarine or dripping. ¾ oz. flour. 1 tablespoonful curry powder. 1 teaspoonful curry paste. Juice of ½ lemon. 2 small onions. ½ sour apple. 1 teaspoonful chutney. 1 tablespoonful tomato pulp, *or* 1 tomato (sliced). ¾ pint stock or water.	6 oz. Patna ri (boiled accor ing to dire tions on p. 14
HASH NO. 1. (BEEF, OR MUTTON OR LAMB.)	1 lb. cooked meat (beef or mutton or lamb, plus suitable flavouring meat).	¾ oz. margarine or dripping. 1 small onion or shallot. 1–2 mushrooms (optional). ¾ oz. flour. ¾ pint stock. Salt and pepper.	2 turnips. 2 carrots. 1 slice of toast.

Frying Batter

¼ lb. flour.
1 tablespoonful melted margarine or oil.
¼ pint water.
Whites of 2 eggs.

Method. Cut meat into pieces about 2 inches square. Put them on a dish and sprinkle with parsley, etc. Leave for about ¼ hour, turning occasionally.

Prepare batter (see p. 257), coat the pieces of meat with it and fry them, two or three at a time, in deep fat. Drain on crumpled paper, pile on a hot dish and serve very hot.

Type II. B. Minced meat bound with sauce or egg and moulded.

Group I. Minced meat bound with sauce.

The stiffness of the starchy binding sauce and its proportion

SHES OF TYPE 1A. HASH, MINCE, ETC.

Making of Gravy.	*Re-heating of Meat.*	*Serving.*
lake the gravy according to method described for curry of n meat (see p. 104), omitting wning meat.	Put the meat and gravy into the inner vessel of a double saucepan. Put boiling water in the outer pan and let the water boil gently for at least 1 hour.	Serve the meat and gravy on a hot dish. Arrange the boiled rice in a border round the curry or serve it separately in a vegetable dish.
) Put carrots and turnips into ing salted water and boil 10–inutes if old, 5–10 minutes if ng, allowing the longer time in case for the carrots; drain cut into thin slices.) Prepare gravy as for stew of e 2 (see p. 106) omitting wning the meat, but frying the pped onion and mushrooms he margarine or dripping. wn the flour, add the stock ually, bring gravy to boil and 3–4 minutes.	Put gravy into the inner vessel of a double saucepan, add prepared meat and parboiled carrot and turnip. Put boiling water into the outer pan and let the water boil for at least 1 hour	Make the toast and cut it into neat triangular pieces. Arrange the meat on a hot dish, strain the gravy over it and arrange the vegetables in little heaps at intervals round the dish. Complete the garnish with the toast.

Dish.	*Meat.*	*Gravy.*	*Additions.*
HASH No. 2. (BEEF OR MUTTON IN TOMATO SAUCE.)	1 lb. cooked beef or mutton, in slices ½ inch thick.	1–2 oz. margarine. ½ oz. flour. ½ pint tomato sauce (see p. 168, omitting thickening of potato flour). ⅛ pint gravy from meat. Salt, pepper and cayenne.	6 oz. rice or ma roni (optio boiled accc ing to di tions on pp. and 144, pectively.
HASH No. 3. (VEAL OR FOWL.)	1 lb. cooked veal or similar quantity of cooked fowl, plus suitable flavouring meat.	1–2 oz. margarine. ½ oz. flour. ½ pint white stock. 1–2 small onions (whole). Blade of mace. 5 peppercorns. 1 bayleaf, 1 sprig parsley. Salt. Yolk of 1 egg. 1 tablespoonful stock. ½ teaspoonful lemon juice.	¼ lb. bacon bacon rolls (roll up sn pieces of bac thread on ske and cook about 5 mins oven or un gas griller).
MINCE. (BEEF, OR MUTTON, OR VEAL, OR FOWL.)	1 lb. cooked meat (beef, mutton, veal, or fowl, plus suitable flavouring meat).	½ pint gravy as for Hash No. 1, *i.e.* ½ oz. margarine or dripping. 1 small onion or shallot. 1–2 mushrooms. ½ oz. flour. ½ pint of stock (brown stock for beef or mutton, white stock and milk for veal or fowl.) Salt and pepper.	*Beef and Mutt* (*a*) 3 poached 3 hard bo eggs (pp. 72 70). *Veal and fowl.* (*a*) Bacon roll lb. bacon, Hash No. 3).

to the amount of meat vary according to the purpose for which the mixture is intended.

For each ½ lb. of cooked meat the ingredients for the sauce are:

No. 1.	*No.* 2.
1 oz. margarine. 1 oz. flour. ⅜ pint stock *or* water.	1 oz. margarine. 1 oz. flour. ¼ pint stock *or* water.

Making of Gravy.	*Re-heating of Meat.*	*Serving.*
Melt margarine, add flour and ok gently for 3–4 minutes with- t letting them colour. Add gra- ally the gravy and tomato ıce, bring to the boil and boil 4 minutes. Add seasonings.	Put gravy into double pan, add pre- pared meat and heat 1 hour, letting water in the outer pan boil gently.	Arrange meat neatly on a hot dish, beat up sauce to make it smooth and pour it over the meat. If rice or macaroni is served arrange it in a border round the dish.
Stage 1. Melt margarine, add ur and cook carefully without louring for 3–4 minutes. Add ck gradually, bring to boil, d onions, herbs and salt. The vy is now ready for the addi- n of the meat. *Stage* 2. When the meat is oked, strain the gravy, return it the pan and re-heat it. Beat up yolk of egg and add 1 table- oonful cold stock or gravy. ıen the gravy is hot but not ling, add the egg and cook efully till it thickens. Flavour gravy with lemon juice.	Transfer gravy to double pan and put with it the prepared meat. Heat for 1 hour, letting the water in the outer pan boil gently. At the end of the time take out the meat and complete the making of the gravy as directed (Stage 2).	Put the meat on a hot dish. Pour the thickened gravy over the meat and garnish the dish with bacon rolls.
Prepare as for Hash No. 1, *i.e.* onion or shallot in margarine dripping, remove from the ı, add flour and cook well, ping it colourless for fowl or l and browning it for beef or tton. Add stock gradually, ng to the boil and boil 3–4 ıutes. Season well.	Put gravy into double pan and add minced meat. Pour boiling water into the outer pan and let it boil gently for ¾ hour.	Serve mince on hot dish, garnished with poached eggs or boiled eggs quartered length- ways, or bacon rolls, whichever are used. If mashed potatoes are served with the mince, arrange them in a border round the meat.

Preparation of Mixtures.

Cut up the meat finely or pass it through a mincing machine. Prepare the sauce exactly as though making white sauce (Method 2, p. 152), *i.e.* melt margarine, add flour, cook carefully without colouring for 2–3 minutes, add stock gradually, bring to the boil and boil for a few minutes. Mix the prepared meat with the sauce, add seasonings and flavourings and cook very gently for 5 minutes. Spread the meat mixture evenly on a plate and let it cool. When it is firm, divide it into equal portions and form each into the required shape. Dip the fingers in flour to do this and sprinkle a little flour on the board. Care must be taken to avoid working flour into the mixture, since the swelling of the starch grains in the cooking will make the croquettes, etc. burst open.

Sauce No. 1, when mixed with the meat, gives a somewhat soft meat paste, suitable for making into croquettes or for enclosing in the pastry. The paste must be cooled for at least an hour or for still longer in summer, to make it sufficiently firm to handle. Except in hot weather when it would be liable to go bad it may conveniently be prepared the day before it is required, so that it may have ample time to become cold and firm.

Sauce No. 2 is a stiffer binding and its use gives a more solid meat paste, which, when time is short, can be substituted for that made with the thinner sauce, No. 1. This more solid paste can be moulded into cork or cutlet shapes or used to form a casing round hard-boiled eggs, as in Scotch Eggs. (See p. 269.)

Comparative Recipes for Minced Meat bound with Sauce.

Name of Dish	*Ingredients*	*Directions*
Croquettes.[1]	½ lb. seasoned and flavoured meat.[2] *Sauce No.* 1 *or No.* 2, *viz.* No. 1. — No. 2. 1 oz. margarine. — 1 oz. margarine. 1 oz. flour. — 1 oz. flour. ⅜ pint stock *or* water. — ¼ pint stock *or* water. Egg and breadcrumbs *or* crushed vermicelli.	Mince the meat by hand, mix it with the sauce and make it into 4 or 5 rolls about 2–2½ inches long and rather thicker than sausages. Coat with egg and breadcrumbs or crushed vermicelli and fry in a bath of fat 3–4 minutes. Reduce the heat slightly almost at once, and fry until the croquettes are a golden brown colour. Drain on crumpled paper, arrange neatly on a hot dish and garnish with parsley.

[1] A slightly thickened gravy, served in a tureen, may accompany these if desired.

[2] For list of suitable combinations of meats and flavourings, etc. see p. 261. The meat of sausages, freed from skin, can also be used.

Name of Dish	*Ingredients*	*Directions*
Scotch Eggs.[1]	½ lb. seasoned and flavoured meat.[2] *Sauce No.* 2, *viz.* { 1 oz. margarine. 1 oz. flour. ¼ pint stock *or* water. } 4 hard boiled eggs. Egg and breadcrumbs *or* crushed vermicelli.	Remove the shell and skin from the eggs, dry with a towel and rub with flour. Make the meat paste in the usual way, divide it into 4 portions and wrap an egg in each, pressing the paste evenly on to the egg. Brush with beaten egg, toss in breadcrumbs or vermicelli and fry in deep fat for 4 or 5 minutes. Cut the eggs in half lengthwise and dish with the cut side uppermost, garnishing with parsley.
Meat Rolls or Patties.	½ lb. seasoned and flavoured meat.[2] *Sauce No.* 1, *viz.* { 1 oz. margarine. 1 oz. flour. ⅜ pint stock *or* water. } *Short or flaky pastry, viz.* { 8 oz. flour, salt. 4 oz. margarine and lard, etc. ½ teaspoonful baking powder (for short crust only). } ¼ pint water. Beaten egg *or* milk for glaze.	Mince meat by hand, mix with the sauce and put to cool. Prepare pastry, roll out thinly, cut into 10 squares and damp the edges of each. Form the meat into 10 rolls and put one on each piece of pastry. Fold the pastry over, pressing the ends together. Brush with egg or milk and bake in a quick oven for 20–25 minutes. *Alternative plan.* Cut the pastry into rounds and line greased patty tins with them. Put a portion of meat on each, cover with a second round of pastry, glaze and bake 20–25 minutes.

Type II. B. *Group* 2. *Minced Meat held together with Egg.*

Meat and Macaroni or Rice Rolls.

Ingredients

¼ lb. cooked ham *or* tongue.
2 oz. macaroni, boiled and chopped finely (p. 144), *or* 2 oz. rice boiled (p. 142).
1 tablespoonful tomato essence or sauce.
} *plus* yolk of 1 egg.

Salt, pepper and cayenne.
White of 1 egg and breadcrumbs.
¼ pint tomato sauce (p. 168).

Method. Mix together the minced meat, macaroni or rice, tomato essence and seasonings and moisten with beaten yolk of

[1] See note 1 opposite. [2] See note 2 opposite.

egg. Divide into four or five equal portions and form into rolls or balls. Beat the white of egg slightly, brush the rolls with it and toss them in breadcrumbs. Fry in deep fat, drain well and arrange on a hot dish garnished with parsley. Serve the tomato sauce in a tureen.

Type III. A. Minced Meat, etc., steamed or baked in Moulds.

Bewitched Veal.

Ingredients

1¼ lbs. cooked minced meat (*e.g.* 1 lb. veal *plus* ¼ lb. ham *or* bacon).
¼ lb. breadcrumbs.
Salt, pepper, cayenne.
½ nutmeg (grated).

plus 4 tablespoonfuls stock *or* gravy and 2 eggs.

Salad or tomatoes for garnish.

Method. Mix meat, bread and seasonings with the stock and beaten eggs; press together well and pack very firmly into a greased mould. Cover the mould with a greased paper and steam for 1½–2 hours. Turn out of the mould and serve cold, garnished with salad or with tomatoes cut into quarters. The mould may be cut into very thin slices, if this is preferred.

Type III. B. Minced Meat, etc. baked in hollowed vegetables.

Examples of the use of cold meat in this fashion will be found in the recipes for Stuffed and Baked Vegetables on pp. 167, 168.

Type III. C. Minced Meat Balls baked in Sauce.

Meat Balls in White Sauce.

Ingredients

1 lb. cooked meat or mixtures of meat.
1½ oz. dried breadcrumbs.
Salt and pepper.
2 teaspoonfuls finely chopped shallot or parsley, if liked.
1 egg.
Stock.
½ pint white sauce (savoury) see p. 151.

Method. Mix minced meat, breadcrumbs, seasonings and shallot or parsley, if used. Moisten with beaten egg and as much stock as is necessary to make the mixture sufficiently firm to form into balls. Place the balls in a fireproof dish.

Make the white sauce in the usual way, seasoning it carefully and pour it over the meat balls. Cover the dish with a lid or with a greased paper and cook in a moderate oven for 20 minutes.

Type IV. Jellied Meat Moulds.

Veal or Chicken Mould.

Ingredients

2 hard-boiled eggs.	¼ oz. gelatine.
2 oz. cooked ham.	⅝ pint of stock.
¾ lb. cooked veal or chicken.	Lemon and parsley for garnish.
Rind of ½ lemon.	Salad.
Salt, pepper, cayenne, nutmeg.	

Method. (1) Slice the hard-boiled eggs, and cut the pink parts of the ham into fancy shapes with a cutter. Rinse the mould with cold water and decorate it with the egg and ham.

(2) Cut the veal or chicken into small pieces, removing gristle, etc. and put it with the remainder of the ham, seasonings and lemon rind into the mould.

(3) Steep the gelatine in the stock; when it is soft, heat it till it dissolves, and pour it over the meat. Cover the mould with a greased paper, put it in a fairly quick oven, heat until the stock just boils. If this heating is omitted the meat may not keep well.

(4) Put the mould into a cold place; when it is set, turn it out and garnish it with slices of lemon and parsley. Serve with salad.

RÉCHAUFFÉS OF FISH

What has already been said as to the desirability of re-heating cold meat applies also to cold fish, which is, on the whole, the less appetising of the two. Cold salmon, halibut and other suitable fish can be served with salad, and salmon can be potted and used for sandwiches, but for most cold fish re-heating is desirable.

In making réchauffés of fish, the same points require attention as in dealing with meat:

(1) Lack of flavour must be made up by additions of good sauce or of small quantities of shrimps or lobster, if these are available, or by the addition of anchovy essence, lemon juice, etc.

(2) Protection from undue heat must be given by mixing the fish with potatoes or sauce, or by covering it with a casing of egg and breadcrumbs, or with pastry.

Réchauffés of fish and meat naturally bear a decided resemblance to one another:

Type I. A. Fish flaked and heated in sauce.

B. Fish flaked, mixed with sauce, protected with a casing of potatoes and baked in a dish.

Type II. Fish flaked, mixed with potato or not, as desired, bound with a starch sauce or egg or both, then moulded and fried.

Type III. Fish flaked, mixed with breadcrumbs, etc. moistened with egg and steamed or baked in a mould.

Making of Réchauffés of Fish.

Preparation of Fish. Before being used, the fish must be freed from all skin and bones and be divided into flakes.

Type I. A. Fish re-heated in sauce.

Fricassee of Fish. (Compare Meat Mince.)

Ingredients

½ lb. cooked fish.
1 oz. shelled shrimps (optional).
½ pint white sauce (p. 151).
¾ teaspoonful lemon juice.
Salt, pepper, cayenne.
1 hard-boiled egg.
2 teaspoonfuls finely chopped parsley.

Method. Free the fish from skin and bones and divide it into flakes. Chop the white of the egg and put the yolk through a sieve. Make sauce, or if cold sauce is to be used, re-heat it with 1–2 tablespoonfuls milk, removing skin and beating out any lumps. Add fish, white of egg and seasoning. Heat the fish gently in the sauce until it is thoroughly hot, taking care it does not burn. Serve heaped up neatly on a hot dish and garnished with yolk of egg and parsley.

Scalloped Fish.

Ingredients. As for Fricassee of Fish, substituting 4 tablespoonfuls breadcrumbs for hard-boiled egg.

Method. Heat prepared fish in the sauce, season it and put it in a greased fireproof dish or on scallop shells. Sprinkle breadcrumbs on top and brown in a quick oven or under the gas or electric griller.

Kedgeree.

Ingredients

½ lb. cooked fish.
½ lb. boiled rice (see p. 142).
2 oz. margarine.
2 hard-boiled eggs.
1 teaspoonful lemon juice.
Salt, pepper, cayenne.
Pinch of ground mace *or* nutmeg.

Method. Chop the white of the egg and put the yolk through a sieve. Melt the margarine in the pan, add the prepared fish, boiled rice, white of egg and seasonings and heat thoroughly. Serve piled up on a hot dish, decorated with the yolk of egg.

Type I. B. Fish flaked, mixed with sauce, protected by casing of potato and baked.

Fish Pie. (Compare Shepherd's Pie.)

Ingredients

½ lb. cooked fish.
Lemon juice.
Salt, pepper, cayenne.
1 lb. mashed potatoes (p. 161).
½ pint sauce (white, anchovy, shrimp, parsley, or egg sauce (pp. 151–153).
1–2 hard-boiled eggs.
Beaten egg *or* milk.

Method. Grease a pie, or other deep fireproof dish. Season the prepared fish and cut the hard-boiled eggs in slices. Arrange the fish, sauce, hard-boiled eggs and potato in layers in the dish, beginning with fish and ending with potato. Score the topmost layer of potato with a fork and brush it with beaten egg or with milk. Put the dish in a moderate oven for 20–30 minutes to heat the pie thoroughly and to brown the potatoes.

An alternative plan is to mix the fish and potato together very thoroughly before putting it into the pie-dish alternately with hard-boiled egg and sauce.

Type II. Fish flaked, bound with sauce or egg, moulded and fried.

Group I. Flaked Fish bound with sauce.

For each ½ lb. of fish the ingredients for the sauce are:

No. 1	*No.* 2
1 oz. margarine.	¾ oz. margarine.
1 oz. flour.	¾ oz. flour.
¼ pint milk.	$\frac{5}{16}$ pint milk.

No. 1 is suitable for croquettes, when ample time can be allowed for the cooling and setting of the fish paste. No. 2 can be substituted for No. 1 when time is short; it gives a firmer mixture, stiff enough to be moulded into cutlet or cork shapes.

The making of the sauce, the mixing with the seasoned and flavoured fish, and the moulding are done in the way already described on p. 267 for meat. The fish mixture is usually made up into croquettes or into cutlet or cork shapes, but it may also be enclosed in pastry as rissoles or patties.

Fish Croquettes. (Compare Meat Croquettes.)

Ingredients

Sauce	*Fish, etc.*
¾ oz. margarine.	½ lb. cooked fish.
¾ oz. flour.	1 oz. picked shrimps, *or*
$\frac{3}{16}$ pint milk.	Few oysters, *or*
	1 teaspoonful anchovy essence.
	Lemon juice.
	Salt, pepper, cayenne.

Egg and breadcrumbs.

Method. Make the sauce in the usual way, *i.e.* melt the margarine, add the flour and cook for 2 or 3 minutes, then add the milk gradually, bring it to the boil and boil for a moment or two. Add to the sauce the prepared fish, chopped shrimps or oysters, etc. lemon juice and seasonings. Mix thoroughly and spread on a plate to cool. When set, divide the mixture into equal portions and mould into sausage-shaped pieces. Coat with egg and breadcrumbs and fry in deep fat. Drain well and serve on a hot dish garnished with parsley and lemon.

Group II. Flaked Fish bound with egg, etc.

Fish Cakes. (Compare Meat and Macaroni or Rice Rolls.)

Ingredients

½ lb. cooked fish.
½ lb. mashed potatoes.
½ oz. margarine.
2 teaspoonfuls finely chopped parsley.
Salt, pepper, cayenne.

plus 1 egg *or* little fish sauce *or* little milk.

Egg and breadcrumbs.

Method. Mix together the prepared fish, potatoes, margarine, parsley and seasonings and add enough beaten egg or fish sauce or milk to hold the ingredients together. Press the mixture well and form into 8 flat cakes or rolls or balls. Coat with egg and breadcrumbs and fry in deep or shallow fat. Drain carefully and arrange neatly on a hot dish. Garnish with parsley.

Type III. Fish flaked, moistened with egg and steamed or baked in moulds.

Fish Pudding. (Compare Bewitched Veal.)

Ingredients

½ lb. cooked fish.
1–1½ oz. margarine.
1 tablespoonful breadcrumbs.
2 teaspoonfuls finely chopped parsley.
1 teaspoonful lemon juice.
Salt, pepper, cayenne.
} *plus* 2 eggs.
½ pint anchovy sauce (p. 153).

Method. Melt margarine, add prepared fish, breadcrumbs, parsley, lemon juice and seasonings, mix well and moisten with the beaten eggs. For a very light pudding, separate the yolks from the whites of the eggs and beat them both, the whites to a stiff froth. Add the yolks to the fish, etc. then fold in the whites carefully. Put the mixture in a greased mould, cover with a greased paper and steam ½–¾ hour, until the mixture is firm in the centre. Turn out on to a very hot dish, pour the anchovy sauce over and serve immediately before the pudding loses its lightness.

RÉCHAUFFÉS OF VEGETABLES

Many cooked vegetables, *e.g.* green peas, potatoes, can be used in salads. Suggestions for other uses to which vegetables may be put are given here.

Potatoes. There are several possibilities for these:
(1) Use in a meat or fish réchauffé already described.
(2) Make into Potato Cakes (see p. 234).
(3) Re-heat in a sauce, as 'Scalloped Potatoes' (see below).
(4) Fry in slices or in a cake (see below).

Scalloped Potatoes.

Ingredients

2 lbs. cooked potatoes.
½ pint white sauce (p. 151).
3 teaspoonfuls finely chopped parsley.
2 oz. ham *or* tongue (optional).
Salt and pepper.

Method. Cut the potatoes into slices ¼ inch thick and cut the ham or tongue, if used, into strips. Grease a fireproof dish and arrange the potatoes, sauce, parsley and ham or tongue in layers, keeping a layer of potatoes for the top. Cover the dish with a greased paper or a second dish and bake in a moderate oven for ½ hour.

Fried Potatoes.

(1) *Whole Potatoes.* Choose firm, unbroken potatoes and cut them into slices about ¼ inch thick. Fry them either in shallow or deep fat till they are a golden brown colour. Lift them out carefully, drain well, sprinkle with salt and finely chopped parsley. Serve at once.

(2) *Mashed Potatoes.* Season the potatoes and press them into a firm flat cake. For each pound of potatoes, heat about 1 oz. dripping in a frying pan until the blue vapour is clearly seen. Then, but not till then, put in the cake of potato; when the first side is browned, turn it over very carefully and brown the second side. Serve on a hot dish.

Cauliflower.

(1) Use in salads.

(2) Convert into Cauliflower au Gratin (Cheese Cauliflower), (p. 166).

Haricot Beans.

(1) Re-heat whole with beef or mutton in hash or curry.

(2) Re-heat whole in parsley or brown or curry sauce.

(3) Substitute for freshly boiled beans in dish of Normandy Eggs (p. 166).

Note. Suggestions for the use of small quantities of stale bread, stale cake, cheese, etc. are given in Chapter V and elsewhere.

CHAPTER XXII

SUMMARY AND CRITICISM

Section I

THE EFFECTS OF COOKING ON FOODS

In the foregoing chapters we have considered the nature and properties of the different foodstuffs found in foods. We have considered also the treatment to which, among civilised races, at any rate, it is customary to subject foods in order to prepare them for eating. It may be well to sum up here the effects on foods of this treatment, if only to justify the amount of thought and labour which the right cooking of food does undoubtedly entail. We may take the term cooking to include the many and varied processes which foods undergo in addition to the actual application of heat and we shall find it well to discuss the results of cooking as they affect (1) the digestibility, (2) the composition and food value, (3) the wholesomeness of foods.

I. Effects of Cooking on the Digestibility of Foods.

A. The Effects of Cooking on the Digestibility of Foods in General.

These may be summarised thus:

(1) Food must be at the temperature of the human body before digestion can begin. The giving of food which is already warm therefore effects a saving of bodily energy which would otherwise be spent in raising the food to the required temperature.

(2) Cooking brings about changes in the appearance and flavour of the food which tend to make it more appetising and hence more digestible. The sight, taste and smell of skilfully prepared food all stimulate the nerves which originate and control the flow of the digestive fluids by whose action foods are prepared for the use of the body.

Cooking makes foods pleasanter to the taste by developing their natural flavours or by allowing of the addition of substances which heighten those flavours. Again, the taste of a food which is naturally insipid or otherwise unpleasant can be disguised by combining it with another with a distinctive and more agreeable flavour. An instance of the first is the development of the natural flavours of meat which takes place as it cooks, an improvement particularly noticeable when the meat is roasted or baked. An example of the emphasising of the natural flavour of a food is the use of sugar in cooking carrots and green peas. Thirdly, gelatine-solution may be taken as an instance of a food which is peculiarly flavourless. When this forms the basis of a jelly, sugar and fruit juice, etc. are added to it, while when it is to be converted into soup, vegetables and herbs are used to give a savoury taste. Again, lemon rind, vanilla and other essences are used to flavour cereals cooked in milk.

Variations in the form as well as in the flavour of foods are made possible by cooking and the same kind of food can be served several times without that monotony of diet which is so fatal to digestion.

(3) Cookery processes frequently aid digestion by increasing the amount of surface exposed to the digestive fluids. Thus meat and fish may be cut up, minced or shredded or pounded and rubbed through a sieve, according to the degree of fineness required. Cheese may be grated and nuts may be ground. Again, the beating of eggs and the aeration of doughs convert what would otherwise be dense compact masses, into which the digestive fluids could penetrate only with difficulty, into light and porous mixtures. Yet another instance of this fine division of foods is the emulsification of oils and fats, familiar in the making of mayonnaise sauce and salad cream.

This exposure of a large surface is particularly desirable in the case of foods whose texture makes it difficult for the digestive fluids to act on them. The grated cheese used in many savoury dishes, for example, is more easily digested than cheese eaten without such preparation. Again, eggs, the yolks and whites of which have been beaten very thoroughly are less of a tax on the digestive organs than eggs in an unbroken mass.

Foods which contain a large proportion of indigestible matter also benefit by being divided into fine particles. Nuts and legumes with their tough cellulose are most readily digested when ground into meal or flour or reduced to a pulp by being put through a sieve after cooking.

Further, the division of food into fine particles is of great importance in the preparation of foods for the very young, the very old and for invalids, all of whom, as far as digestion is concerned, may rank together. The digestive organs of babies have not developed fully and those of old people and invalids are in an enfeebled condition. The most casual glance at a book of recipes for invalid cookery will show how much use is made of the fine division of foods as an aid to digestion.

B. Effects of Cooking on the Digestibility of Individual Foodstuffs.

The effects of cooking and particularly of the application of heat on individual foodstuffs are very varied and often very complex.

Protein Foods. When animal flesh is cooked the connective tissues which bind together the muscle fibres are gelatinised. By this change, helped by the formation of steam between them the fibres are loosened and made more accessible to the digestive fluids. To this extent, therefore, cooking makes animal flesh more digestible but it has the opposite effect on the fibres themselves and on the 'juices' they contain, both of which, as we have seen, are coagulated and made less soluble by heat. This is true of the majority of both animal and vegetable proteins. It is for this reason that when, as in cases of illness, it is essential to give proteins in their most digestible form, we have recourse to meat juice, raw beef tea, sandwiches of finely shredded raw meat or eggs very lightly boiled. The decrease in digestibility which protein foods undergo as a result of heating is, as we have seen, counterbalanced to a large extent by increased attractiveness of taste and appearance and by other beneficial effects. None the less, we should do well to bear in mind at all times the importance of not over-cooking protein foods.

Bones and Gristle. Here the effects of cooking are wholly valuable. Bones and gristle in their natural state are useless as food for man, but by cooking, the nutriment they contain is made available in the form of a gelatin solution which becomes stock or jelly, according to the manner in which it is treated.

Carbohydrates. The digestibility of these foodstuffs, which, it will be remembered, occur almost wholly in vegetable foods, is increased by cooking. Cooking, as we have seen, bursts the cellulose coverings of the starch-grains and sets free the starch so that it is exposed to the action of the digestive fluids. Hence, starchy foods of all kinds would lose greatly in nutritive value if they were eaten raw and, as we have seen in some cases, cooking increases digestibility still further by changing starch into dextrin. When starch is heated to a high temperature it is converted into dextrin, a soluble substance which is readily digested. Starch in the crust of well-baked bread, in toast, in browned breadcrumbs has been dextrinised thus. A common recognition of the increased digestibility of dextrinised starch is the use in cases of weak digestion of rusks, or of thin slices of bread either toasted very slowly or baked in the oven, and the use of baked flour as food for infants.

Experience goes to prove that, as a whole, vegetables and fruits also are made more digestible by cooking, because the softening which the stiff, tense framework of cellulose undergoes causes them to be more readily broken down in the course of digestion. When the cells contain starch, as do those of potatoes, the softening and rupturing of the cellulose coverings of the cells is undoubtedly valuable.

Fats. In so far as fats are made more palatable or are emulsified by cooking, its effects may be said to be beneficial. Apart from these changes, cooking does not increase the digestibility of fats to any great extent, except perhaps inasmuch as it softens the connective tissues of raw fat and causes the fat to melt.

When fats are cooked in combination with other foods in their capacity as shortening, for example, or are used in frying to heat foods, they coat its particles so that the digestive juices cannot reach them easily. This naturally retards the digestion of the foods, especially as the digestion of fats themselves is one of the last processes to be undertaken by the digestive organs. Hot buttered toast, muffins, rich pastry and cakes and all fried foods are notoriously unsuited to people with weak digestions. The indigestibility of the last named is probably due in part to certain irritating substances formed when fat is heated to a high temperature.

II. Effects of Cooking on Composition and Food-Value of Foods.

When we remember to what a large extent water is used in cooking and how powerful a solvent it is, we shall understand that cooking must frequently result in the loss of some of the constituents of foods. Indeed, we have seen that in making such meat extracts as beef-tea, meat-stock, water is used for this very purpose. The same extractive action occurs, though to a lesser degree, whenever meat, fish, vegetables and other foods are cooked in or by means of water. Thus meat and fish, as we know, lose albumen, salts and 'extractives', while vegetables and cereals part with salts, sugar and starch grains.

Meat, again, loses water and fat as it cooks. The shrinkage which occurs in a 'roast' joint and the quantity of dripping which accumulates in the average household give some indication of this loss.

The effect of cooking on the vitamin value of foods has also to be considered. Vitamin C in green vegetables is readily affected by heat and oxidation and by alkalies. Vitamins A and D of fats can resist quite high temperatures as long as air is excluded, while B is not destroyed to any extent by the ordinary processes of cooking.

We may point out here that cooking frequently gives an

opportunity of adding to a food the foodstuff in which it is deficient, thus neutralising the effect of an undue proportion of any one foodstuff. Bacon, for example, is cooked with such lean meats as veal and chicken and margarine or dripping with pulse.

III. The Effects of Cooking on the Wholesomeness of Foods.

Cooking has an important influence on the wholesomeness of foods, inasmuch as it tends to destroy parasites and micro-organisms present in them. It is not clear exactly how far cooking brings about this desirable end; as we have seen, complete sterilisation is probably seldom achieved by the ordinary processes of cookery and the same is probably true of the destruction of parasites. But as far as it goes, cooking certainly makes foods more wholesome and delays for a time the onset of decay.

Section II.

CRITICISM OF COOKING PROCESSES AND THEIR APPLICATION TO DIFFERENT FOODS

At the risk of repetition, it may be well in conclusion to summarise what has been said as to the suitability of the different cookery processes to the various foods and to estimate the particular merits and demerits of each process.

Roasting and Grilling are used for the cooking of meat and poultry of good quality, tender and juicy. Roasting, adapted to joints, poultry and game, is now seldom used except in the modified form of pot-roasting. Grilling is useful for steaks, chops and other comparatively small thin pieces of meat, and for sections of poultry and game. It is also used for small fish and sections of fish.

Grilling cannot be considered conspicuously economical. Not only must the meat be of good quality, but the expenditure of fuel is great as compared to that necessary for other processes. Against this we have to set the results of the cooking, which are undoubtedly good. The high degree of radiant heat to which the meat is subjected sets the albumen rapidly and browns the surface. Further, the high temperature in combination with the free movement of air round the meat develops its flavour well, decomposing some of its constituents and producing new and more savoury substances.

Baking, a process which also requires a rather large amount of fuel, is suited for the cooking of a far greater variety of foods than roasting or grilling and is, of course, much used not only for meat, fish, and certain vegetables but also for bread, cakes, pastry and many puddings.

For reasons already given, meat and poultry are now very generally baked rather than roasted. The oven reaches a moderate temperature and the appearance, flavour and texture of baked meat approach very nearly those of meat which has been roasted in front of the fire.

Baking, as applied to fish and certain vegetables has again good results, giving them a crisp brown surface and developing their flavours well. Moreover, all three foods, meat, fish and vegetables can be made still more savoury by the addition of stuffing. A further advantage of baking is that as the process does not involve the use of water, the loss of substance is slight.

With regard to vegetables, it must be remembered that baking alone does not always make the cellulose completely tender and that a preliminary boiling is in many cases necessary.

Baking is the chief means of cooking bread, cakes, pastry and many puddings. The starch these contain is cooked thoroughly, some of it, as we have seen, being converted into dextrin, giving the loaf or cake a brown surface.

Frying, cooking in a medium of oil or liquefied fat, is a quick method of cooking requiring no great outlay on fuel or apparatus and adapted to a wide variety of foods. The high temperature at which frying is carried on makes the process suitable for small portions of meat and fish which require rapid cooking and which, boiled, would be sodden and tasteless, and baked, would be hard and dry. Frying is much used for réchauffés which require rapid heating rather than a second cooking and for pancakes, fritters and other forms of batter.

To be a success, frying perhaps demands greater attention to detail than other methods of cooking, but it is not difficult, once certain essentials are grasped. Over-cooking the outer layers of the food before the heat has had time to reach the centre is somewhat liable to happen in spite of the beaten egg, etc. with which the food is usually protected. It is important to take pains to drain the food thoroughly, but however carefully this is done it is almost inevitable that some fat should cling to the food, and for this reason, as we have seen, fried foods should not be given to invalids or others with weak digestions.

Steaming. By many people steaming is still considered as a process to be employed only in cooking for invalids, but this is to take a narrow view of its possibilities. Many foods can be steamed very satisfactorily. The penetrative power of steam ensures the food being cooked thoroughly, while the slowness of the process makes over-cooking a rare occurrence. The amount of substance lost from the food is relatively small and what *is* extracted mingles with the condensed steam, which, being small in quantity, can generally be served with the food in some way or other. Moreover, wastage seldom occurs through breaking of the food by the movements of water. The fact that foods are surrounded by steam and not by water means also that light pudding and other mixtures can expand to their full extent and that they are not made sodden and heavy by the absorption of water. Finally, steaming does not add to the food substances such as fat which make it indigestible.

It follows, therefore, that steaming is eminently adapted for the cooking of:

(*a*) Small pieces of meat and fish, especially pieces with a good deal of cut surface in proportion to their size.

(*b*) Various pudding and other light mixtures, *e.g.* suet, batter, custard and cake-pudding mixtures.

(*c*) Food for invalids for whom digestibility and delicacy of taste are of great importance.

(*d*) Foods which require to be re-heated either in their original or in a new form.

Steaming has the further advantage of being an inexpensive way of cooking. The apparatus is not costly and is simple in construction and easily managed. Only a small quantity of fuel need be burnt to keep up the necessary supply of steam and when a regulation steamer is used several dishes can be cooked at the same time with one expenditure of fuel.

Like other cookery processes, steaming has its demerits as well as its merits. Many people consider that steamed foods are insipid as to taste and unattractive as to appearance. This is perhaps particularly the case with meat and fish. Coating the food with a good well-flavoured sauce is one way of dealing with this defect; another plan, used for meat, is to complete the cooking by a short baking. This method answers well for old fowls or joints of meat of doubtful tenderness.

It will be remembered that steaming takes a considerable time, from one-half to one-third as long again as the time reckoned for boiling. This, also, is frequently a drawback.

Boiling. The term boiling covers both the boiling of liquids *e.g.* gravy, sauce, and the so-called 'boiling' of solids by placing them in either direct or indirect contact with heated water or other liquids. Hence the process is one which is used for the cooking of a wide variety of foods, among which are:

(*a*) Bones, gristle and connective tissues, whose gelatin is extracted by this means.

(*b*) Joints of meat, the quality of which is not sufficiently good to allow of their being roasted or baked. Such joints, as we have seen already, need water or steam to gelatinise the large amount of connective tissue and sinew. Joints which are small enough to go into the steamer should be steamed rather than boiled.

(*c*) Fish, large whole fish or cuts of fish, which are too big for steaming to be practicable.

(*d*) Vegetables and cereals, etc. whose cellulose is readily softened and ruptured by the boiling water.

(*e*) Suet puddings (especially rich plum puddings) which would take a long time to steam, and roly-poly puddings which are frequently too large to fit into a steamer.

(*f*) Soups, gravies, sauces, etc.

As compared to baked foods, boiled foods are inferior in appearance, in texture and in flavour. The temperature of boiling water is comparatively low and does not develop the flavour of the food as well as does the radiant heat used in baking and, in the case of meat and fish, does not seal up the pores so rapidly. Further, in the case of meat and fish, the water, as we have seen, simmers rather than boils. The solvent action of water is partly responsible for the insipid taste of boiled foods and, further, diminishes their nutritive value considerably. The actual waste of food substance can in many cases be lessened by using the water in which the food has boiled for stock or for making sauce or gravy. Water in which meat, poultry, rice, macaroni, haricot beans, lentils, celery have been cooked can be used thus. The bulk of the water is sometimes so great that it is difficult to utilise it completely and to find a use for the water in which such foods as fish or suet puddings have been boiled is still less easy.

The appearance of boiled meat, fish and vegetables can be made somewhat more interesting by covering them with sauce, the plan adopted for steamed foods. The taste of meat can be improved by cooking in the same water herbs and vegetables, the latter frequently being served with the meat.

Stewing is an eminently successful and economical method of cooking. To stew foods only a small amount of heat is necessary and the stew can be cooked in the oven or on the hot plate of a gas or electric cooker, as well as over a fire. The long, slow cooking softens tough foods and the liquid medium makes it easy to flavour them. Thus meat and sometimes fish are stewed with herbs and vegetables, and fruits with lemon rind or cinnamon stick. If the food is not very nutritious it can be stewed in stock or milk as the case requires, instead of in water. Moreover, there is practically no waste, since any substance dissolved out forms part of the liquid in which the food stews. This liquid, in the shape of gravy, sauce, or syrup according to the nature of the food, is almost invariably eaten as part of the dish and serves the double purpose of preventing waste and of disguising the appearance of the food when, as sometimes happens, this is not all that could be desired.

Stewing is applied chiefly to:

(*a*) Meat, especially meat which is tough and somewhat flavourless or is in irregularly-shaped, unsightly pieces. Stewing is also the means of extracting the substance of meat (and also of fish) in the form of beef-tea, meat-stock, fish-stock, etc.

(*b*) Fish, notably small fish and cutlets or fillets of fish for which boiling would be totally unsuitable.

(*c*) Vegetables, *e.g.* celery, onions, old peas, etc. which need long slow cooking to make them tender.

(*d*) Fruits of all kinds which need careful cooking at a low temperature to make them tender without loss of shape.

The chief drawbacks to stewing are the length of cooking (resulting in the case of meat and vegetable stews in a lessening of the vitamin C value of the latter) and the amount of attention needed to maintain the low even temperature which is so important. Especially is this the case in stewing meat which otherwise becomes 'cooked to rags', and in stewing fish and fruit which break easily.

QUESTIONS AND PRACTICAL TESTS

Chapter I

The Bearing of Micro-organisms on Food and Cookery.

(1) To what causes may attacks of food-poisoning be due? What steps may (*a*) the housewife, (*b*) the general public, take with a view to the prevention of food-poisoning?

(2) On which foods and under what conditions do moulds form? Give reasons for the statements you make. What practical steps would you suggest to prevent the growth of moulds?

(3) Compare and contrast bacteria and moulds as regards (*a*) nature and structure, (*b*) conditions favourable to growth, (*c*) means of preventing growth.

(4) Explain in detail the relation between (1) cleanliness and micro-organisms, (2) micro-organisms and food.

(5) 'A study of micro-organisms is of great value as the foundation of a course of training in housekeeping.'

Discuss this statement fully.

PART I. KITCHEN ORGANISATION

Chapter II

Kitchen Equipment and Management.

(1) Describe an ideal kitchen for a small house in a town *or* for a small cottage in the country in which the housewife works single-handed.

(2) Describe shortly an electric cooker with which you are familiar. If the household electricity bill is unduly high and the electric cooker is thought to be the cause, what means would you suggest of economising in electricity?

(3) Explain clearly as to an inexperienced person, the purpose, construction and management of the flues and dampers connected with the boiler and oven of a coal range. On which points do you consider special stress should be laid?

(4) Give some account of the measures taken in the manufacture of modern cooking stoves to facilitate cleaning.

(5) Discuss the merits and demerits of the different pans in common use, arranging your answer under suitable headings.

Chapter III

The Cleaning of Kitchen Equipment and Utensils.

(1) Describe the plan followed in *all* forms of cleaning, irrespective of the nature of the thing to be cleaned. Give examples from any kind of domestic work you have done.

(2) Classify according to their actions the agents commonly used to remove grease from kitchen equipment and utensils. Write brief notes on the use of each.

(3) By what means would you remove grease from (*a*) frying basket, (*b*) enamel-lined saucepan, (*c*) aluminium frying pan, (*d*) hot plate of an electric cooker, (*e*) cake tins, (*f*) wooden rolling-pins? Justify your choice of cleaning agents in each case and suggest alternatives whenever possible.

(4) Discuss the use of acids and substances containing acids as cleaning agents. Why should special care be taken in preparing a brass or copper preserving pan for use?

(5) Give full instructions for the disposal of kitchen refuse and explain the importance of its right treatment.

PART II. FOODS AND COOKERY

Chapter IV

The Buying of Foods.

(1) Discuss the statement 'The buying of food . . . if indifferently done, involves much waste, not only of money but also of time and labour.'

(2) Describe the general plan followed in the division into joints of the different animals used as food. Which parts, generally speaking, provide (*a*) the most tender, juicy meat, (*b*) the most lean and close meat, (*c*) the most sinewy meat? Give the average cost of the meat included in each group.

(3) Give your own views on personal shopping versus shopping by telephone.

Write short notes as for a Guide to Shopping on:

(*a*) Hams and gammons.
(*b*) Chops and cutlets.
(*c*) Herrings and mackerel.
(*d*) Beef suet and mutton suet.

(4) Explain *in words* from which part of an ox the following are cut: (*a*) aitchbone, (*b*) sirloin, (*c*) silverside, (*d*) fillet,

(*e*) gravy-beef. What is the average price per pound and for what purposes is each used?

(5) By what signs would you judge the quality and good condition of (*a*) green vegetables, (*b*) fish, (*c*) butcher's meat?

Chapter V

The Storage of Foods.

(1) Make a simple plan to show the construction and arrangement of any larder (or substitute for a larder, other than a refrigerator) with which you are acquainted. Write a short critical report on it and, as far as possible, suggest remedies for any defects you mention.

(2) Give general directions for the care and management of (*a*) a larder and (*b*) a refrigerator, arranging your answer under the headings (*a*) daily, (*b*) weekly treatment.

(3) Give directions for the keeping in the larder of (*a*) meat, (*b*) butter, (*c*) milk, (*d*) stock, (*e*) bread. Explain the reasons for the directions you give. Why is it necessary to protect food from flies?

(4) Discuss the exercise of economy in the administration of the kitchen departments of the household.

Chapter VI

The Processes of Cooking Foods.

(1) What do you understand by the terms (*a*) water vapour, (*b*) condensation of steam, (*c*) convection currents, (*d*) simmering?

(2) Explain in your own words what you understand by the 'latent heat' of steam. Describe fully the process of cooking food by means of steam.

(3) Compare and contrast the processes of boiling and stewing, arranging your answer under suitable headings.

(4) What do you understand by (*a*) direct, (*b*) indirect heat? Give some account of *two* methods of cooking by indirect heat.

Chapter VII

Foodstuffs and Food.

(1) Classify the foodstuffs which constitute the foods commonly eaten by human beings. Give as many examples as possible of foods in which each foodstuff may be found.

(2) For what reasons do human beings require food? Explain briefly how and why the food necessary to the existence of human beings differs from that needed by plants.

(3) Say, as far as you can, what foodstuffs are found in the ingredients required for the following dishes:

(1) Oatmeal Porridge and Milk (for Recipe see p. 144). (2) Fried Eggs and Bacon (for Recipe see p. 172). (3) Lentil Soup (for Recipe see p. 128). (4) Haricot of Mutton (for Recipe see p. 102). (5) Fried Potatoes (for Recipe see p. 276). (6) Apple Charlotte (for Recipe see p. 183).

(4) Write out the menus of the meals you have eaten on the day on which you answer this question. Show what vitamins these meals have, in all probability, contained. Explain shortly what effect the vitamins named may be expected to have on your health and well-being.

(5) Say what you know of the following: (*a*) a first-class or 'A' protein; (*b*) cellulose; (*c*) vitamin D. Explain, as far as you can, the value of each in a diet.

Chapter VIII

The Cooking of Protein Foods: Eggs.

(1) Say what you know of the nature and properties of egg-albumen. Show in detail how the methods of (1) poaching eggs, (2) making 'boiled' egg custards, are based on these properties.

(2) What do you consider to be the food-value of shell eggs? Suggest ways of cooking shell eggs (*a*) as substitutes for meat or fish, (*b*) for a convalescent.

(3) Describe briefly the preparation and cooking of the different forms of plain custards, explaining clearly the mistakes an inexperienced cook would be likely to make.

(4) What do you understand by the term 'cabinet' custard-pudding? Give two *original* recipes for puddings of this type, one suitable for children, the other for a dinner sweet. Give clear directions for preparing and cooking either one *or* the other.

(5) Discuss the use and treatment of eggs in cookery, dealing with *either* shell eggs *or* dried eggs.

Practical Tests

(1) Prepare eggs in four different ways showing as wide a variety of method and purpose as possible.

(2) Make (*a*) 'boiled' custard, (*b*) a plain custard to be turned out, (*c*) a 'cabinet' custard-pudding. Use 1 egg for each dish.

(3) Show how eggs may be prepared, (*a*) as a breakfast dish, (*b*) as a sweet dish, (*c*) as a luncheon or supper dish, (*d*) as a dish for a convalescent. Cook sufficient for one person in each case.

(4) Show 4 different ways (other than boiling) of preparing eggs for breakfast. Use 1 egg for each dish.

Chapter IX

The Cooking of Protein Foods: Milk and Cheese.

(1) Explain, as far as possible, the following mishaps:

(*a*) A dish of junket does not set as it should.

(*b*) A milk and egg mixture, *e.g.* 'boiled' custard, curdles during cooking.

(*c*) A cornflour mould made with dried milk tastes burnt.

(*d*) Some milk, thought to be fresh, unexpectedly turns sour.

(2) Why is cheese usually considered to be difficult to digest? What can be done in preparing dishes from cheese to make it less so?

Illustrate your answer by reference to any two dishes you have prepared at school or at home; estimate the food-value of each.

Practical Tests

(1) (*a*) Prepare a dish of junket and two other dishes in which milk is an important ingredient; one of the two should be suitable for a convalescent.

(*b*) Show a simple way of serving raw grated cheese.

(2) (*a*) Prepare and cook two dissimilar cheese dishes, one of which can be served at short notice.

(*b*) Prepare a sample cheese sandwich suitable for a picnic lunch.

Chapter X

The Cooking of Protein Foods: Meat.

(1) Say what you know of (*a*) the nature of meat, (*b*) the properties of its proteins. Show by reference to any practical work you have done the bearing of the information you give on the cooking of meat.

(2) Discuss in general terms the value of home-made meat extracts in (*a*) serious illness, (*b*) convalescence. Give directions for making beef-tea, explaining clearly the purpose of each step.

(3) Compare and contrast the processes of baking and boiling meat, arranging your answer under suitable headings.

(4) Discuss the stewing of meat. What are the features which make this method of cooking particularly good for meat of indifferent quality and what conditions do you consider essential to its success?

(5) (*a*) Indicate in general terms the nature of the cuts of meat suitable for cooking by the different methods. Give examples.

(*b*) What time is allowed for cooking joints of meat by each of the usual methods and what conditions regulate these times?

Practical Tests

(1) Cook the two pieces of meat provided so as to show (*a*) how to extract, (*b*) how to retain as much nutriment as possible.

(2) A piece of the upper part of leg of mutton (or rump steak) is provided. Cook part of it as a luncheon dish and prepare the remainder for an invalid.

(3) A portion of fillet of veal (or rump steak) is provided. Make two luncheon dishes from it.

Chapter XI

The Cooking of Protein Foods: Fish.

(1) Classify the different kinds of fish. Name the different ways in which fish can be cooked and the kind and cuts of fish for which each is suitable.

(2) (*a*) Estimate briefly the relative food values of fish and meat.

(*b*) Show by reference to any experimental work you have done that the principles underlying the cooking of fish and meat are essentially the same.

(3) Compare and contrast the boiling of fish and meat (unsalted) accounting fully for any differences you mention.

(4) Discuss the preparation of stews of fish and meat respectively, showing wherein the processes (*a*) resemble, (*b*) differ, from each other.

(5) Compare the processes of steaming and baking fish having regard to (*a*) economy of material, (*b*) digestibility, (*c*) palatableness, (*d*) attractiveness of appearance.

Practical Tests

(1) (*a*) A plaice (or a lemon sole) is provided. Prepare it in such a way as to make the most of all the nutriment it contains.

(*b*) Cook the finnan haddock provided.

(2) Three fillets or cutlets of fish are provided. Cook them by three different methods, showing as wide a variety as possible.

(3) Two cutlets of cod or hake are provided. Cook them by whatever method you think best, the first for an invalid, the second for a person with a capricious appetite.

(4) (*a*) Bake 2 fillets of fish, showing how stuffing may be introduced.

(*b*) Boil the piece of fish provided and serve with sauce.

Chapter XII

The Cooking of Protein Foods: Bones, Gristle, etc.

(1) Define 'stock' in your own words; give brief directions for making stock from knuckle of veal, explaining as far as you can the action of the process on each of the principal constituents of the stock.

(2) How does the nature of the materials which form the basis of stock regulate the cooking? What other ingredients are (*a*) essential, (*b*) not essential, but desirable? What undesirable materials are sometimes utilised in stock-making?

(3) Discuss the use of the stock-pot from the point of view of economy.

(4) Describe briefly the different types of soup and say what determines the choice of soup when planning a meal. Give a typical recipe for *one* type of soup.

(5) What is gelatin and what are its properties? Describe the forms in which it is eaten and estimate its food value.

Practical Tests

(1) Make two kinds of soup, one with and one without stock.

(2) Prepare two soups to show (1) the use of vegetables as the foundation of a purée soup; (2) the preparation of a typical 'thickened' soup.

(3) Make two dishes to illustrate the use of gelatine.

(4) Prepare two dishes with gelatine, one suitable for a convalescent, the other for a dinner sweet.

Chapter XIII

The Cooking of Carbohydrate Foods: Cereals.

(1) What are one's aims in cooking starchy foods? How would you fulfil these aims in cooking (1) semolina, (2) arrowroot, (3) macaroni, (4) tapioca? Account for any difference in treatment.

(2) Say what you know of the foodstuff starch, its nature and properties, the foods in which it is found and the changes which it must undergo to prepare it for eating.

(3) What is meant by the 'dextrinisation' of starch? Illustrate your explanation by reference to your practical work.

(4) Discuss the making of sauces of which starch forms a part.

Practical Tests

(1) Prepare four different cereals as food for convalescents.

(2) Illustrate the preparation of starchy foods by making from three different cereals (1) a pudding or sweet, (2) a savoury, (3) a sauce.

(3) Show the cooking of cereals by making dishes from (*a*) cornflour, (*b*) semolina, (*c*) macaroni. Show in one of the dishes how eggs may be cooked in combination with starchy foods.

(4) (*a*) Prepare two beverages from cereals.

(*b*) Prepare white foundation sauce by two methods; 'garnish' one sauce for serving with fish and the other for serving with meat.

Chapter XIV

The Cooking of Carbohydrate Foods: Vegetables.

(1) Classify the different vegetables usually eaten and indicate the food value of each class.

(2) What special difficulties does the cooking of green vegetables present? Describe and account for the measures usually taken to cope with these difficulties.

(3) Give detailed directions for the preparation of (*a*) fresh green materials, *e.g.* lettuce, and (*b*) cooked vegetables for salads; give, also, some account of other materials used in salad-making.

(4) Discuss fully the cooking of potatoes.

(5) Estimate the value of legumes in a diet, and describe briefly any methods of cooking them you have practised.

Practical Tests

(1) (*a*) Cook potatoes in two different ways, choosing those methods which involve least loss of substance.

(*b*) Cook a green vegetable and prepare a simple, seasonable green salad.

(2) Three vegetables, one of each class are provided. Prepare

them by the method you think best, showing as wide a variety of treatment as possible.

(3) (*a*) Cook new potatoes and green peas. (*b*) Prepare mint sauce.

(4) Prepare (*a*) a cauliflower, (*b*) some tomatoes, as vegetable entrées or savouries.

Chapter XV

The Cooking of Carbohydrate Foods: Fruits.

(1) Contrast nuts and sugary fruits with regard to constituents, nutritive value and digestibility.

(2) What changes does cooking cause in sugary fruits? Describe a method of stewing fresh fruits and say how it differs from that employed for dried fruits.

Practical Tests

(1) Cook apples in three different ways, (1) as a dinner sweet, (2) as a dish for a nursery dinner, (3) in the form of a sauce.

(2) Three kinds of fruit provided. Stew two of them and make a fruit sauce of the third.

(3) Prepare three fruit dishes suitable for a simple vegetarian luncheon.

Chapter XVI

The Cooking of Fats: The Preparation of Fats for Use in Frying and the Frying of Foods.

(1) Describe shortly the method of preparing the different kinds of fats for use as mediums for frying foods. What are the merits and demerits of each kind?

(2) Give full directions for the clarifying of raw beef or mutton fat, explaining the changes the fat undergoes at each stage of the process.

(3) What changes take place in clarified fat when it is heated and what practical bearing have these changes on the frying of foods? How do you account for the fact that fried foods so often look greasy and unattractive?

(4) How are foods prepared for frying and why do most foods need such preparation? What foods do *not* need this preparation?

(5) Give instructions for two methods of frying foods, showing in what respects they are (*a*) similar, (*b*) dissimilar.

Which method would you yourself advise for general use and on what grounds?

Practical Tests

(1) Show your skill in frying by preparing one meat dish suitable for breakfast and one suitable for luncheon. Serve a vegetable with the latter.

(2) (*a*) Clarify 1 lb. raw fat.

(*b*) Fry (1) a plaice or lemon sole and (2) a whiting to show two methods of preparing and two methods of frying fish.

(3) (*a*) Clarify dripping by two methods.

(*b*) Fry mutton cutlets and serve with gravy; fry raw potatoes. Two methods of frying should be shown.

(4) Cook dishes of (1) beefsteak and onions, (2) liver and bacon to show two methods of preparing meat for frying.

Chapter XVII

The Cooking of Fats: The Use of Fats as Shortening.

(1) Name the ingredients used in pastry-making and state the proportions required for the different kinds of pastries. Give *general* directions for pastry-making.

(2) Describe the making of an inexpensive short crust and explain how it differs from suet crust. For what purposes is each used?

(3) Give an *original* recipe for a suet pudding in which the suet is distributed throughout the pudding. Group the ingredients according to their functions and give directions for preparing and cooking the pudding.

(4) By what methods can suet puddings be cooked? Comment on each method and give directions for cooking puddings by *one* of them.

Practical Tests

(1) Make two dishes to show the making of short pastries (*a*) with margarine and lard or dripping, (*b*) with suet.

(2) Make one sweet and one savoury dish to show the making and cooking of (*a*) short crust, (*b*) flaky crust.

(3) (*a*) Prepare a dish to show the making of short crust.

(*b*) Make a suet pudding to use up breadcrusts.

(4) Make two suet puddings, one with and one without suet crust; show two methods of cooking the puddings.

Chapter XVIII

The Aeration of Doughs: (1) Baking Powder and its Constituents.

(1) Discuss fully the part bicarbonate of soda plays in the aeration of doughs; illustrate your answer by reference to your practical work.

(2) Give a recipe for baking powder and instructions for its keeping and use. On what does its success as a means of aeration depend?

(3) Suggest substitutes for baking powder and give directions for their use. What exactly is the effect of baking powder (or substitutes for baking powder) on cake and pudding mixtures?

(4) Give *original* recipes for (1) small cakes (2) scones. Give *general* instructions for preparing scones and for two methods of cooking them.

Practical Tests

(1) Make (*a*) small cakes, (*b*) scones, to show the use of baking powder and substitutes for baking powder respectively.

(2) Make two kinds of scones and show two methods of cooking them.

(3) Make (*a*) an inexpensive plain cake, (*b*) afternoon tea scones.

(4) Make (*a*) a gingerbread cake, (*b*) buns to show two methods of aerating doughs.

Chapter XIX

The Aeration of Doughs: (2) Yeast.

(1) Enumerate the conditions necessary for the growth of yeast. Show in detail how these conditions are provided when yeast is used to aerate doughs.

(2) Give a brief account of the processes of bread-making, explaining clearly the purpose of each.

(3) Give full instructions for the baking of bread and describe the changes the dough undergoes in the process.

(4) Explain *exactly* how yeast brings about the aeration of doughs, comparing and contrasting its action with that of baking powder.

(5) Explain the relation between temperature and the growth of yeast. Illustrate your answer by reference to some usual defects in bread.

Practical Tests

Practical tests involving the use of yeast will be found among the general tests given at the end of the questions on Chapter XXII.

Chapter XX

The Aeration of Doughs: (3) The Mechanical Inclusion of Air.

(1) Discuss the use of air in 'raising' doughs. Compare and contrast its use with that of baking powder.

(2) What is the distinction between 'pound' cakes and 'plain' cakes? Give a typical recipe for a cake of each kind and show how the proportion the ingredients bear to one another influences the method of making and baking the cake.

(3) Give exact directions for the making of the different types of batter and describe the purposes for which each is used.

(4) Discuss fully the aeration of doughs, comparing and contrasting the different methods.

Practical Tests

(1) Make two kinds of small cakes which depend wholly or mainly on the inclusion of air for their aeration.

(2) Make cakes of two types to show the use of air as a 'raising' agent.

(3) Prepare two dishes to show two methods of making and two methods of cooking batters.

Chapter XXI

The Utilisation of Cooked Foods.

(1) Discuss the re-heating of foods from the point of view of economy, using the word in its widest sense.

(2) Indicate briefly the different forms in which cold meat may be re-heated. How do you determine which form is best for a given piece of meat?

(3) Give some account of the making of réchauffés of meat and fish, indicating the conditions which you consider essential to their success.

(4) Describe any practical work you have done in connection with re-heating or otherwise using cooked vegetables.

Practical Tests

(1) Use the cold meat provided in two different ways, making one dish to be eaten hot and one to be eaten hot *or* cold.

(2) Prepare three dishes from cold fish, making one réchauffé suitable for breakfast and two for luncheon.

(3) Use the cooked meat, fish and potatoes provided to make a meal for one person. Show as wide a variety of method as possible.

(4) Use cold potatoes in three ways. (Credit will be given for variety of method.)

(5) Prepare three réchauffés from the cooked potatoes, cauliflower and haricot beans provided.

Chapter XXII

Summary and Criticism.

Section I.

(1) Discuss cooking as it affects the digestibility of foods.

(2) In what ways is cooking a source (*a*) of loss, (*b*) of gain to foods?

(3) Discuss the preparation of food for invalids.

Section II.

(4) Classify the different cookery processes and indicate in general terms the nature of the foods for which each is suitable.

(5) Compare and contrast water and fat as mediums for cooking foods.

(6) Discuss the possibilities of frying and stewing from the point of view of hard-pressed housewives. What means can you suggest of simplifying cooking for them?

(7) What use is made of steam as a means of cooking foods? For what purposes do you consider it is peculiarly suited?

(8) Contrast stewing and grilling with special reference to economy of time, fuel and food materials.

Section III. The Arrangement of Menus.

(9) Draw up a list of meals for three days for people who are camping out. What cooking equipment would you advise ?

(10) Suggest meals for four days for a delicate child, ten years of age, who dislikes fat in any shape or form and who is ordered to eat a good quantity of it.

(11) Give a menu for a choice but not unduly expensive dinner of four courses suitable for the present month. Give the approximate cost.

(12) Arrange breakfasts for one week for a girls' boarding school.

(13) Draw up menus for a week's dinners in which meat and fish are used sparingly.

(14) Plan a fairly substantial hot evening meal for three travellers, the exact time of whose arrival is uncertain. Describe the measures you would take to have it ready to serve at very short notice and in as good condition as possible.

General Practical Tests

(1) Cook a meal consisting of (1) fish, (2) a vegetable entrée or savoury, (3) a sweet dish, to show the possibilities of baking as a method of cooking.

(2) Prepare a simple but attractive luncheon for a convalescent.

(3) (*a*) Cook three cutlets of fish by three different methods.

(*b*) Prepare a vegetable entrée or savoury.

(4) Prepare a vegetarian lunch of two courses for two people for the summer (or winter) months. Eggs may be used, if desired.

(5) Cook a breakfast for two people suitable for a cold winter (or a hot summer) morning.

(6) Three fillets of fish are provided. (*a*) Show three ways of cooking them, then (*b*) prepare a réchauffé from them.

(7) Prepare scones, small cakes, etc. to show three ways in which doughs can be aerated.

(8) Cook three dishes containing eggs to show respectively their power of (1) binding together different ingredients, (2) holding air when beaten, (3) thickening a liquid or semi-liquid substance.

INDEX